1010 SERMON ILLUSTRATIONS
FROM THE BIBLE

1010

SERMON ILLUSTRATIONS

FROM THE BIBLE

Edited by Charles L. Wallis

BAKER BOOK HOUSE
Grand Rapids, Michigan

Special acknowledgment is made for permission to reprint copyrighted materials from the following translations: *The Bible, A New Translation* by James Moffatt, copyright 1935 by Harper & Row, Publishers, Incorporated; *The Complete Bible, An American Translation* by J. M. Powis Smith and Edgar J. Goodspeed, copyright 1939 by the University of Chicago; *The New English Bible: New Testament,* copyright © 1961 by the Delegates of the Oxford University Press and the Syndics of the Cambridge University Press; *The New Testament in Modern English* by J. B. Phillips, copyright © 1958 by J. B. Phillips and reprinted by permission of The Macmillan Company; *The New Testament in Modern Speech* by Richard Francis Weymouth, copyright 1903 by Harper & Row, Publishers, Incorporated; *Revised Standard Version,* copyright 1946, 1952 by the Division of Christian Education of the National Council of the Churches of Christ in the United States of America.

Reprinted 1975 by Baker Book House Company
with the permission of
Harper & Row, Publishers, Incorporated
Library of Congress Catalog Card Number: 63-7610
ISBN: 0-8010-9552-2

To three teachers

VERL F. SMURTHWAITE
JOSEPH H. BACCUS
JAMES R. BRANTON

with appreciation and affection

CONTENTS

PREFACE

The editing for pastors of a book of this character requires a few words of explanation, for pastors are specialists in biblical literature and know—or surely should know—the contents of the Bible. Yet the unlimited illustrative materials to be gleaned from Bible study are too often neglected in much preaching.

For more than a decade it has been my privilege to edit *Pulpit Preaching,* a homiletical journal, and so month by month I have had the opportunity to read and evaluate sermons which are representative of the Christian pulpit in English-speaking countries. By conservative estimate, more than 75 per cent of these sermons use the Bible in an incidental manner and often as little more than a point of departure and return. These sermons come from high and low pulpits, the traditionally-oriented and the evangelical communions. The sermons contain an abundance of illustrative matter but generally from the daily press, secular periodicals and literature, and pastoral experience. As pastors we miss our most important, pertinent, and life-centered resource—the Bible in which the proclamation of the gospel must find its stimulus and inspiration.

I am confident that sermons which are rich in interpretations of, and allusions to, the Bible will more strongly appeal and benefit —and be remembered longer—than those which have origins and explications from secular sources. By recalling and making immediately available the content of the Bible, this volume will have fulfilled its purpose. In addition to adding verve, color, substance, and meaning to sermons, biblical references will also help in the important responsibility of educating parishioners in the vast range of biblical history.

The illustrations are in abbreviated form. A specific textual reference follows quoted materials. Paraphrased materials are identified by contextual reference. The illustrations are listed under relevant subject headings. An extensive cross index identifies a particular illustration according to a variety of related topics. The special day index lists illustrations according to emphases of the Christian and civil calendars.

Biblical books are identified by the following abbreviations:

Genesis	Gen.	Micah	Mic.
Exodus	Ex.	Nahum	Nah.
Leviticus	Lev.	Habakkuk	Hab.
Numbers	Num.	Zephaniah	Zeph.
Deuteronomy	Deut.	Haggai	Hag.
Joshua	Josh.	Zechariah	Zech.
Judges	Judg.	Malachi	Mal.
Ruth	Ruth		
Samuel	Sam.	Matthew	Matt.
Kings	Kings	Mark	Mk.
Chronicles	Chron.	Luke	Lk.
Ezra	Ezra	John	Jn.
Nehemiah	Neh.	Acts	Acts
Esther	Es.	Romans	Rom.
Job	Job	Corinthians	Cor.
Psalms	Ps.	Galatians	Gal.
Proverbs	Prov.	Ephesians	Eph.
Ecclesiastes	Eccl.	Philippians	Phil.
Song of Solomon	S. of S.	Colossians	Col.
Isaiah	Isa.	Thessalonians	Thess.
Jeremiah	Jer.	Timothy	Tim.
Lamentations	Lam.	Titus	Tit.
Ezekiel	Ezek.	Philemon	Phm.
Daniel	Dan.	Hebrews	Heb.
Hosea	Hos.	James	Jas.
Joel	Joel	Peter	Pet.
Amos	Amos	John (epistles)	Jn.
Obadiah	Obad.	Jude	Jude
Jonah	Jon.	Revelation	Rev.

Unidentified scriptural citations are from the King James Version. Other translations or paraphrases are identified by the following designations:

AMNT	*The Amplified New Testament* (1958)
AT	*The Complete Bible: An American Translation* (1939)
BARCLAY	*The Daily Study Bible Series* by William Barclay (1953–1960)

BARRETT	*A Commentary on the Epistle to the Romans* by C. K. Barrett (*Harper's New Testament Commentaries*) (1957)
FILSON	*A Commentary on the Gospel According to St. Matthew* by Floyd V. Filson (*Harper's New Testament Commentaries*) (1960)
GOODSPEED	*The New Testament: An American Translation* by Edgar J. Goodspeed (1923)
JOHNSON	*A Commentary on the Gospel According to St. Mark* by Sherman E. Johnson (*Harper's New Testament Commentaries*) (1960)
LESLIE	*The Psalms* by Elmer A. Leslie (1949)
MOFFATT	*A New Translation of the Bible* by James Moffatt (1922)
NEB	*The New English Bible* (1961)
PHILLIPS	*The New Testament in Modern English* by J. B. Phillips (1952–1958)
RSV	*The Holy Bible: Revised Standard Version* (1946–1952)
RIEU	*The Four Gospels* by E. V. Rieu (1953)
TORREY	*The Four Gospels* by Charles Cutler Torrey (2nd ed., 1947)
WEYMOUTH	*The New Testament in Modern Speech* by Richard Francis Weymouth (1903)
WILLIAMS	*The New Testament* by Charles B. Williams (1937)
C. S. C. WILLIAMS	*A Commentary on the Acts of the Apostles* by C. S. C. Williams (*Harper's New Testament Commentaries*) (1957)

CHARLES L. WALLIS

Keuka College
Keuka Park, New York

ACTION

1 THE LORD SAID ARISE   Joshua rent his clothing and flung himself before the ark after Israel had been defeated at Ai, but the Lord told Joshua that his self-abasement should come to an end: "Arise, why have you thus fallen upon your face?" (Josh. 7:10, RSV).

2 THEY REMAINED TO TALK   Concerning the tribe of Reuben, Deborah sang, "But in the shires of Reuben were divisions and debates. Why did you lounge in shepherds' cotes, with only an ear for pastoral notes?" (Judg. 5:15–16, MOFFATT). When the call to battle was sounded, the Reubenites organized, not a military force, but lively debates and discussions—a counterpart, perhaps, of in-effectual committee meetings of our day.

3 WHEN DISCUSSION IS FATAL   After hearing Paul's eloquent defense, Festus and Agrippa "retired to discuss the affair" (Acts 26:31, MOFFATT)—and apparently they never moved beyond the point of discussion.

4 A WORK TO BE FINISHED   Many a good work, undertaken with resolution and enthusiasm, dwindles to inaction. Paul advised the Corinthians, "You were the first not only to do anything about this, but to want to do anything, and that was last year. Now finish doing it, so that your readiness to undertake it may be equaled by the way you finish it up" (2 Cor. 8:10–11, GOODSPEED).

5 WORDS OR ACTION?   Words come easily; actions more slowly. Yet a man is measured, not by what he says, but by what he does. A farmer asked his sons to work in the vineyard. "He went to the first and said, 'Go and work in my vineyard today, my son.' He said, 'All right, sir'—but he never went near it. Then the father approached the second son with the same request. He said, 'I won't.'

But afterward he changed his mind and went." Jesus' question is rhetorical: "Which of these two did what their father wanted?" (Matt. 21:28–31, PHILLIPS.) "Let us not love in word, neither in tongue; but in deed" (1 Jn. 3:18).

6 *ALIEN ACTIONS*   Of those who piously speak the name of the Lord when their actions are alien to his will, Jeremiah says, "Thou art always on their lips, but far, far from their hearts" (Jer. 12:2, MOFFATT).

7 *TRANSLATING BELIEF INTO ACTION*   Jesus spoke of those who professed to believe what he said but neglected to translate their beliefs into action by describing two houses: one without a strong foundation was unable to withstand flooding waters, and the other set firmly upon a rock base remained unmoved when torrents came. (Lk. 6:46–49.)

AGE

8 *BEYOND TODAY'S HORIZONS*   No life is ever completed. Always beyond today's horizons lie challenging and unfinished opportunities and responsibilities. "When Joshua was old, well advanced in years, the Eternal said to him, 'You are old, well advanced in years, and yet much land still remains to be occupied'" (Josh. 13:1, MOFFATT). However long and faithfully a man has served, "old age hath yet his honour and his toil" and "'tis not too late to seek a newer world" (Tennyson).

9 *CONTINUING CONFIDENCE*   Caleb returned from scouting Palestine to say that God would enable the children of Israel to overcome the Anakim, or giants, who possessed the land. Years later, when Moses was parceling out the land to the tribes, Caleb, now eighty-five and still confident of God's sustaining power, claimed the very territory where he had seen the giants. "Now therefore give me this mountain, whereof the Lord spake in that day; for thou heardest in that day how the Anakim were there, and that the cities were great and fenced: if so be the Lord will be with me, then I shall be able to drive them out, as the Lord said" (Josh. 14:12).

10 *EXPERIENCED COUNSELORS*   When the Levites had completed the years of their service in the tent of meeting, their experience and devotion were not completely bypassed. Rather, they were then to "minister to their brethren in the tent of meeting" (Num. 8:26, RSV). Here is a lesson for those who, wishing to serve beyond their more active years, may become counselors, advisers, and encouragers to Christians of the new generation.

ALTAR

11 *ALTARS THAT CHALLENGE*   "And Abram went up out of Egypt . . . even to Bethel . . . unto the place of the altar, which he had made there at the first: and there Abram called on the name of the Lord" (Gen. 13:1, 3–4). Every man has stood before an altar where an initial confession of faith was made, where cleansing baptismal waters flowed, where marriage vows were exchanged. By returning the soul is braced for the dangers and challenges that still lie ahead.

12 *LIFE'S PRIORITY*   Isaac "built an altar [at Beer-sheba] and called upon the name of the Lord, and pitched his tent there. And there Isaac's servants dug a well" (Gen. 26:25, RSV). The sequence is exemplary. That life is blessed which invokes God before settling a new home or undertaking a new responsibility.

13 *PERSONAL INVESTMENT*   After the pestilence which threatened Jerusalem was lifted by the Lord, David sought to purchase the threshingfloor of Araunah the Jebusite in order to build an altar. Araunah wished to give the king all that was needed for the sacrifice of thanksgiving, but David protested, "No, but I will buy it of you for a price; I will not offer burnt offerings to the Lord my God which cost me nothing" (2 Sam. 24:24, RSV).

14 *FIRST AN ALTAR*   After a four-month pilgrimage across the desert sands, the Exiles returned to the city of their fathers; but the desolation seemed to mock their dream of rebuilding the temple. How did they begin their formidable task? "They set up the altar in its place" (Ezra 3:3, RSV).

15 *A LASTING REMINDER*   When the children of Israel heard rumors that the Reubenites, the Gadites, and the half-tribe of Manasseh had erected a strange altar near the Jordan, they presumed that sacrilege was being committed and they armed for war. Bloodshed was averted only after they paused long enough to be told that the altar was raised to remind later generations of their faithfulness. (Josh. 22:10–29.)

AMBITION

16 *THEY SOUGHT A REPUTATION*   "Go to, let us build us a city, and a tower, whose top may reach unto heaven; and let us make us a name" (Gen. 11:4). Ambition is praiseworthy if the purposes and motives of men are consistent with God's will, but the building of Babel was an effort of proud men to win a presumptive reputation. "Except the Lord build the house, they labour in vain that build it" (Ps. 127:1).

17 *THE TOOLS OF AMBITION*   Although Gideon refused to become king, saying that such an appellation belonged only to the Lord, his unscrupulous son Abimelech shared no such humility. To realize his unwary ambition, Abimelech employed cunning propaganda techniques and ruthlessly slew all of his brothers except Jotham. (Judg. 9:1–6.)

ANGER

18 *THE HIGH COST OF ANGER*   Annoyed and perplexed by the continual complaining of the children of Israel who were without water, Moses twice struck a rock with his rod and exclaimed, "Hear now, ye rebels; must we fetch you water out of this rock?" (Num. 20:10). And his anger and disbelief cost him dearly. God denied him that which for so long Moses had cherished, the privilege of leading the people into the land of promise.

19 *THE DEVIL'S FOOTHOLD*   A formula for healthy Christian living requires that we clear our minds and hearts of irritating thoughts and malignant hatreds before we "retire" each night.

"Never go to bed angry—don't give the devil that sort of foothold" (Eph. 4:27, PHILLIPS), or "Do not let sunset find you still nursing [your anger]; leave no loop-hole for the devil" (NEB).

20 *CLOSED DOORS*   When the brother of the prodigal son heard the joyful music and dancing, "he was angry and refused to go in" (Lk. 15:28, RSV) even after his father had invited him to share the festivities. Anger always shuts tightly the doors that open to abundant life.

ANTICIPATION

21 *THE DREAM WAS IN HIS HEART*   David well understood the impossibility of realizing the fulfillment of all one fondly anticipates. "It was in the heart of David my father to build an house for the name of the Lord God of Israel. And the Lord said unto David my father, Whereas it was in thine heart to build an house unto my name, thou didst well that it was in thine heart" (1 Kings 8:17–18). Yet it was because David treasured so noble a dream that Solomon was enabled to bring it to fruition.

22 *AWAITING THE GOLDEN MOMENT*   During the third year of the reign of King Cyrus of Persia a vision came to Daniel as he stood near the Tigris River. "I Daniel alone saw the vision: for the men that were with me saw not the vision" (Dan. 10:7). Why was this vision, so clearly perceived by Daniel, unseen by those at his side? The context records that Daniel had prepared himself for three weeks in anticipation of the golden moment. Preparation and expectation brought to Daniel that which was denied to the unexpectant and unprepared.

23 *COUNTING THE COST*   "For which of you, intending to build a tower, sitteth not down first, and counteth the cost, whether he have sufficient to finish it?" (Lk. 14:28). Whether we build a house or a meaningful Christian life, we must realize that anything worthwhile demands sober forethought, a relinquishing of the trivial to make possible the more desirable, and a willingness to make required sacrifices.

24 *LIVING EXPECTANTLY* The story of Anna, the aging prophetess who was in the temple on the occasion of the presentation of Jesus, is briefly told: a widow now, she was in the temple by day and night where she engaged in the pious disciplines of fasting and praying. Having recognized the Child as God's Messiah, "she kept speaking about Him to all those who were waiting expectantly for the deliverance of Jerusalem" (Lk. 2:38, BARCLAY).

25 *RECEIVED WITH JOY* Is Jesus enthusiastically welcomed into our hearts, homes, communities? After the curing of the demoniac, the Gadarenes besought him to depart from them, and Jesus returned to Capernaum where "the people received him with joy, for they were all waiting for him" (Lk. 8:40, TORREY).

26 *HEARTS TOWARD HEAVEN* "Ye men of Galilee, why stand ye gazing up into heaven?" (Acts 1:11). Their hearts, like those of Christians of every generation, were oriented toward heaven whence they had seen their Lord ascend. The Christian's anticipation of Christ's return, as he promised, has been an undergirding of faith and a stimulus for labors in the Kingdom.

APPEARANCE

27 *WHAT THE LORD SEES* Looking for a successor to Saul, Samuel went to the house of Jesse where "he looked on Eliab, and said, Surely the Lord's anointed is before him." In bearing and stature Eliab was presumably not unlike Saul, whom the Lord had rejected. But Eliab was not the Lord's choice. The Lord said, "Look not on his countenance, or on the height of his stature; because I have refused him: for the Lord seeth not as man seeth; for man looketh on the outward appearance, but the Lord looketh on the heart." (1 Sam. 16:6–7.) Christ said, "Judge not according to the appearance" (Jn. 7:24).

28 *NOT BY HEARSAY* The Lord, who discerns correctly the heart of man, judges in equity and truth. "He will not judge by appearances, nor decide by hearsay" (Isa. 11:3, MOFFATT).

29 *DECEPTIVE APPEARANCES* "Why do bad men prosper? why are scoundrels secure and serene?" (Jer. 12:2, MOFFATT).

Perhaps they aren't, for appearances may deceive. But what if they are? "Better is a little with righteousness than great revenues with injustice" (Prov. 16:8, RSV).

30 *FALSE FACES*   False-face Christians make the most of a proper "Christian appearance." Anyone can see that everything is done with punctilious care. Yet the plumbline of Christ never touches their hearts. "You clean the outside of the cup and dish, while the inside is full of greed and self-indulgence" (Matt. 23:25, PHILLIPS).

31 *FAÇADE PIETY*   After a Pharisee was askance when Jesus did not follow the traditional practice of washing before eating, Jesus denounced façade piety and said that it is better that a man be pure within than that he be too fastidious about outer manifestations of cleanliness (Lk. 11:38–40).

APPRECIATION

32 *TO SPEAK WITH UNDERSTANDING*   The men of Ephraim, their pride sorely taxed, upbraided Gideon for having gone to war without calling upon them for help. A capable military strategist, Gideon was not lacking in those psychological understandings which are essential for leadership. He recalled their past achievements and said, "What have I done now in comparison of you?" (Judg. 8:2). So genuine was his appreciation of their former accomplishments that the anger of the men of Ephraim abated.

33 *DELAYED COMMENDATION*   When Haman was snubbed by Mordecai, he built a gallows on which to hang his enemy. But the approval of King Ahasuerus was not forthcoming. During the night, sleep being a stranger to the king, "the book of records of the chronicles" was read by request in the royal chamber. The records recalled to the king that Mordecai had never received appropriate commendation for having at a previous time saved the king's life. And so the man whom Haman sought to destroy the king delighted to honor. (Es. 5:9–6:11.)

34 *NO PAYMENT NEEDED*   Having been healed of leprosy, Naaman sought ways to repay Elisha. "Now therefore, I pray thee, take a blessing of thy servant." But Elisha adamantly refused: "As the Lord liveth, before whom I stand, I will receive none." (2 Kings 5:15–16.)

35 *TO WHOM APPRECIATION IS DUE*   Every church leader is supported by little-known partners to whom great appreciation is due. "I never think of you without thanking my God, and always whenever I pray for you all I do it with joy, over your co-operation in the good news from the day you first received it until now" (Phil. 1:3–5, GOODSPEED).

ARGUMENT

36 *CONTROVERSY WITH GOD*   "I would speak to the Almighty, and I desire to argue with God" (Job 13:3, AT). And why not? No one else really matters, and if we do not find God's answers, of what value are the words of another?

37 *THE IMPERTINENT CLAY*   Speaking of the impertinence of mortals who quarrel with God, Isaiah said, "Woe to him who strives with his Maker, an earthen vessel with the potter! Does the clay say to him who fashions it, 'What are you making'? or 'Your work has no handles'?" (Isa. 45:9, RSV).

38 *HE AVOIDED CONTENTION*   Water is essential for the maintenance of all life. No less essential—and especially in a nuclear age—is harmony among men and the spirit of conciliation. When Isaac settled in Gerar, his herdsmen dug a well. But the native herdsmen claimed it, saying, "The water is ours." Isaac surrendered his claim. A similar contention followed the digging of a second well. Again Isaac avoided quarreling. But the digging of a third well was uncontested. (Gen. 26:17–22.)

39 *AN ADVERSARY'S GOOD WILL*   The fundamental practicality of the gospel is illustrated in Jesus' teaching that it is better to possess the good will than the ill will of an adversary: "Be quick and make terms with your opponent, so long as you and he are on the way to court, in case he hands you over to the judge, and the judge to the jailer, and you are thrown into prison; truly I tell you, you will never get out till you pay the last halfpenny of your debt" (Matt. 5:25–26, MOFFATT).

40 *THEY MUMBLED ABOUT CHRIST*   "And there was a great deal of grumbling about Him among the crowds, some saying that He was a good man, and others that He was not, but was misleading the masses" (Jn. 7:12, WILLIAMS). These words have a modern echo, for do we not similarly judge any man who tries to invigorate an ancient belief with the transfusion of new truth?

ARROGANCE

41 *THE BOASTING DREAMER*   Jacob's evident preference for Joseph exasperated his brothers beyond measure, yet the bad blood within Jacob's family was intensified, not by any overt action of the father, but by the arrogant boastfulness of Joseph when he related to them his dreams in which they were pictured as weak supplicants bowing before him. (Gen. 37:5–11.)

42 *THE CONSEQUENCE OF INDULGENCE*   "Then Adonijah . . . exalted himself, saying, I will be king: and he prepared him chariots and horsemen, and fifty men to run before him." This behavior is explained by the historian: "His father had not displeased him at any time in saying, Why hast thou done so?" (1 Kings 1:5–6). The son's arrogance apparently increased in proportion to David's indulgence.

43 *THE HOLLOW MEN*   Isaiah described Moab in a manner appropriate not only for proud nations but also for arrogant men: "They are so proud, so insolent, so haughty, so hollow and so loud" (Isa. 16:6, MOFFATT).

44 *DOWNFALL OF THE HAUGHTY*   Uzziah's remarkable achievements, both in war and in peace, spread far his fame, "but when he attained power, he became haughty, and that ruined him" (2 Chron. 26:16, MOFFATT). An old, old story! "Though thou exalt thyself as the eagle, and though thou set thy nest among the stars, thence will I bring thee down, saith the Lord" (Obad. 1:4).

45   THE FOOLISH AXE   The arrogant man, proud in his self-sufficiency and oblivious to the providential care of the Lord, is chided by Isaiah: "Is the axe to boast over the woodman? Is the saw to decry the sawyer? 'Twould be like a club swinging him who lifted it, a staff brandishing a man!" (Isa. 10:15, MOFFATT).

AWARENESS

46   MISSING THE POINT   "Saul's uncle asked, 'Now tell me what Samuel said to you.' And Saul said to his uncle, 'Why, he told us that the asses had been found!' He said nothing about the matter of the kingdom" (1 Sam. 10:15–16, MOFFATT). Saul had been anointed king, but because he was afraid, unimpressed, or skeptical, he spoke only of the animals.

47   SPIRITUAL DIFFIDENCE   Concerning the spiritual diffidence of Judah, Isaiah wrote, "Thou [the Eternal] art in action, and they see nothing" (Isa. 26:11, MOFFATT).

48   AWARENESS OF NEED   Neither wealth nor poverty guarantee spiritual perceptiveness, but either may sharpen a man's awareness of his deeper needs. "The brother who is poor may be glad because God has called him to the true riches. The rich may be glad that God has shown him his spiritual poverty" (Jas. 1:9–10, PHILLIPS).

49   I SAW YOU   No individual is beyond the range of Jesus' heart and eyes. "When Jesus saw Nathanael coming, he said, 'Here is an Israelite worthy of the name; there is nothing false in him.' Nathanael asked him, 'How do you come to know me?' Jesus replied, 'I saw you under the fig-tree before Philip spoke to you'" (Jn. 1:47–48, NEB).

50   NO TOUCH UNNOTICED   Even when crowds of people pressed close to Jesus, he was aware of individuals who had need of him. One woman, plagued for twelve years by sickness, hesitantly reached for the hem of his garment. Jesus turned and said, "Who touched me?" (Lk. 8:45).

BACKSLIDING

51 *HIS WIVES TURNED HIS HEART*   In defiance of the will of God, "Solomon loved many strange women . . . [and] when Solomon was old . . . his wives turned away his heart after other gods: and his heart was not perfect with the Lord his God, as was the heart of David his father" (1 Kings 11:1, 4).

52 *WEAK WITHOUT GOD*   After Delilah had gleaned from Samson the secret of his strength and then had his long locks cut, Samson rose as on previous occasions to defend himself against the Philistines but he was powerless, for "he wist not that the Lord was departed from him" (Judg. 16:20). Few tragedies equal that moment when a man, once strong in the Lord, discovers that his backsliding has left him weak.

BARTER

53 *CONTRASTING PRAYERS*   One of the least-worthy prayers in the Bible was Jacob's offer of loyalty and a tithe in exchange for food, clothing, and an eventual safe homecoming (Gen. 28:20–22). More becoming to an unworthy suppliant was his later petition: "I am not worthy of the least of all thy mercies, and of all the truth, which thou hast shewed unto thy servant" (Gen. 32:10).

54 *A RASH VOW*   Jephthah, sorely pressed by the Ammonites, bartered with God, vowing, "If thou shalt without fail deliver the children of Ammon into mine hands, then it shall be, that whatsoever cometh forth of the doors of my home to meet me, when I return in peace from the children of Ammon, shall surely be the Lord's, and I will offer it up for a burnt offering" (Judg. 11:30–31). Jephthah paid dearly for his foolish vow by which he wished to curry divine favor, for as he returned from battle his daughter and only child came joyously from the door of his home to greet him.

BEAUTY

55 *SHORT-LIVED BEAUTY*   The historian wrote extravagantly concerning the beauty of Absalom—"from the sole of his foot even to the crown of his head there was no blemish in him"— and added that when, at the end of each year, he cut his hair, its weight was 200 shekels by the king's weight. But it was this very head of hair about which he was so vain that at last brought his downfall: "Absalom was riding upon his mule, and the mule went under the thick branches of a great oak, and his head caught fast in the oak, and he was left hanging between heaven and earth, while the mule that was under him went on." (2 Sam. 14:25; 18:9, RSV.)

56 *UNFADING LOVELINESS*   Do clothes make the man? Must beauty be only skin deep? Why do we adorn our bodies according to Fifth Avenue dictates and neglect our souls? "Your beauty should not be dependent on an elaborate coiffure, or on the wearing of jewelry or fine clothes, but on the inner personality—the unfading loveliness of a calm and gentle spirit, a thing very precious in the eyes of God" (1 Pet. 3:3–5, PHILLIPS).

57 *CAMOUFLAGED UGLINESS*   Anointed as king of Israel by an embassy of Elisha, Jehu instigated the downfall of the house of Ahab. Jezebel, knowing that she would be killed, "painted her eyes, and adorned her head" (2 Kings 9:30, RSV), so that in death she might be as physically attractive as possible. But no toiletry could camouflage her inner ugliness, and as Elijah had prophesied, her body was torn apart by dogs.

58 *PROPRIETIES OF BEAUTY*   King Ahasuerus, having become intoxicated at his festive banquet, requested that Queen Vashti come in to exhibit her rare beauty. Sensitive to proprieties, she adamantly refused, although she no doubt knew that her refusal would bring a loss of her crown and position. (Es. 1:10–12.)

BEGINNING

59 *DAY OF SMALL THINGS*   Small beginnings seldom inspire confidence or solicit commendation, and yet no great work is wrought which did not begin as a modest undertaking. To re-build the temple seemed to some people to be incredibly ambitious, but "any who despised the day of small things shall rejoice" when the work is completed and they "behold the final plumb-line in Zerubbabel's hands" (Zech. 4:10, MOFFATT).

60 WATERED GARDENS   The best-laid plans of men topple, that which formerly delighted us becomes ashes on our tongues, and that to which we surrendered our talent and effort is ravished by the despoiler. "I looked, and lo! the garden land was desert" (Jer. 4:26, AT). Then having watched the collapse of the things we gave our lives to, we must "stoop and build 'em up with worn-out tools" (Kipling). But with God's help life may once more "be like a watered garden" (Isa. 58:11).

BENEVOLENCE

61 MARGIN FOR THE NEEDY   An attitude of benevolence toward a man's less fortunate neighbor is encouraged in the Holiness Code wherein the farmer is counseled, "When ye reap the harvest of your land, thou shalt not wholly reap of the corners of thy field" (Lev. 19:9). The rest of the harvest the farmer may claim as the rightful fruit of his labors, but that margin is set aside for the needy.

62 COLD COMFORT   To say "I'm interested, but—" is hollow benevolence. An empty-handed expression of concern is cold comfort. Would you have another person know where your heart lies? Then open wide your hand. "If a fellow man or woman has no clothes to wear and nothing to eat, and one of you say, 'Good luck to you, I hope you'll keep warm and find enough to eat,' and yet give them nothing to meet their physical needs, what on earth is the good of that?" (Jas. 2:15–16, PHILLIPS).

63 GOOD FOR GOODNESS' SAKE   In charitable work persons often do that which is right for the wrong reasons—because charity is expected of them, to win the plaudits of those whom they tell, or perhaps so they won't be pestered further. To do good for goodness' sake was commended by Jesus: "When you do good to other people, don't hire a trumpeter to go in front of you—like those play actors in the synagogues and streets who make sure that men admire them. . . . No, when you give to charity, don't even let your left hand know what your right hand is doing, so that your giving may be secret. Your Father who knows all secrets will reward you" (Matt. 6:2–4, PHILLIPS).

64 *BROADHEARTEDNESS*   A Christian—to employ words from Robert Frost's "Mending Wall"—is a person who "doesn't love a wall" and does not believe that good fences necessarily make good neighbors. More than any other people, Christians have sought to break down or to transcend parochial walls of race and creed. In an instance of broadheartedness worthy of emulation to this day, Peter welcomed the Gentile Cornelius with these words: "Of a truth I perceive that God is no respecter of persons: but in every nation he that feareth him, and worketh righteousness, is accepted with him" (Acts 10:34–35). But the benevolence of Peter did not spring from some sort of natural or spontaneous goodness on his part; it came, rather, from his reading of the mind of humanity's heavenly Father.

BIBLE

65 *REDISCOVERED BOOK*   During the repairing of the temple, the ancient book of the law, so long neglected and now well-nigh forgotten, was brought to light and Josiah made it the foundation stone upon which was built one of the great religious reformations in history (2 Kings 22:8–10). The experience of old has always brought beneficent results to the church and to individuals who rediscover the Word of God and apply it to their immediate circumstance.

66 *BOOK BURNING*   When Jeremiah's scroll was read to King Jehoiakim, he cut it piece by piece with his penknife and threw the scraps into the fire (Jer. 36:20–23). Did he thereby presume to cancel God's Word and judgment?

67 *FOR BIBLE INTERPRETERS*   Long ago Ezra and his associates set a pattern for the interpreting of the Bible. "They read from the book, from the law of God, translating as they went and explaining the meaning, so that the people understood what was read" (Neh. 8:8, MOFFATT).

68 *FAMINE OF THE WORD*   Few more perturbable trage-
dies can beset a people than that of having their Bibles taken from them, and few tragedies equal that of a people who, possessing God's Word, turn from it with obdurate hearts. After Israel had con-
tinually ignored his message and his messengers, God foretold of a famine, not of bread or water, but of hearing the words of the Lord. And at that time the people "shall wander from sea to sea, and from the north even to the east, they shall run to and fro to seek the word of the Lord, and shall not find it" (Amos 8:12).

69 *ONE THOUSAND TONGUES*   The miracle of Pentecost, expressed in the question, "How is it then that we hear them, each of us in his own native language?" (Acts 2:8, NEB), foreshadowed the day when the words of the Bible would be translated into more than one thousand tongues.

70 *LIFE'S MIRROR*   The Bible holds a mirror up to life and reveals our true characters. "The man who simply hears [the Word] and does nothing about it is like a man catching the reflection of his own face in a mirror. He sees himself, it is true, but he goes on with whatever he was doing without the slightest recollection of what sort of person he saw in the mirror. But the man who looks into the perfect mirror of God's Law . . . and makes a habit of so doing, is not the man who sees and forgets" (Jas. 1:23–25, PHILLIPS).

71 *ANY WORD FROM GOD?*   After his counselors and ad-
visers had failed him, King Zedekiah brought Jeremiah from prison and "questioned him secretly in his house, and said, 'Is there any word from the Lord?' " (Jer. 37:17, RSV).

BLAME

72 *THE SOLDIERS DID IT*   Strongly criticized by Samuel for taking spoils after his attack on the Amalekites, Saul answered by weakly throwing the blame upon his soldiers and attributing to them a lame motivation: "The people took of the spoil, sheep and oxen, the chief of the things which should have been utterly destroyed, to sacrifice unto the Lord thy God in Gilgal" (1 Sam. 15:21).

73 BLAMING OTHERS   The ritual of the scapegoat which bore the sins of the people (Lev. 16:7–22) represents a mentality that is strange to us, but not strange to our behavior is our disposition to reject responsibility for our sins and by rationalizing to place blame on others.

BLESSING

74 BLESS ME, TOO!   To Isaac, Esau made this plea: "My father, is that your only blessing? O my father, bless me, bless me too!" (Gen. 27:38, MOFFATT). But Isaac had unwittingly given his blessing to Jacob and, unlike our heavenly Father who blesses each of his children, he had no further blessing to bestow.

75 HOME BLESSING   David wished to take the ark to Jerusalem, but en route, at the threshing floor of Nachon, Uzzah died after he had inadvertently touched the sacred object. Unable to fathom the mystery of Uzzah's death, David left the ark at the home of Obed-edom the Gittite. "And the ark of the Lord continued in the house of Obed-edom the Gittite three months: and the Lord blessed Obed-edom, and all his household" (2 Sam. 6:11). A similar blessing attends him who makes room in his home and heart for God.

76 SATAN'S QUESTION   When the Lord spoke of the goodness of Job, Satan in a jaunty manner—born of a profound understanding of human beings—asked whether Job's steadfastness would continue were God to withdraw his protecting arm. "Hast not thou made a hedge about him, and about his house, and about all that he hath on every side? thou hast blessed the work of his hands, and his substance is increased in the land" (Job 1:10). Remove these blessings and would Job—or we—curse God to his face?

77 FROM CURSES TO BLESSINGS   Balak was mightily annoyed by Balaam. "What is this you have done? . . . I brought you to curse my foes, and here you have done nothing but bless them!" (Num. 23:11, MOFFATT). The love of God transforms our curses into blessings. "The Lord thy God turned the curse into a blessing unto thee, because the Lord thy God loved thee" (Deut. 23:5).

78 *GOD BLESSED HIM*   "The spirit of the Lord came upon David from that day forward. . . . But the spirit of the Lord departed from Saul" (1 Sam. 16:13–14). By disobeying God, Saul lost divine favor, but whatever David did was attended by God's blessings.

79 *RICH FRUIT*   All humanity is indebted to the Jews for their contributions to all fields of endeavor. The promise God made to Abraham has borne rich fruit: "Through you shall all the families of the earth invoke blessings on one another" (Gen. 12:3, AT).

BROTHERHOOD

80 *HIS BROTHER'S KEEPER*   In response to the Lord's question, "Where is Abel thy brother?" Cain replied with casual diffidence, "Am I my brother's keeper?" His question was his indictment, for Abel's blood "crieth unto me from the ground," the Lord said. (Gen. 4:9–10.)

81 *DEEP KINSHIP*   Moses' slaying of an Egyptian who had beaten a Hebrew underscored his instinctive sympathy toward those of his own race. Raised in the palace of Pharoah while his people languished in slavery and given every privilege while they were denied all freedom, Moses nonetheless felt a deep kinship toward his brethren. (Ex. 2:11.)

82 *BUT THEY WERE BROTHERS*   Moses, seeking entry into Canaan by way of Edom, dispatched messengers who made this request of the king of Edom: "Let us pass . . . through thy country: we will not pass through the fields, or through the vineyards, neither will we drink of the water of the wells: we will go by the king's high way, we will not turn to the right hand nor to the left, until we have passed thy borders" (Num. 20:17). The coldhearted rejection was doubly cruel, for Edom and Israel were brothers!

83 *STRANGE LOGIC*   A strange and not uncommon logic concerning brotherly responsibility was expressed by Joseph's brother Judah: "What is the good of killing our brother. . . . Come on, let us sell him to the Ishmaelites, instead of doing him violence! He is our brother, our own flesh!" (Gen. 37:26–27, MOF-FATT).

84 *IDENTIFIED WITH HIS BRETHREN*   After David had sinned against Bath-sheba, he ordered her husband Uriah to return to his home from battle. Uriah refused to enter his home, saying, "The ark, and Israel, and Judah, abide in tents; and my lord Joab, and the servants of my lord, are encamped in the open fields; shall I then go into mine house? . . . as thou livest, and as thy soul liveth, I will not do this thing" (2 Sam. 11:11). He had so greatly identi-fied himself with the lives of his brethren that he would not accept privileges denied to them.

85 *MORE THAN A SLAVE*   The brotherhood of Christ tran-scends and obliterates secular distinctions of race and class. Writing to Philemon in behalf of his runaway slave Onesimus, Paul asked that he receive him back "no longer [as] a mere slave but something more than a slave—a beloved brother; especially dear to me but how much more to you as a man and as a Christian!" (Phm. 16, MOFFATT).

86 *BROTHER SAUL*   Ananias thought is was incredible that the Lord should send him to assist Paul. "Lord," he said, "I have heard by many of this man, how much evil he hath done to thy saints at Jerusalem." But the Lord explained, "He is a chosen vessel unto me." Obediently Ananias sought out Paul and addressed him in a manner becoming to those within the Christian fellowship: "Brother Saul." (Acts 9:13, 15, 17.)

87 *THE BRIDGE*   The elders of the Jews, bridging traditional racial animosities, petitioned Jesus in behalf of a sick servant of a certain centurion who had himself exhibited a brotherliness tran-scending barriers of creed and clan. The elders said of the cen-turion, "He loveth our nation, and he hath built us a synagogue" (Lk. 7:5).

BURDEN

88 *BURDEN BEARERS*   The Lord told Moses to select seventy men to assist in his arduous duties. "I will come down and talk with thee there: and I will take of the spirit which is upon thee, and will put it upon them; and they shall bear the burden of the people with thee, that thou bear it not thyself alone" (Num. 11: 17). Not only was Moses thus enabled to share his responsibilities but an opportunity was also given to capable men to become vessels for the Lord's ministry. Many hands not only make work lighter but enrich and broaden the base of operations.

89 *GRIEVOUS YOKE*   The magnificence of Solomon's reign was forged from the great labors and unbearable taxation of the people. When Solomon had died, the Israelites said to Rehoboam, "Thy father made our yoke grievous: now therefore make thou the grievous service of thy father, and his heavy yoke which he put upon us, lighter, and we will serve thee." Rehoboam then consulted his father's advisers who said, "If thou wilt be a servant unto this people this day, and wilt serve them, and answer them, and speak good words to them, then they will be thy servants for ever." But he accepted the advice of a group of his own age who insisted that Solomon's yoke had been too easy. (1 Kings 12:4, 7.)

90 *CAST THY BURDEN*   When the king of Assyria sent a message to Hezekiah, saying that God would not deliver his people, "Hezekiah received the letter of the hand of the messengers, and read it: and Hezekiah went up into the house of the Lord, and spread it before the Lord" (2 Kings 19:14). He did that which God most desires: he shared his problem with the Eternal and his first step was to enter the house of prayer. "Cast thy burden upon the Lord, and he shall sustain thee" (Ps. 55:22).

91 *PRECIOUS CARGO*   "The sons of Kohath . . . were charged with the care of the holy things which had to be carried on the shoulder (Num. 7:9, RSV). Some things are too precious to be assigned to beasts of burden. The good shepherd laid the lost sheep on his shoulder, and the Shepherd of our salvation bore on his shoulder the cross.

CHANCE

92 *NOT BY CHANCE*   Ahab's struggle to capture Ramoth-gilead was his last battle, for "a certain man drew a bow at a venture, and smote the king of Israel between the joints of the harness" (1 Kings 22:34). Yet not by chance did Ahab fall, but according to the will of God as spoken by his prophet Micaiah.

93 *OCCASIONS FOR SERVICE*   When a traveler on the road to Jericho had been ravaged by thieves, it was "by chance" (Lk. 10:31) that a priest, a Levite, and a Samaritan passed the place where he lay. Occasions for loving service are happenstances, not planned nor prepared for except insofar as a man is ever ready to respond to any exigency.

94 *GOD OR CHANCE?*   Such disasters followed the capture of the ark by the Philistines that they prepared a cart that would carry it away from their territory. But to determine whether the ark had actually caused their troubles it was decided that if the cart, drawn by two cows, "goeth up by the way of his own coast to Beth-shemesh, then he hath done this great evil: but if not, then we shall know that it is not his hand that smote us: it was a chance that happened to us" (1 Sam. 6:9). Their dilemma still confronts us: Is life directed by the hand of God or by chance?

95 *CHOOSING A LEADER*   The apostles were unwilling that the choice of Judas' successor be left to chance. Rather, they prayed, "Thou, Lord, which knowest the hearts of all men, shew whether of these two [Barsabas and Matthias] thou hast chosen" (Acts 1:24). Their prayer was followed by the casting of lots. Their method may seem primitive to us, but their emphasis was spiritually invigorating and a worthy example for all who seek leadership for Kingdom tasks.

96 *WHEN MEN TURN FROM GOD*   When men turn from God, superstition often replaces faith and life is surrendered to the caprice of fortune's wheel or the toss of dice. "But ye . . . have forsaken the Eternal, ye . . . ignore his sacred hill, spreading tables to Good Luck, pouring libations to Fate" (Isa. 65:11, MOFFATT).

CHILD

97 *A CHILD'S PROMISE*   God grant that we may see the oak in the acorn—or a forthright Christian leader in the towheaded rascal who pulls the tail of the neighbor's cat or in the freckle-faced girl who whispers annoyingly in church. No child is without some promise. There were those who spoke disparagingly of the Lord of life: "He's only the carpenter's son" (Matt. 13:55, PHILLIPS).

98 *THE MOTHER'S RESPONSE*   When Solomon was confronted by two women who claimed a single child, he determined which was the true mother by proposing to divide the child so that each might claim her share. Then the child's true mother said, "O my lord, give her the living child, and in no wise slay it," but the pretender said, "Let it be neither mine nor thine, but divide it" (1 Kings 3:26).

99 *THE BOY GOD CHOSE*   Goliath taunted the Israelites and challenged them to select a man to engage in combat with him. Saul and his men "were dismayed, and greatly afraid," for they knew none equal to the giant. But tending sheep at Bethlehem was the boy David whom God had appointed to silence the threats of Israel's enemy. (1 Sam. 17:8–11.)

100 *THE KINGDOM'S CHILDREN*   When eager parents pressed forward that Jesus might bless their little children, the disciples rebuked them—"frowned upon them" (PHILLIPS)—thinking, no doubt, that the Master's time was too full to be wasted on children. Even today an individual's value is too often measured by his size, age, or ability to contribute to the church budget. To the first-generation and present-day disciples, Jesus responds, "Let the little children come to me . . . do not hinder them; for it is to those who are childlike that the Kingdom of God belongs" (Lk. 18:16, WEYMOUTH).

101 *IN MY NAME*   When the disciples got into a dispute concerning their individual status, Jesus took the hand of a small child and said, "Whoever receives this child in my name receives me"

(Lk. 9:48, NEB). To help any of God's children is far more important than foolishly and vainly to measure one's greatness.

102 *THE CHILD GROWS*   As a child Samuel "ministered before the Lord" and "grew before of the Lord." Under the tutelage of Eli, "the child Samuel grew on, and was in favour both with the Lord, and also with men." (1 Sam. 2:18, 21, 26.)

103 *SAFE PLACES FOR PLAYING*   To the exiles returning to Jerusalem, the Lord pictured a community wherein "the streets . . . shall be full of boys and girls playing" (Zech. 8:5). Such a description contrasts sharply to the war-ravaged lands of our generation where many children find no safe places for play and are neglected, forgotten victims of man's inhumanity.

104 *FAVORITISM*   Of the factors which contrived to alienate Esau and Jacob, one was paramount: the ill-advised and flamboyant favoritism of the parents: "And Isaac loved Esau, because he did eat of his venison: but Rebekah loved Jacob" (Gen. 25:28).

CHOICE

105 *THE LORD'S SIDE*   Moses' anger was kindled when, descending from the mountain, he found his people worshiping before a golden calf. Moses required a purging of those who had given themselves to a false god. "Then Moses stood in the gate of the camp, and said, Who is on the Lord's side? let him come unto me. And all the sons of Levi gathered themselves together unto him" (Ex. 32:26). His challenge that men make an immediate and decisive choice was not unheeded.

106 *CONFRONTED BY CHOICE*   Every man is confronted by the choice offered by Moses to his people: "Behold, I set before you this day a blessing and a curse; a blessing if ye obey the commandments of the Lord your God, which I command you this day: and a curse, if ye will not obey the commandments of the Lord your God, but turn aside out of the way which I command you this day, to go after other gods, which ye have not known" (Deut. 11:26–28).

107 *ENIGMATIC ALTERNATIVES*   After David had proudly called for a census of his people, the Lord sent the prophet Gad to offer three choices by which his sin should be punished: "Shall seven years of famine come unto thee in thy land? or wilt thou flee three months before thine enemies, while they pursue thee? or that there be three days' pestilence in thy land?" (2 Sam. 24:13). Life sometimes requires that we make a choice from enigmatic alternatives. And with David we can do little more than to make a choice and depend upon the mercies of God.

108 *STRANGE CHOICE*   "Will ye therefore that I release unto you the King of the Jews? Then cried they all again, saying, Not this man, but Barabbas. Now Barabbas was a robber" (Jn. 18:39–40). Is it strange that they chose a contemptible breaker of the peace, who made their very lives perilous and insecure, and rejected the Lord of life? No stranger than when we choose the low road, not the high, or the road leading to death by rejecting the road of life.

CHRIST

109 *CHRISTIANITY MEANS CHRIST*   Christianity means many things to many people, but supremely Christ is Christianity and apart from him Christianity is hopelessly diluted. "Christ is the visible expression of the invisible God. . . . He is both the first principle and the upholding principle of the whole scheme of creation" (Col. 1:15, 17, PHILLIPS).

110 *HIS MISSION*   The mission of Jesus was to rout the devil and to see that he was no longer uncontested and unchallenged; this is our work, too. "The Son of God came to earth with the express purpose of liquidating the devil's activities" (1 Jn. 3:8, PHILLIPS), or "This is why the Son of God appeared, to undo the devil's work" (WILLIAMS).

111 *NO LIMITATIONS POSSIBLE*   The evangelist John did not presume to confine the story of Jesus to the limitations of his manuscript: "There are many other things which Jesus did, the which, if they should be written every one, I suppose that even the

world itself could not contain the books that should be written"
(Jn. 21:25). Nor can we confine Jesus within a book, a creed, or the
walls of a church. He is greater than our small hearts, and each new
generation experiences wonders sufficient to confound the most
skeptical person.

112 SHARING HIS THOUGHTS   No more salutary experience may be claimed by Christians and none charged with greater
obligation than is found in Paul's exclamation, "Our thoughts
are Christ's thoughts" (1 Cor. 2:16, MOFFATT), or "We share the
thoughts of Christ" (GOODSPEED).

113 DO WE KNOW HIM?   How well do we know Jesus? Do
we know him as he wishes to be known? Do we know him personally or only according to the experience of others? "So you have
not come to know me, Philip, in all the time we have been together?" (Jn. 14:9, RIEU).

114 CHRIST'S COMPANIONS   The elders of Israel, amazed
by the boldness of Peter and John whom they knew to be "un-
learned and ignorant men"—that is, untutored according to rab-
binical disciplines—recognized them as being former companions of
Jesus (Acts 4:13). Here is a question to ponder: Do our words and
deeds identify us as men who have found strength and courage
through our association with the living Lord?

115 HIS ATTRACTIVENESS   "The whole town was there,
crowding at the door" (Mk. 1:33, RIEU). The attractiveness of Jesus,
described here by the second Evangelist, prefigures that day when
before him every knee shall bend.

116 WHEN CHRIST CONFRONTS US   "And suddenly all
the town turned out to meet Jesus, and as soon as they saw Him,
they begged Him to move on and leave their neighborhood" (Matt.
8:34, WILLIAMS). Surely this is one of the strangest verses in the gospels, and yet it has an authentic ring. Jesus attracts both the devout
and the curious, and when many hear his stern commands and his
call for spiritual transformation, the merely curious do not wish
him to upset their easy routines. When a man confronts Christ—or
is confronted by him—live-and-let-live is no longer possible.

117 *CROWDED OUT*   Jesus, in whom our faith and hope of eternal salvation resides, is crowded out of our busy lives. "The man who had been cured did not know who it was; for Jesus had passed out unnoticed, there being a crowd in the place" (Jn. 5:13, WEYMOUTH).

118 *HE CANNOT BE HID*   Evil-intentioned men have tried to blot Jesus' name from history, and well-meaning persons have unintentionally obscured him in the labyrinths of theological speculation. But the ageless testimony is that neither time nor circumstance can escape his presence. When Jesus entered a home, hoping to find solitude for rest and meditation, a needy woman found him for "he could not be hid" (Mk. 7:24).

119 *HIS INITIATIVE*   Jesus made a suggestion which Zacchaeus would have felt unworthy to make for himself. "Zacchaeus . . . I must be your guest today" (Lk. 19:5, PHILLIPS). When in unworthiness men hold back, Jesus takes the initiative.

120 *BLESSED ARE THE EMBARRASSED*   From his birth in a manger to his death on a cross, Jesus must surely have been an embarrassment to many whose names were in the social register or who thought that God must do things with a divine punctiliousness. Even today there are those who would, had they been Jesus, have done things differently. Jesus was aware of such reservations: "Blessed is he who is repelled by nothing in me!" (Matt. 11:6, MOFFATT), or "Happy the man who finds no fault in me" (RIEU).

121 *WE SAIL WITH HIM*   "[Jesus] saith unto them, Let us pass over unto the other side. . . . And there were also with him other little ships" (Mk. 4:35–36). On the seas of life we, like the other little ships, may claim Jesus as our companion.

CHRISTIAN

122 *SLAVES OF CHRIST*   "It was in Antioch that the disciples were first given the name of 'Christians'" (Acts 11:26, PHILLIPS). The labors of Paul and Barnabas at last bore fruit, and the fellowship became recognized by outsiders as a distinct group and given a nickname—for millions since then a badge of highest honor—which identified them as "slaves of Christ." Dr. Goodspeed reminds us that to be a Christian meant to be a partisan of Christ or a member of Christ's party.

123 INVESTMENT IN CHRIST   A Christian, after a manner of speaking, puts all his eggs in one basket; he invests his time and strength—his whole life and living—in Christ and his Kingdom. "The Realm of heaven is like treasure hidden in a field; the man who finds it hides it, and in his delight goes and sells all he possesses and buys it" (Matt. 13:44, MOFFATT).

124 WORLD UPSETTERS   The opponents of Paul and Silas hurled at them words which seem especially befitting of all Christians: "These men . . . have turned the world upside down" (Acts 17:6, RSV). Christians should not be those who conform to worldly behavior. Their responsibility is to turn the world right side up.

125 RULE OF THE SAINTS   To the Corinthian Christians, who were having difficulty keeping their own house in order, Paul said, "Do you not know that the saints [Christians] are to manage the world?" (1 Cor. 6:2, MOFFATT). Who can estimate how greatly the lives of noble Christians have permeated human experience and influenced even the counsels of nations?

126 INTERRELATED LIVES   The mutual and interrelated responsibilities and privileges of Christians are suggested by Paul: "The God of all comfort . . . comforts me in all my distress, so that I am able to comfort people who are in any distress by the comfort with which I myself am comforted by God" (2 Cor. 1:4, MOFFATT).

127 WHAT MOST COUNTS   Treadmill spiritual behavior, bereft of living meaning, is an inadequate substitute for vigorous Christianity. "Circumcision counts for nothing, uncircumcision counts for nothing; obedience to God's commands is everything" (1 Cor. 7:19, MOFFATT).

128 ALL OR NOTHING   We are Christians—or we are not. One-day-a-week Christianity or Christian behavior in one area of life and not in another is a privilege we may not claim. "Whoever obeys the whole law, except to slip in a single instance, is guilty of breaking it all" (Jas. 2:10, WILLIAMS), or "Remember that a man who keeps the whole Law but for a single exception is none the less a Law-breaker" (PHILLIPS).

129 *CHRIST WILL REMEMBER THEM* Within the Kingdom are innumerable saints who do not ostentatiously parade their achievements nor claim credit or praise, but Christ will remember them: "I will give him a white stone inscribed with a new name, unknown to any except him who receives it" (Rev. 2:17, MOFFATT).

CHURCH

130 *FRONTIER SETTLEMENT* Paul wrote to the Philippian Christians, "We are a colony of heaven" (Phil. 3:20, MOFFATT). Each church is a frontier settlement in the divine expansion which shall continue until "Jesus shall reign where'er the sun does his successive journeys run" (Watts).

131 *A HOUSE UNTO THY NAME* So completely engaged was David in wresting a strong kingdom from his warring neighbors that he was forced to bequeath to Solomon the building of a house unto the Lord. Solomon determined to fulfill his father's work: "Behold, I propose to build a house unto the name of the Lord my God, as the Lord spake unto David my father, saying, Thy son, whom I will set upon thy throne in thy room, he shall build a house unto my name" (1 Kings 5:5).

132 *MEASURING THE CHURCH* By what measuring rod and by whose calculations are our churches to be judged? "Then I was given a measuring rod like a staff, and I was told: 'Rise and measure the temple of God and the altar and those who worship there'" (Rev. 11:1, RSV). How do we measure up?

133 *MISSED OPPORTUNITY* Jotham "did what was right in the eyes of the Eternal . . . except that he did not make his way into the temple of the Eternal. (The nation still went wrong.)" (2 Chron. 27:2, MOFFATT.) The historian's parenthetical judgment might well have been otherwise had the just king regularly attended services in God's house and thereby through his example have persuaded his people to attend.

134 *EXPRESSION OF FELLOWSHIP* From the daily life of the early Christians comes a pattern worthy of emulation by Christians of every generation: "They met constantly to hear the apostles teach, and to share the common life, to break bread, and to pray. . . . With one mind they kept up their daily attendance at the temple, and, breaking bread in private houses, shared their meals with unaffected joy, as they praised God and enjoyed the favour of the whole people" (Acts 2:42, 46–47, NEB). So comprehensive an expression of fellowship and faith makes pale the halfhearted witness of men in our day who often tend to limit their spiritual concerns to the eleven o'clock hour on Sundays.

135 *HOUSE FOR ALL PEOPLE* The church of an all-loving God frequently becomes a sanctuary for those who measure up to such-and-such standards or are "my kind of people." An ancient law declared vindictively, "No Ammonite or Moabite shall enter the gathering of the Eternal; no one belonging to them, even down to the tenth generation, shall ever enter the gathering of the Eternal" (Deut. 23:3, MOFFATT). But Isaiah—in words which Christ repeated—said, "Mine house shall be called an house of prayer for all people" (Isa. 56:7; cf. Mk. 11:17).

136 *NO FRONT RUNNERS* A Christian is a VIP in the eyes of the Lord, but he should make no such claim for himself. The church is no place for social climbers and seekers after status, authority, prestige, and power. No individual should seek to be front runner. "Christ is the head of the church" (Eph. 5:23). Within the early church there was a disruptive person: "Diotrephes, who likes to put himself first" (3 Jn. 9, RSV).

137 *ARE WE SAFE?* Christians who attend church, perhaps regularly, and yet give no evidence of spiritual cleansing make a mockery of the hymns they sing and the prayers they recite. The Lord condemned the people of Israel who "steal, murder, and commit adultery, swear falsely, offer sacrifices to the Baal, and run after other gods . . . and then come and stand before me in this house which bears my name, and say, 'We are safe'" (Jer. 7:9–11, AT).

138 *MINIMAL REQUIREMENTS*   The Kingdom of Christ is wide open to all who will accept the responsibilities which membership entails. In the parable of the wedding guests, the king came upon one man who was not dressed for the occasion: "My friend . . . how did you get in here without wedding clothes?" (Matt. 22:12, RIEU). We ought not to make admission to Christ's fellowship so easy that a man does not meet the minimal requirements of a change of heart and an unswerving love of the Master.

139 *CONGENIAL TO HIS NATURE*   Joseph and Mary, having lost track of Jesus in Jerusalem, wondered where they might find him. He was in the place which was most congenial to his nature. In the temple he was speaking with the learned men, for they were the keepers of his Father's house. (Lk. 2:42–49.)

140 *BEYOND CHURCH WALLS*   Solomon wished that the house of God might be magnificent, "for great is our God above all gods." But Solomon realized that God could not be confined to four upright walls. "Who is able to build him a house, seeing the heaven and heaven of heavens cannot contain him?" (2 Chron. 2:5–6.) The king's spiritual perspective was right, for "the whole earth is full of his glory" (Isa. 6:3) and even the human heart may be his temple (1 Cor. 3:17).

COMMITMENT

141 *NO INWARD COMMITMENT*   The outward display of splendor of Solomon's kingdom was such that the Queen of Sheba said, "It was a true report that I heard . . . of thy acts and of thy wisdom. Howbeit I believed not . . . until . . . mine eyes had seen it" (1 Kings 10:6–7). Yet lacking an inward commitment to God, his kingdom lost its glitter and Solomon became at last a morally bankrupt individual.

142 *THEY COMMITTED THEMSELVES*   "You have become a model for all believers in Macedonia and in Achaia. From Thessalonica the word of the Lord rang out; and not in Macedonia and Achaia alone, but everywhere your faith in God has reached men's ears" (1 Thess. 1:7–8, NEB). These radiant words show not only that

Paul was not hesitant to give credit where warranted but also that these Christians—"you turned from idols, to be servants of the living and true God" (v. 9)—took seriously the life to which they had committed themselves.

143 *WITH WHAT RESPONSE?* Not everyone who hears the proclamation of the gospel is permanently enriched. For some there is a momentary stir of excitement, but soon they return to their former routines; others accept the gospel joyfully, but the word finds no lasting rootage in their hearts; still others cannot really become too interested, for their lives are encumbered with transitory concerns; but there are those who, having embraced the gospel heart and soul, find in it a meaning and purpose for life. These various responses are characterized by Jesus in the parable of the soils. (Lk. 8:4–8.)

144 *ACCORDING TO THY WORD* When told by an angel concerning the Child to be born to her, Mary of Nazareth doubted not and humbly accepted the privilege of becoming God's vessel. "Behold the handmaid of the Lord," she said; "be it unto me according to thy word" (Lk. 1:38).

COMMONPLACE

145 *ONLY MANNA* The Lord never guarantees that faithfulness will be rewarded by an abundance of sensual delights. In the wilderness the children of Israel complained, "There is nothing at all, besides this manna, before our eyes" (Num. 11:6). The ordinariness of the diet which God provided became wearisome and commonplace. They hankered for the delicacies of Egypt. They had yet to realize that the rewards of living in their promised land would become more palatable to their hearts than the fleshpots of the Nile.

146 *COME AND SEE* "Nazareth! . . . can anything good come from Nazareth?" (Jn. 1:46, NEB). Nathanael's question reveals the kind of thinking that identifies goodness with spectacular origins, favorable circumstances, and the blare of trumpets. Yet from the least likely and most common situations God brings forth beauty and purpose, like a mighty tree from a worthless-looking seed, a gorgeous sunrise from the dull morning skies, and a man mighty in power from a squatter's hovel. Philip's answer is sufficient: "Come and see."

147 JOSEPH'S SON   After Jesus had read from the prophet Isaiah in the synagogue at Nazareth, "there was a general stir of admiration; [the people] were surprised that words of such grace should fall from his lips. 'Is not this Joseph's son?' they asked" (Lk. 4:22, NEB). Willing to laud the achievements of those who come from afar, we suspect that something has gone awry when a home-town boy makes good.

148 TAKEN FOR GRANTED   In their day-by-day associations with Jesus, the disciples took for granted many things. Only with later reflection did they fully comprehend that to which they had given slight attention. "When Jesus was glorified, then they remembered" (Jn. 12:16, RSV).

149 MISSING THE OBVIOUS   The things to which Paul testified in his defense before the Roman governor Festus and King Agrippa seemed incredible to the Roman, but Paul said that surely Agrippa as a Jew should have understanding of them. Said Paul, "I do not believe that he can be unaware of any of these facts, for this has been no hole-and-corner business" (Acts 26:26, NEB). Often that which is most obvious is least closely observed.

COMPASSION

150 HEART OF A FATHER   However greatly God was pained by the sin and disobedience of Adam and Eve, his fatherly heart responded to their need and "unto Adam also and to his wife did the Lord God make coats of skins, and clothed them" (Gen. 3:21). With loving-kindness he tailored their wardrobes for their new life east of Eden.

151 WHEN A BABY WEPT   The mother of the child Moses read well human nature. Although ruthless hands were killing all Hebrew children, she knew that neither race nor color would keep the daughter of Pharoah from being compassionate when a baby wept. (Ex. 2:5–6.)

152 GROWTH IN COMPASSION   A seemingly coldhearted and highhanded governmental policy is recorded in Gen. 47:14–26 wherein Joseph exchanged bread and seed for the cattle, land, and labor of the victims of an Egyptian drought. A comparison of that ancient practice with the present-day concern of government for the welfare of people testifies eloquently to the growth of Christian compassion.

153 THE CHRISTIAN'S RESPONSE   "Men at ease sneer at the unfortunate; when a man falters, there are blows for him" (Job 12:5, MOFFATT). This is true along Main Street. Empathy is the Christian's response to another's difficulties. "Who is weak, and I am not weak? who is offended, and I burn not?" (2 Cor. 11:29). "Be ye all of one mind, having compassion one of another, love as brethren, be pitiful, be courteous" (1 Pet. 3:8).

154 THE SHEPHERD REJOICES   Having been criticized for eating with sinners, Jesus told of a shepherd who left ninety-nine sheep that he might seek for the one hundredth that had been lost. So overjoyed was he when his efforts were rewarded that he invited his neighbors to share his good fortune. (Lk. 15:4–10.) The Good Shepherd rejoices whenever a sinner repents.

155 LET ME DO THIS MUCH   When the mob came to arrest Jesus, his friends asked, "Master, shall we use our swords?" Forthwith, one of them brandished his sword and cut off the ear of a servant of the high priest. Jesus, whose compassion was not left in Galilee nor shown only toward those who loved him, said, "Let me do this much!" and he touched the ear and healed it. (Lk. 22:49–51, GOODSPEED.)

COMPLAINT

156 IF THE LORD BE WITH US   When the Lord called him, Gideon complained that the Lord had apparently abandoned his children. "O my Lord, if the Lord be with us, why then is all this befallen us? and where be all his miracles which our fathers told us of?" And the Lord responded as though to say that Gideon's call was proof of God's watchful care. "Go in this thy might, and thou shalt save Israel from the hand of the Midianites: have not I sent thee?" (Judg. 6:13–14.)

157 GOD'S REBUTTAL   "Your words have been hard against me," the Lord said to his people. They asked how, and the Lord enumerated three specific criticisms which wrong-headed people—then and now—make. " 'It is useless to serve God,' and 'What gain is it to do his bidding, to walk in penitent garb before the Lord of hosts? It is the worldly, we find, who are well off; evildoers prosper, they dare God—and they escape!' " (Mal. 3:13–15, MOFFATT.)

158 CALL ME MARA   At times most individuals know the distress of Naomi: "Call me not Naomi [pleasant], call me Mara [bitter]: for the Almighty hath dealt very bitterly with me. I went out full, and the Lord hath brought me home again empty" (Ruth 1:20–21).

159 COMPETING WITH HORSES   Everything seemed to be going all wrong for the young prophet Jeremiah: his life had been threatened, the wicked seemed to be prospering, and the unrighteous were not punished. When he complained, the Lord said, "If you have raced with men on foot, and they have beaten you, how will you compete with horses?" (Jer. 12:5, AT). How could the prophet in later years withstand mightier adversaries if he now so easily became downhearted?

COMPROMISE

160 SERVING TWO MASTERS   The historian wrote concerning the emigrants placed in the Northern Kingdom by the king of Assyria, "They worshipped the Eternal and they also served their own gods" (2 Kings 17:33, MOFFATT). Perhaps they knew no better, but present-day Christians who in a similar fashion attempt to serve two masters usually give a perfunctory lip service to God and give their hearts and their hands to the strange gods of vanity, profit, and social fashion.

161 *ONE GOD OR ANOTHER* One difficulty which confronted Jeroboam when he attempted to strengthen his hold on the Northern Kingdom was the desire of the people to worship at Jerusalem. So the king "made two calves of gold, and said unto them, It is too much for you to go up to Jerusalem: behold thy gods, O Israel, which brought thee up out of the land of Egypt" (1 Kings 12:28). To say that one god is as efficacious as another is not dissimilar to the manner of many who compromise genuine values for the sake of self-interest.

CONFIDENCE

162 *BASED ON EXPERIENCE* The young shepherd David confronted Goliath with a confidence born of experience: "The Lord that delivered me out of the paw of the lion, and out of the paw of the bear, he will deliver me out of the hand of this Philistine" (1 Sam. 17:37).

163 *SONGS IN THE NIGHT* "Where is God my Maker, who gives men songs of gladness in the night?" (Job 35:10, MOFFATT). When life is shrouded with turmoil and despair—the dark nights of the soul—the faithful man is confident. "Thou hast visited me in the night" (Ps. 17:3). "In my heart there rings a melody . . . with heaven's harmony . . . of love" (Roth).

164 *WE WILL BUILD* Though the walls of Jerusalem lay in ruins, Nehemiah was confident that God would bless the efforts of his people: "The God of heaven, he will give us success; so we his servants will start to build" (Neh. 2:20, MOFFATT).

165 *GOD'S CONFIDENCE IN US* Satan protested that Job reverenced God because of the many advantages religion offered. Given another circumstance and Job would blaspheme. And God took up the gauntlet! "Behold all that [Job] hath is in thy power" (Job 1:12). Would God have an equal confidence in us? Our candle flickers. Our arrow ricochets. "The evil which I would not, that I do" (Rom. 7:19). "I am not worthy that thou shouldest come under my roof" (Matt. 8:8). "God be merciful to me a sinner" (Lk. 18:13).

166 *SERENITY BORN OF FAITH*   Neither fear, apprehension, pain, nor regret was discernible in the face of Stephen as he gave his courageous testimony to the members of the Sanhedrin. "All that sat in the council, looking steadfastly on him, saw his face as it had been the face of an angel" (Acts 6:15). Such serenity is born of deep faith and confidence.

CONSECRATION

167 *THE ROD IN HIS HAND*   When the Lord commissioned him, Moses began to recite his inadequacies. The Lord said, "What is that in thine hand?" Moses replied, "A rod." (Ex. 4:2.) So it was that the Lord chose a shepherd's staff to be an instrument for the saving of the Hebrew people. God asks only that a man put into use those things which he possesses. By a holy transformation such things become divine vessels.

168 *HERE AM I*   After Isaiah accused himself of being a man of unclean lips, a seraphim touched his lips with a glowing coal from the altar, and the prophet, his sins forgiven, responded to the Lord's words, "Whom shall I send, and who will go for us?" by exclaiming, "Here am I; send me" (Isa. 6:8).

169 *NOT MY FEET ONLY*   To be completely Christian is to consecrate heart, flesh, spirit, time, talents, pocketbook, purposes, and goals to God. After Peter had perceived the deeper significance of Jesus' washing of his feet, he exclaimed, "Lord, not my feet only, but also my hands and my head" (Jn. 13:9).

170 *A GOD-MADE SIGN*   Paul emphasized the inwardness of true religion: "The true Jew is one who belongs to God in heart, a man whose circumcision is not just an outward physical affair but is a God-made sign upon the heart and soul, and results in a life lived not for the approval of man, but for the approval of God" (Rom. 2:29, PHILLIPS).

CONTENTMENT

171 *TIME TO MOVE ON*   Contentment with the status quo discourages progress. After the children of Israel had tarried over-long in the relative security of Mount Horeb, the Lord said, "Ye have dwelt long enough in this mount: turn you, and take your journey. . . . Behold, I have set the land before you: go in and possess the land" (Deut. 1:6, 8).

172 *THINGS-AS-THEY-ARE*   Amos condemned self-centered and proud leaders who were content with things-as-they-are and were unmindful of the needs of the people. "Woe to those who are at ease in Zion, and to those who feel secure on the mountain of Samaria, the notable men of the first of the nations, to whom the house of Israel come!" (Amos 6:1, RSV).

173 *OPPORTUNITY FOR SERVICE*   Contentment is not the absence of difficulty and trouble but rather the opportunity of doing worthwhile things and finding a place in the sun for work and service. "I know how to live humbly; I also know how to live in prosperity. I have been initiated into the secret for all sorts and conditions of life . . . in Him who strengthens me, I am able for anything" (Phil. 4:12–13, MOFFATT).

CONVERSION

174 *A NEW HEART*   After Samuel anointed Saul, the prophet said, "The spirit of the Lord will come upon thee, and thou . . . shalt be turned into another man." And when Saul "had turned his back to go from Samuel, God gave him another heart." (1 Sam. 10:6, 9.) God always gives a new heart to those who commit themselves to his Kingdom.

175 *THE MASTER'S TOUCH*   A halfway conversion will not give a spiritual vision of 20-20. After Jesus had touched the eyes of the blind man of Bethsaida, the man said, "I see men; but they look like trees, walking." A second time Jesus touched his eyes and "he looked intently and was restored, and saw everything clearly."

(Mk. 8:24–25, RSV.) Christian conversion may come with sudden splendor and then soon wane. The second touch of the Master's hand, and the third and fourth, may be needed before the heart is completely illumined.

176 *READY TO RECEIVE*   To close one's mind to the testimony of another may be to shut out God from life. The Jews in Beroea were more openhearted than many whom Paul and Silas encountered, for when the apostles had spoken of their confidence that salvation was in Christ, "they were perfectly ready to receive the Word and made a daily study of the scriptures to see if it was really as Paul said" (Acts 17:11, MOFFATT).

CONVICTION

177 *GOD OF OUR FATHERS*   When God spoke to Moses "out of the midst of the [burning] bush," he identified himself by saying, "I am the God of thy father, the God of Abraham, the God of Isaac, and the God of Jacob" (Ex. 3:4, 6). Our confidence in God is according to the faith of our fathers and our trust is a lengthened shadow of their convictions.

178 *BECAUSE OF HIS CONVICTIONS*   Among a strange people Daniel maintained the integrity of his faith and "retained his position till the first year of King Cyrus" (Dan. 1:21, AT), or for a period exceeding threescore years. He prospered, not in spite of his convictions, but because of them.

179 *THE HOPE YOU CHERISH*   Hiding one's Christian convictions under a bushel will extinguish them. Faith grows and becomes vibrant when it is interpreted and explained to others, defended, and propagated. Be "always ready to make your defence to any one who asks from you a reason for the hope which you cherish" (1 Pet. 3:15, WEYMOUTH).

180 *ALMOST PERSUADED?*   During his defense before Festus and Agrippa, Paul rose to the opportunity of winning them to Christ. Responding to Paul's eloquent plea, Agrippa, speaking perhaps words of biting sarcasm, responded, "Almost thou persuadest me to be a Christian" (Acts 26:28), or "At this rate . . . it won't be long before you believe you have made a Christian of me!" (MOFFATT), or "You think it will not take much to win me over and make a Christian of me" (NEB), or "Much more of this, Paul . . . and you will be making me a Christian!" (PHILLIPS). Agrippa may have been deeply moved, but not sufficiently enough to share Paul's magnificent obsession.

CO-OPERATION

181 *EACH INDIVIDUAL IMPORTANT*   The tribes of Reuben and Gad, discovering fertile grazing lands on the near side of the Jordan, petitioned Moses for permission to settle there. Moses said that the welfare of the community is dependent upon the co-operative energies of each individual: "Shall your brethren go to war, and shall ye sit here?" He further recognized the psychological truth that the enthusiasm of the group diminishes when individuals withdraw their assistance: "Wherefore discourage ye the heart of the children of Israel from going over into the land which the Lord hath given them?" (Num. 32:6–7).

182 *HEARTS AND HANDS TOGETHER*   Wishing to flee from inevitable disaster, "the sailors sought to escape from the ship and lowered the dinghy into the sea under the pretext of stretching out anchors from the prow, [but] Paul said to the centurion and to the soldiers, 'If these men do not stay in the ship, you cannot be saved' " (Acts 27:30–31, C. S. C. WILLIAMS). Weathering a calamity of whatever kind requires co-operation and the binding together of all hearts and hands.

183 *CO-OPERATION FOR EVIL—AND GOOD*   Because of their co-operation in evil—the making of idols—Isaiah described as stupid and inconsequential the effort of his people: "Every one helps his neighbor, and says to his brother, 'Take courage!' The craftsman encourages the goldsmith, and he who smooths with the hammer him who strikes the anvil, saying of the soldering, 'It is good'; and they fasten it with nails so that it cannot be moved" (Isa. 41:6–7, RSV). Christians are called to a higher co-operative movement: "We are labourers together with God" (1 Cor. 3:9).

184 *MANY MEN NEEDED*   The work of the Kingdom, like the construction of a Gothic cathedral, requires the labors of many men, extending perhaps through many generations: "I laid the foundation of the house like an expert master-builder; it remains for another to build on this foundation" (1 Cor. 3:10, MOFFATT).

185 *IN JESUS' NAME*   When John, claiming for the disciples an exclusive use of Jesus' name, spoke of one outside of their number who in Jesus' name was casting out evil spirits, Jesus said, "You must not stop him. The man who is not against you is on your side" (Lk. 9:50, PHILLIPS). Help from whatever quarter is needed, and broad-heartedness makes possible the co-operation of all of God's children.

COURAGE

186 *BE OF GOOD COURAGE*   When David's commander, Joab, "saw that the battle was set against him both in front and in the rear," he and his brother Abishai pledged mutual support, shored up their moral courage, and left the final decision in the hands of God: "If the Syrians are too strong for me, then you shall help me," Joab said, "but if the Ammonites are too strong for you, then I will come and help you. Be of good courage, and let us play the man for our people, and for the cities of our God; and may the Lord do what seems good to him" (2 Sam. 10:9, 11–12, RSV).

187 *EXPRESSION OF REVERENCE*   Obadiah, overseer in the house of Ahab, was like a saint in Caesar's household, for when Jezebel was destroying the Lord's prophets he "hid them . . . in a cave, and fed them with bread and water" (1 Kings 18:4). Uncontaminated by an evil environment, Obadiah expressed his reverence with courage and self-sacrifice.

188 *I WILL NOT GO*   The enemies of the Jews did everything imaginable to impede the rebuilding of Jerusalem. They sought to destroy the reputation of Nehemiah by advising him to seek safety within the temple, for this would be an evidence of cowardice. Without knowing of their stratagem, Nehemiah refused their counsel: "Is a man like me to run away? Besides, who would go into the temple, simply to save his life? I will not go in!" (Neh. 6:11, MOF-FATT).

189 *STANDING SIDE-BY-SIDE*   When at last Paul, who had given his life for the Christian fellowship, approached Rome, "the brethren . . . came to meet us as far as Appii forum, and the three taverns." The apostle must surely have been enheartened to know that there would be those to stand at his side when he would appear before Caesar. "When Paul saw [them], he thanked God, and took courage." (Acts 28:15.)

CRITICISM

190 *A PROPHET'S HONOR*   The spirit of God so came upon the young Saul that he joined a company of prophets and prophe-sied among them. "When all that knew him beforetime saw . . . the people said one to another, What is this that is come unto the son of Kish? Is Saul also among the prophets?" (1 Sam. 10:11). Jesus said that "a prophet is not without honour, save in his own country, and in his own house" (Matt. 13:57). The last person in whom we are likely to recognize remarkable achievement is he whom we best know.

191 *CENSORIOUS COMPANIONS*   A new life in Christ re-quires new orientation, direction, and emphasis in thought and be-havior, and this may make former companions restive and abusive. "It astonishes pagans that you will not plunge with them still into the same flood of profligacy" (1 Pet. 4:4, MOFFATT), or "Your former companions may think it very queer that you will no longer join with them in their riotous excesses, and accordingly say all sorts of unpleasant things about you" (PHILLIPS).

CROSS

192 *NO CROSS, NO CROWN*   Paul coveted for King Agrippa, and for all who heard his defense of the gospel, a faith in Christ equal to his own with one reservation—"except for these chains" (Acts 26:29, RSV). But the trials and hardships which Paul did not scorn have become identifications of the Lord's disciples in every generation. The words "No cross, no crown" are written indelibly into Christian experience.

193 JESUS IN THE CENTRE   "They crucified him, and with him two others, one on either side with Jesus in the centre" (Jn. 19:18, RIEU). Between two criminals—how ghastly! and yet how like him to take his place between wretched sinners whom he came to save.

194 CHALLENGE OF THE CROSS   To see Jesus die for the faith his lips proclaimed gave boldness to Joseph of Arimathea and has given heroic courage and derring-do to Christ's followers ever since. After the crucifixion, the "secret" disciple "summoned up courage" (Mk. 15:43, WEYMOUTH) to ask permission to give Jesus a proper burial.

195 HARBINGER   Pilate ordered that the inscription on Christ's cross should proclaim in three tongues—Hebrew, Latin, and Greek—the words "Jesus of Nazareth the King of the Jews" (Jn. 19:19)—a harbinger of that time when the poet's words "O for a thousand tongues to sing my great Redeemer's praise" (Wesley) should be more than realized.

196 CURIOUS BYSTANDERS   The cross of Christ was not raised to arouse a morbid curiosity; it is rather a call to discipleship, commitment, and action. "And they crucified him. . . . And sitting down they watched him there" (Matt. 27:35–36). Having perfunctorily done the job assigned to them, the soldiers sat down and watched him die.

197 PREACHING EMPHASIS   Paul's preaching emphasis was not centered in himself as an interpreter but in the message he proclaimed: "When I came to you, brothers, I did not come and tell you the secret purpose of God in superior, philosophical language, for I resolved, while I was with you, to forget everything but Jesus Christ and his crucifixion" (1 Cor. 2:1–2, GOODSPEED).

CURIOSITY

198 *IRREVERENT PRYING*   When the Philistines restored the ark to the people of God, there was great rejoicing among the men of Bethshemesh. But the Lord "smote the men of Bethshemesh, because they had looked into the ark of the Lord" (1 Sam. 6:19). Their unwarranted curiosity and irreverent prying into that which no man should look upon were indications of a distrust of the Lord's providence. Is it not true that curiosity, a hallmark of an energetic mind, may also lead to skepticism and faithlessness?

DEATH

199 *BORROWED YEARS*   Sick and at the point of death, Hezekiah prayed that God might lengthen his life. And God said, "I will add unto thy days fifteen years" (2 Kings 20:6). What mortal would not cherish a similar reprieve from inevitable death? And did Hezekiah thereafter serve well his gracious and benevolent Creator? No, for in those borrowed years he did that which was displeasing to the Lord.

200 *HOME BURIAL*   Migration into Egypt meant survival for Jacob and his sons. Yet when the hour of his death approached, Jacob caused Joseph to swear that his body would be returned to the land of his fathers for burial among his own people. (Gen. 47:29–31.)

DECEIT

201 *TWISTED MEANINGS*   Not only did Abraham disguise the truth from Abimelech, inferring that his relationship to Sarah was that of sister, not wife, he heightened his guilt by lamely attempting to justify his sin, saying, "Yet indeed she is my sister; she is the daughter of my father, but not the daughter of my mother" (Gen. 20:12).

202 *LEST I DIE FOR HER*   Rebekah was fair to look upon. Her husband Isaac, fearful lest the Philistines, desiring her, would

kill him, made it known that she was his sister. When Abimelech
called upon Isaac to account for his deception, saying, "Behold, of
a surety she is thy wife: and how saidst thou, She is my sister?" Isaac
said, "Lest I die for her" (Gen. 26:9). Perhaps in the flush of new
love, Isaac had pledged to love and to honor her in all exigencies
and under all circumstances. By what strange reasonings does he
now become fearful that he may be called upon to die for her
honor?

203 *OPPORTUNITY FOR PROFIT*   Elisha refused to accept
gratuities from Naaman who had been healed of his leprosy, but
the prophet's servant Gehazi, seizing an opportunity for personal
profit, pursued Naaman who generously bestowed upon him both
silver and garments. When Gehazi returned, Elisha asked, "Where
have you been?" The servant replied, "Your servant went nowhere."
And Elisha, who read accurately weak human nature, said, "Did I
not go with you in spirit when the man turned from his chariot to
meet you?" (2 Kings 5:25–26, RSV.)

204 *ROAD OF DECEIT*   Driven from Judah, David and his
warriors fled into Philistia where he made peace with the Philistine
king, Achish, and led him to believe that he had joined in fighting
the Judahites. So when Achish asked, "Whither have ye made a
road today?" David would enumerate the names of Philistine
enemies. This he did not in fact do, but he did slay any who might
report otherwise to Achish—"Lest they should tell on us, saying, So
did David." (1 Sam. 27:10–11.)

205 *WORKING IN THE DARK*   Isaiah spoke of those who
thought they could obscure their actions from the all-seeing eye of
God: "Woe to the men who hide their plans from the Eternal, working in the dark, and thinking, 'No one sees or knows!' " (Isa. 29:15,
MOFFATT).

206 *ALL'S WELL*   Treating lightly the spiritual sickness of the
people, the false prophets of Israel chanted, "All's well, all's well,"
when, as Jeremiah said, "all is not well" (Jer. 6:14, MOFFATT).

207 *FALSE CLAIM*   When members of the early Christian fellowship voluntarily brought to the apostles what they had and

owned, Ananias retained a portion of the profit from the sale of his property but behaved as though he had withheld nothing. What he owned was, of course, his to share as he wished. He sinned by claiming that everything had been surrendered to the common treasury. (Acts 5:1-7.)

DECISION

208 *I WILL GO* The family of Rebekah desired to keep her with them for at least ten days before she should depart to become Isaac's bride. They asked, "Wilt thou go with this man?" She responded instantly and unequivocally, "I will go." (Gen. 24:58.) Hesitance and procrastination would have been understandable, but her decision was undeterred.

209 *FOOLISH DECISION* After Gideon's worthless son Abimelech had persuaded the men of Shechem to make him king, his brother Jotham in a fable pointed to the folly of their decision. The trees urged in turn the olive tree, the fig tree, and the vine to become king, and each refused, but finally the trees capitulated to the solicitations of the useless bramble that he be named king. (Judg. 9:7-15.)

210 *NOW OR NEVER* Paul received a mixed reception on Mar's Hill. Some, mocking, turned from him; others, intrigued, curious, or diffident, said, "We will hear you again about this" (Acts 17:32, RSV). But those who for whatever reasons delayed their decisions were never given a second opportunity.

211 *HALF AND HALF* Men who lack wholeheartedness refuse to make up their minds and wish for safety's sake to keep a foot in every door. "I hate double-minded men" (Ps. 119:113, RSV), or "I hate men who are half and half" (MOFFATT).

212 *FATEFUL INDECISION* Plagued by indecision and harried by voices that demanded the blood of Jesus, Pilate said limply, "Take ye him, and crucify him: for I find no fault in him" (Jn. 19:6). But his indecision was a momentous decision, and Pilate is the more to be condemned for his failure to insist on the right as he saw it.

DELAY

213 *REST ALONG THE WAY*   "When the cloud tarried long upon the tabernacle . . . then the children of Israel . . . journeyed not" (Num. 9:19). The Israelites were guided through the wilderness by a fiery cloud, but there were days for them, as for us, when pauses for rest, reflection, instruction, and recreation were essential.

214 *HE PAID DEARLY*   "Jacob came safely to the city of Shechem, which is in the land of Canaan . . . and he camped before the city. . . . And . . . he bought . . . the piece of land on which he had pitched his tent" (Gen. 33:18–19, RSV). Before him lay Bethel and reconciliation with Esau, but Jacob delayed his journey and tented near a pagan people. By accepting the company of unbelievers Jacob paid dearly, for Shechem defiled his beloved daughter Dinah.

215 *HIGHER CLAIMS*   After Elijah had cast his mantle upon him, Elisha said, "Pray let me kiss my father and my mother, and then I will follow you." Recognizing the claims of filial devotion, Elijah nonetheless reminded Elisha of the higher claims of God. "Go, but—consider what I have done for you!" (1 Kings 19:20, MOFFATT.)

216 *GOD'S DELAYS*   Nothing in the gospels seems less characteristic of Jesus than his response to the message that his friend Lazarus was sick: "When he heard that he was ill, he stayed two days longer in the place where he was" (Jn. 11:6, RSV). Why this seemingly unkind procrastination? Did Jesus think it was now too late to be helpful? Incredible. Was he exhausted from the pressures made on his strength and time? Never was he too preoccupied to respond to human need. Was he fearful lest his journey to Jerusalem would precipitate his death? Already he had determined to go to Jerusalem, come what may. He delayed only that the power of God might be more vigorously demonstrated. We who want answers *pronto!* to our prayers must also learn that there is an appropriate season and that God's delays are within the context of his greater purpose for our lives.

217 *WHEN I HAVE TIME*   Paul no doubt touched sensitive nerves when he spoke to Felix about righteousness, self-control, and the judgment to come. Felix procrastinated, saying, "For the present, go your way. When I have time I will send for you" (Acts 24:25, BARCLAY). But within a short time he was replaced by Portius Festus, and his opportunity for repentance was forever gone.

218 *NOW IS THE TIME*   The messenger of God speaks deliberately concerning the requirements of the present hour, but some who hear him assume an attitude of after-us-the-deluge as though the message were without pertinence to them. Ezekiel wrote of men who said, "The vision he sees is for a long time ahead; he is predicting about a far-off age" (Ezek. 12:27, MOFFATT). Procrastination within the spiritual realm is fatal. Today's necessities cannot await tomorrow's deliberations. "Now is the accepted time; behold, now is the day of salvation" (2 Cor. 6:2).

DESPAIR

219 *GOD WAS WITH THE LAD*   After Abraham had sent Hagar and the child Ishmael into the wilderness of Beer-sheba, Hagar despaired for the boy's life. She cast him under a bush and went off that she might not see him die. But "God was with the lad" (Gen. 21:20) and not only provided for his needs but also promised that he should one day become the father of a great nation.

220 *HOUSES AND GARDENS*   Surely our generation, during which so many people have been displaced persons, ought to understand the despair of the children of Israel when they were made captives of the Babylonians. All was lost and hope had become a diminished thing! Jeremiah told them that one day they would return to their homeland, but for the meanwhile he prescribed an occupational therapy which is valid for all seasons of unrest and trouble: "Build ye houses . . . and plant gardens" (Jer. 29:5).

221 *WHO CARES?*   The prodigal was in despair in the distant country, for he was in need and "no one gave him anything"

(Lk. 15:16, MOFFATT). If the Christian gospel had reached the people in that country, would they have cared for him?

DIFFICULTY

222 *WHAT COULD HE DO?*   One of the darkest days in David's life was when during his absence the Amalekites raided Ziklag and carried off his wives and the families of his warriors. "David was in serious difficulties; the men spoke of stoning him, for their souls were sore, every man for his sons and daughters." What could he now do? "But David relied on the Eternal his God and took courage." (1 Sam. 30:6, MOFFATT.) And once more the families were reunited.

223 *I AM WITH YOU*   At the time Jeremiah was commissioned to be a prophet the Lord warned him of the difficulties ahead but also promised divine support: "Behold, I make you this day a fortified city, an iron pillar, and bronze walls, against the whole land. . . . They will fight against you; but they shall not prevail against you, for I am with you, says the Lord, to deliver you" (Jer. 1:18–19, RSV).

224 *ON A SNOWY DAY*   The real measure of a hero is his willingness to do a job that needs to be done, not on sunny afternoons only, but also when circumstances are uninviting, difficult, and discomfortable. "Benaiah . . . went down and slew a lion in a pit in a snowy day" (1 Chron. 11:22).

225 *UNCHOSEN CROSSES*   Many times we are burdened with crosses that are not of our choosing. "They found a man of Cyrene, Simon by name: him they compelled to bear his cross" (Matt 27:32). Like Simon, who with his sons embraced the Christian faith, we find that difficulties may become bridges to a great future.

226 *RESISTING GOD*   On the road to Damascus, Paul, breathing fire against the Christians, was confronted by Christ who said, "It is hard for thee to kick against the pricks" (Acts 26:14). Other versions read, "You hurt yourself by kicking at the goad"

(MOFFATT) and "It is not easy for you to kick against your own conscience" (PHILLIPS). Concerning this proverb William Barclay has written:

> When a young ox was first yoked it resented it and tried to kick his way out of the yoke. If it was yoked to a one-handed plough, the ploughman held in his hand a long staff with a sharpened end which he held close to the ox's heels so that every time it kicked it was jagged with the spike. If it was yoked to a wagon, at the front of the wagon there was a bar studded with wooden spikes and if it kicked it only hurt itself. The young ox had to learn submission to the yoke the hard way and so had Paul.*

How difficult it is to resist the will of God!

DISAGREEMENT

227 *RELEVANT COUNSEL*   Discord and disagreement are bound to arise within any group of free individuals and this, of course, includes the church. To such a situation in the Philippian church Paul offered counsel which is still relevant: "I entreat Euodia and I entreat Syntyche to agree in the Lord. And you, my true comrade, lend a hand to these women, I beg of you" (Phil. 4:2–3, MOFFATT).

228 *LIKE CHILDREN PLAYING*   The lack of logic in the criticisms of those who described John the Baptist as being beside himself when he required strictest austerity and yet condemned Jesus for seeming to enjoy life was described by Jesus in terms of small children playing in the market place. One group calls upon another group to play "wedding," but they refuse, wishing rather to play "funeral," and finding themselves unable to play at all because of their silly disagreements. (Lk. 7:31–32.)

DISCIPLESHIP

229 *FISHERS OF MEN*   Jesus appealed to men in a language they could best understand. To Galilean fishermen he said, "Come ye after me, and I will make you to become fishers of men" (Mk.

---

* Barclay, *The Acts of the Apostles* (Philadelphia: Westminster Press, 1953), p. 195.

1:17). To each individual he speaks according to the pattern of his life and the character of his vocation.

230   WHO ARE YOU?   Credentials, please! Having denied that he was the Messiah, Elijah, or a prophet, John the Baptist was asked, "Then who are you? . . . tell us, so that we can give some answer to those who sent us. What have you to say for yourself?" What response should a follower of Christ give? This was John's: "I am the voice of one who cries in the desert, 'Level the way of the Lord.'" (Jn. 1:22–23, MOFFATT.)

231   THE DIFFERENCE CHRIST MAKES   When Christ enters a man's life, deep waters are troubled. There is no such thing as an even-keeled discipleship. If great enthusiasm, deep stirrings, and spiritual revolutions are not indicated, surely he enters in vain. "And as he entered Jerusalem a shock ran through the whole city" (Matt. 21:10, PHILLIPS).

232   ENTRUSTED WITH A MISSION   "Rabbi, we wish you would grant us whatever request we make of you" (Mk. 10:35, WEYMOUTH), or "Master, we should like you to do us a favour" (NEB). The request of James and John has been repeated by Christians ever since, but following Christ offers no guarantee that bagatelles will be given to us on demand. Rather, we are entrusted with a mission and a purpose requiring that we forego unessentials in order that we may claim the world for Christ.

233   NEW IN ALL RESPECTS   More often than not, discipleship calls for a rejection of old, inadequate ways of living, for a new life in Christ must be new in both major outlines and minor details. "Nobody sews a patch of unshrunken cloth onto an old coat, for the patch will pull away from the coat and the hole will be worse than ever" (Matt. 9:16, PHILLIPS).

234   A DISCIPLE BUT SECRETLY   The Evangelists speak generously of Joseph of Arimathea, who contributed a rock-hewn tomb which no doubt he had prepared for himself as the spot where the mortal remains of Jesus might be laid. Yet as we read the chronicle we wonder if perhaps he was the least fortunate of Christ's followers, for he kept his light under a bushel and refrained from an all-out profession of faith. He was "a disciple of Jesus, but secretly for fear of the Jews" (Jn. 19:38).

235 *BADGE OF DISTINCTION*   Paul claimed for himself a spiritual badge of distinction. As Christ's man, he considered himself to be Christ's slave who had struggled valiantly to be worthy of his master. So he boasted, "I carry on my scarred body the marks of my owner, the Lord Jesus" (Gal. 6:17, PHILLIPS), or "I bear the marks of Jesus branded on my body" (NEB).

236 *SYNTHETIC DISCIPLESHIP*   "For we are not, like so many, peddlers of God's word" (2 Cor. 2:17, RSV). Trafficking in spiritual truth, whether for profit or for promotion, represents a sinister and synthetic discipleship in the name of One who "died for all, that they which live should not henceforth live unto themselves, but unto him which died for them" (2 Cor. 5:15).

DISCOURAGEMENT

237 *ONLY I AM LEFT*   After having fled for forty days and nights from the wrath of Jezebel, Elijah went to Mount Horeb where he entered a cave and bemoaned his circumstance: "I, even I only, am left; and they seek my life, to take it away." But the Lord revealed to him, "I have left me seven thousand in Israel, all the knees which have not bowed unto Baal." (1 Kings 19:10, 18.)

238 *GIANTS AND GRASSHOPPERS*   In any worthy endeavor there are difficulties to be faced, hazards to be overcome, and obstacles to surmount—and the fainthearted will fall by the wayside. The majority report of those who surveyed the promised land was discouraging: "And there we saw the giants . . . and we were in our own sight as grasshoppers, and so we were in their sight" (Num. 13:33).

239 *CALLING IT QUITS*   Stung by the hardheartedness and hostility of those whom he sought to save, Jeremiah at least momentarily wished to call it quits. "O that I had in the desert a wayfarers' lodging place, that I might leave my people and go away from them!" (Jer. 9:2, RSV). But he could not abandon the work to which God had called him—nor can we. "We then that are strong ought to bear the infirmities of the weak, and not to please ourselves" (Rom. 15:1).

240 *SHE LOST HEART*   The stories of the splendors of Solomon's kingdom were so extravagant that the Queen of Sheba went to verify them for herself. When she "had seen all Solomon's wisdom, and the house that he had built, and the meat of his table, and the sitting of his servants, and the attendance of his ministers, and their apparel, and his cupbearers, and his ascent by which he went up unto the house of the Lord; there was no more spirit in her" (1 Kings 10:4–5).

241 *FUTILE WARNINGS*   The remnant of Judah, now living in Egypt, said to Jeremiah, "As for the word which you have spoken to us in the name of the Lord, we will not listen to you. But we will do everything that we have vowed, burn incense to the queen of heaven and pour out libations to her, as we did, both we and our fathers . . . in the cities of Judah and in the streets of Jerusalem; for then we had plenty of food, and prospered, and saw no evil." Knowing that God's corrections and punishments had neither humbled nor chastened the people and perceiving the futility of further warnings, in despair and resignation Jeremiah exclaimed, "Then confirm your vows and perform your vows!" (Jer. 44:16–17, 25, RSV.)

DISGUISE

242 *NO HIDING POSSIBLE*   The wife of Jeroboam disguised herself when she went to the blind prophet Ahijah to ask what would become of their sick child Abijah. As she approached, the prophet said, "Come in, thou wife of Jeroboam; why feignest thou thyself to be another?" (1 Kings 14:6). No man can hide his identity when he approaches that Truth who "knoweth the secrets of the heart" (Ps. 44:21).

243 *SAUL AT ENDOR*   Saul disguised himself when he sought guidance from the medium at Endor. (1 Sam. 28:8.) Invariably a person who turns from the ways of true religion feels a need for a disguise of his face and personality.

244 *BATTLE DRESS* After Micaiah had prophesied failure for the attempt of Ahab and Jehoshaphat to take Ramoth-gilead, Ahab sought to frustrate God's will by exchanging clothing with the king of Judah. "I will disguise myself, and enter into the battle; but put thou on thy robes" (1 Kings 22:30).

245 *VESTED INTERESTS* To protect their lucrative trade, self-interested Ephesian businessmen, concerned lest the persuasiveness of Paul should bring to an end their traffic in silver images of Diana, instigated a riot and claimed that their goddess was being brought into disrepute. (Acts 19:23-29.) So their vested interests were garbed in piety.

DOUBT

246 *BAITING A TRAP* During their seige of Samaria the Lord "made the host of the Syrians to hear a noise of chariots, and a noise of horses, even the noise of a great host" (2 Kings 7:6). Fearful that other armies had come to aid the Israelites, they fled pellmell; but Israel's king was disbelieving when he heard of the evacuation. Instead of recognizing God's protecting care of his people, he believed that the Syrians were merely baiting a trap for the destruction of Israel.

247 *TOO GOOD TO BE TRUE* The gracious words which the angel spoke unto Zecharias seemed too good to be true, and he questioned their authenticity. Because of his disbelief, he was denied the privilege of speech until such time as the angel's words should become true. (Lk. 1:18-20.)

248 *HE LOST HIS NERVE* When Peter saw Jesus walking upon the waters, he was emboldened to make a similar attempt and Jesus encouraged him. "Peter stepped down from the boat and did walk on the water, making for Jesus. But when he saw the fury of the wind he panicked and began to sink, calling out, 'Lord save me!' At once Jesus reached out his hand and caught him, saying, 'You little-faith! What made you lose your nerve like that?' " (Matt. 14: 29-31, PHILLIPS). By lack of trust and by surrendering to our doubts, we often miss faith's possibilities.

249 *LIFE'S ANSWERS*   Doubts, apprehensions, perplexities, and fears confound even Christ's most mature servants. To them Paul writes, "Let the peace which Christ gives settle all questionings in your hearts" (Col. 3:15, WEYMOUTH).

250 *FAITH WITH RESERVATIONS*   Faith is a built-in gyroscope which gives stability to life. "The man who trusts God, but with inward reservations, is like a wave of the sea, carried forward by the wind one moment and driven back the next" (Jas. 1:6, PHILLIPS), or "He who oscillates between doubts is like a surge of the sea, wind-driven and blown hither and thither" (BARCLAY).

DUTY

251 *WE HAVE DONE OUR DUTY*   Nothing that man does places an obligation on God; what man does is a duty which he owes to his Maker. Jesus illustrated this truth by telling of a slave who, returning from the fields where he had long labored, did not for a moment think that his master would prepare the evening meal. The most befitting attitude of men, even when they have labored earnestly in the Lord's vineyards, is expressed in these words: "We are unworthy servants; we have only done what was our duty" (Lk. 17:10, RSV).

ENCOURAGEMENT

252 *CONTRARY WINDS*   "Seeing [the disciples] labouring at the oars against a head-wind, [Jesus] came towards them" (Mk. 6:48, NEB). We too must row on rough seas and against contrary winds—but Jesus comes to encourage and assist us. "Just when I need him most . . . Jesus is near to comfort and cheer" (Poole).

253 *FAITH'S ENCOURAGEMENT*   Paul, Christ's great servant, recognized his need for encouragement from those whom he had encouraged. To the Roman Christians he wrote, "I long to see you; I want to bring you some spiritual gift to make you strong; or rather, I want to be among you to receive encouragement myself through the influence of your faith on me as of mine on you" (Rom. 1:11–12, NEB).

ENTHUSIASM

254 *WE ARE ABLE*   Jesus asked the sons of Zebedee, "Are you able to drink the cup that I am to drink?" Unhesitantly, they responded, "We are able." (Matt. 20:22, RSV.) Foolish young men! Little did they understand the portion of sacrifice which would fall to Jesus—and to them. Yet who would begrudge them their enthusiasm? How much more Christlike to be enthusiastic and wholehearted than to pussy-foot and offer all manner of qualifications and reservations.

255 *WHERE HIS ENTHUSIASM LAY*   "Impetuosity" is a word frequently used to describe Peter and thereby, perhaps, to underscore his human weaknesses. For instance, "when Simon Peter heard that it was the Lord, he . . . sprang into the sea" (Jn. 21:7, RSV). None questioned, however, where Peter's enthusiasm lay, and there is something wholesome and invigorating about his spontaneous responses. In our churches we need more, not fewer, persons who possess Peter's impetuosity.

256 *ONE THING MATTERS*   The enthusiasm of the Seventy was at white heat when they returned to Jesus and exclaimed, "Lord, even the devils are subject unto us through thy name." Jesus checked the radiant flush of their initial victories by saying, "In this rejoice not, that the spirits are subject unto you; but rather rejoice, because your names are written in heaven." (Lk. 10:17, 20.) One thing only matters: that God is honored.

257 *SOBER TRUTH*   Festus interrupted Paul's eloquent defense of his faith by shouting "at the top of his voice, 'Paul, you are raving; too much study is driving you mad.'" Paul responded, "I am not mad, Your Excellency . . . what I am saying is sober truth." (Acts 26:24–25, NEB.) Nor was Festus the last to call Christian enthusiasm mere fanaticism or to fail to perceive that the wisdom of God is at variance with worldly logic.

258 *SHORT-LIVED ENTHUSIASM*   "The gods are come down to us in the likeness of men" (Acts 14:11), the people at Lystra said when Paul had healed a lame man, but their enthusiasm was short-lived. Jews from Antioch and Iconium soon persuaded the people to cast stones at Paul and his companion Barnabas.

EQUALITY

259 *FALSE STANDARDS*   In Christ there is neither high nor low, rich nor poor, honored nor dishonored. Such distinctions within the church are foreign to Christ's inclusive love and an evidence that the spirit of the world has corrupted his fellowship. Why then the stir when the high and the mighty promenade down the center aisle? The ancient admonition is still applicable: "My brothers . . . you must never show snobbery. For instance, two visitors may enter your place of worship, one a well-dressed man with gold rings, and the other a poor man in shabby clothes. Suppose you pay special attention to the well-dressed man and say to him, 'Please take this seat,' while to the poor man you say, 'You can stand; or you may sit here on the floor by my footstool,' do you not see that you are inconsistent and judge by false standards?" (Jas. 2:1–4, NEB).

260 *CHRIST LIVES IN ALL*   Christianity recognizes none of the arbitrary designations and labels of class or race. We are one in Christ, or else we do not belong to him. "In this new man of God's design there is no distinction between Greek and Hebrew, Jew or Gentile, foreigner or savage, slave or free man. Christ is all that matters, for Christ lives in them all" (Col. 3:10–11, PHILLIPS).

ESCAPE

261 *NO ESCAPE FROM GOD*   Having fled from the wrath of his brother Esau, Jacob spent a night in a strange wilderness where he dreamed of God's presence. "Surely the Lord is in this place," he said, "and I knew it not" (Gen. 28:16). Neither sinner nor saint may escape from God.

262 *WHAT DOEST THOU HERE?*   His mind beclouded by fears of what the wrathful Jezebel might do to him, Elijah fled to

Mount Horeb where he went into hiding in a cave, an unlikely spot for God's prophet. And the Lord called to him, "What doest thou here, Elijah?" (1 Kings 19:9). Elijah relinquished his fears of the arrow that flieth by day, and the Lord sent him to anoint Hazael as king of Syria, Jehu as king of Israel, and Elisha as his own successor.

263 *AT A DISTANCE*   "Peter followed at a distance, and sat down among some people who had lighted a fire in the middle of the courtyard and were sitting round it" (Lk. 22:54–55, PHILLIPS). In the hour of crisis, when Jesus' need of companionship was greatest, Peter sought comfort and safety. How like those in our generation who sometimes seek even the comfort of the pew or the relative safety of the pulpit when life's roughest struggles are in the market place and on the highway!

264 *ESCAPE IN A BASKET*   Jewish authorities were stung that Paul, who had so vigorously co-operated with them in destroying Christians, should have linked his life with the "enemy." They placed guards at the gate that Paul might be captured, but "the disciples took him by night, and let him down by the wall in a basket" (Acts 9:25). So began the heroic endeavors of the Great Adventurer whose missionary zeal was to face incredible perils and dangers. (2 Cor. 11:16–28.)

EXAMPLE

265 *WITNESS TO THE NATIONS*   Moses appealed to his people to follow the commandments of God so that they might be a witness and example to other nations: "Keep therefore and do them; for this is your wisdom and your understanding in the sight of the nations, which shall hear all these statutes, and say, Surely this great nation is a wise and understanding people" (Deut. 4:6).

266 *NAKED AND BAREFOOT*   Casting aside whatever compunctions he may have had, Isaiah walked through the streets of Jerusalem naked and barefoot for three years that the people might know to what condition they would be reduced if Judah traded reliance upon other nations for dependence on God (Isa. 20:1–6).

267 *STRENGTHENING WEAK BROTHERS*   Most Christians would not point to themselves as being examples worthy of emulation, yet by word and precept we should strive toward a Christlikeness which will encourage and strengthen weaker brothers. To the new Christians in the Philippian church, Paul, a man of genuine humility, wrote, "Let me be your example here, my brothers: let my example be the standard by which you can tell who are the genuine Christians among those about you" (Phil. 3:17, PHILLIPS).

268 *RIGHT AND WRONG*   Whether he cherishes the responsibility or not, the professing Christian by his example sets standards of "right" and "wrong" for his non-Christian brethren. "See that the exercise of your right does not prove any stumbling-block to the weak. Suppose anyone sees you, a person of enlightened mind, reclining at meat inside an idol's temple; will that really 'fortify his weak conscience'? Will it not embolden him to violate his scruples of conscience by eating food that has been offered to idols? He is ruined, this weak man, ruined by your 'enlightened mind,' this brother for whose sake Christ died!" (1 Cor. 8:9–11, MOFFATT).

EXCUSE

269 *"GOOD" REASONS*   Having been beguiled by the serpent to taste the fruit from the tree of knowledge, Eve rationalized that the fruit was appealing as food, aesthetically attractive, and a source of certain wisdom (Gen. 3:6). Usually we can find "good" reasons for doing what our moral sense prohibits.

270 *SEND SOMEONE ELSE*   When the Lord called Moses to lead the children of Israel out of bondage, Moses begged off in words which commonly identify the timid, preoccupied, or indifferent person: "Oh, my Lord, send, I pray, some other person" (Ex. 4:13, RSV).

271 *PROCRASTINATION MEANS DEATH*   To Jesus' invitation that he engage in Kingdom work, one man responded, "Lord, suffer me first to go and bury my father." By this he meant that at some future time, when his father's death would free him from domestic obligations, he would answer Christ's call. Jesus warned that procrastination would bring spiritual death. "Let the dead bury their dead: but go thou and preach the kingdom of God." (Lk. 9:59–60.)

EXPERIENCE

272 *PROVEN WEAPONS*   When David prepared to fight Goliath, "Saul clothed David with his armor; he put a helmet of bronze on his head, and clothed him with a coat of mail." David took up a sword and "he tried in vain to go, for he was not used to them." Removing the king's armor, David "chose five smooth stones from the brook, and put them in his shepherd's bag, in his wallet; his sling was in his hand, and he drew near to the Philistine." (1 Sam. 17:38–40, RSV.)

273 *THE VICTORY EXPERIENCE BRINGS*   Paul spoke of the love that never diminishes nor fades: "What can separate us from the love of Christ? Can affliction or hardship? Can persecution, hunger, nakedness, peril, or the sword?" The apostle had dipped his pen into the ocean of experience and knew whereof he wrote. So with a sense of victory he exclaimed, "I am convinced that there is nothing in death or life, in the realm of spirits or supernatural powers, in the world as it is or the world as it shall be, in the forces of the universe, in heights or depths—nothing in all creation that can separate us from the love of God in Christ Jesus our Lord." (Rom. 8:35, 38–39, NEB.)

274 *SET UP GUIDEPOSTS*   How may we remember the roads by which we have traveled so that in our further journeyings we benefit from our experience? "Put up waymarks, set up guideposts, bethink you of the high road, by which you have travelled hence" (Jer. 31:21, MOFFATT).

275 *SHALL WE QUIT?*   "In this world the race is not won by the swift, nor battles by the brave, nor bread by the wise, nor wealth

by the clever, nor honour by the learned" (Eccl. 9:11, MOFFATT).
Well, not always at any rate. But then no guarantees are woven into
the fabric of our experience, and the deserving are often bypassed
while evil men prosper. What shall we make of such a situation?
Shall we quit the race? "Be thou faithful unto death, and I will
give thee a crown of life" (Rev. 2:10).

EXPLOITATION

276 *EXPLOITING OR STRENGTHENING*   Returning from
a weary day in the fields, Jacob pleaded with his brother, "Feed me,
I pray thee, with that same red pottage; for I am faint," and Esau
replied, "Sell me this day thy birthright" (Gen. 25:30–31). And so,
perhaps in less candid and calloused ways, all men may be separated
between those who take advantage of the needs of their fellows,
exploiting them in their weakness, and those who wish only to
strengthen and to serve.

277 *DOUBLE STANDARD*   To build the house of God, Solomon inflicted bondage upon great numbers of people, "but of the
people of Israel Solomon made no slaves; they were the soldiers,
they were his officials, his commanders, his captains, his chariot
commanders and his horsemen" (1 Kings 9:22, RSV). The double
standard by which Solomon wrought his kingdom is a far cry indeed from the words of Heb. 13:3: "Remember them that are in
bonds, as bound with them."

278 *GOD'S INNOCENT CHILDREN*   "Man's inhumanity to
man" (Burns) is a sorry page in the human story. Not only in faraway generations but also in our times, and not only under foreign
tyrannical rule but also within our nation, God's innocent children
are exploited and sometimes by those who claim the name of Christian. "They sell honest folk for money, the needy for a pair of
shoes" (Amos 2:6, MOFFATT).

279 *PIGS OR MEN?*   After Jesus had purged the demoniac of
Gadarene of evil spirits, the spirits then inhabited a drove of swine.
Startled by the power Jesus demonstrated and acutely aware of
their loss of marketable livestock, the people "began to urge Him

to get out of their territory" (Mk. 5:17, BARCLAY). Did they place a higher premium on the pigs than on rehabilitated human life?

280 PROFITS OR PERSONALITY?   Having more desire for profits than respect for personality, the owners of a slave girl, who possessed the ability to foretell the future, exploited her deficiency. When Paul cast out the evil spirit from the girl, her masters were wrathful and caused the apostle to be cast into prison. (Acts 16:16–24.)

FAILURE

281 THREEFOLD FAILURE   The failure of Judas was three-fold, for he not only betrayed his Lord and his own higher instincts but he also betrayed his brethren who had confidence in him and needed his assistance in their labors. "For he was numbered among us, and was allotted his share in this ministry" (Acts 1:17, RSV). The work of no church member is expendable in the economy of heaven. When we fail to shoulder our share, always there is a vacuum.

282 FAILURE AS A FATHER   The Bible contains few scenes of such heart-rending pathos as when David is informed of the death of Absalom. David lamented, "O my son Absalom, my son, my son Absalom! would God I had died for thee, O Absalom, my son, my son!" (2 Sam. 18:33). In that hour David realized the enormity of his failure as a father.

283 BROKEN SHIPS   Man's best-laid plans often fall short of fulfillment. One such disappointment is recorded in scarcely more than a score of words: "Jehoshaphat made ships of Tharshish to go to Ophir for gold: but they went not; for the ships were broken at Ezion-geber" (1 Kings 22:48).

284 WEAK PEGS   Great hope was expressed for Eliakim when he succeeded Shebna as steward of Hezekiah's palace; but Isaiah, who read clearly human weaknesses, predicted his failure: "The peg that was fastened in a sure place will give way" (Isa. 22:25, RSV).

285 LIVED AND DIED   Tola, who ruled more than a score of years, is commemorated in the Bible with no further words than these: "And he judged Israel twenty and three years, and died, and was buried in Shamir" (Judg. 10:2).

FAITH

286 *COURAGEOUS ADVENTURING*   Faith is not a blind and reckless leap into the black unknown. Rather, it is a truth-seeking and courageous adventuring into untried territory in the confident knowledge that we are guided by One who knows whence we came and whither we go. So it was with trustful assurance that "faith enabled Abraham to obey when God summoned him to leave his home for a region which he was to have for his own, and to leave home without knowing where he was going" (Heb. 11:8, GOODSPEED).

287 *BRIDGE TO GOD*   Nebuchadnezzar told his wise men that they must give him an interpretation of his dream, although he had forgotten what the dream was about. To do this, they said, was impossible. "The king is asking a hard thing, which none can tell him except the gods who dwell not with mortal men" (Dan. 2:11, MOFFATT). But Daniel was able both to tell the dream and to explain its meaning, not because he had more wisdom than other men, but because his faith was a bridge into the presence of God.

288 *BUT IF NOT—*   Because of the refusal of Shadrach, Meshach, and Abednego to worship Nebuchadnezzar's golden image, the king ordered them to be cast into a burning fiery furnace. The Jewish exiles trusted that their God would deliver them, but they determined to remain faithful whatever the consequences. "Our God . . . is able to deliver us. . . . But if not, be it known unto thee, O king, that we will not serve thy gods, nor worship the golden image which thou hast set up" (Dan. 3:17–18).

289 *THE REWARD OF FAITH*   "The disciples returned to their lodgings. But Mary stayed by the tomb and stood weeping outside it" (Jn. 20:10–11, RIEU). We do not know why the disciples left, but we do know that Mary's faithfulness was rewarded, for in a short time a familiar voice was heard, saying, "Mary."

290 *I AM NOT WORTHY* Jesus described the faith of a Gentile centurion as being greater than the faith he had found in all Israel, for when Jesus approached the centurion's house, the centurion bade him say only a word of healing, adding, "Lord, trouble not thyself: for I am not worthy that thou shouldest enter under my roof" (Lk. 7:6).

291 *WHERE IS YOUR FAITH?* Faith in God gave confident stability to Jesus even in the most distressing of circumstances. When a storm raged on the Sea of Galilee, the disciples panicked, but Jesus slept peacefully. The terrified disciples awakened him and exclaimed, "We are perishing!" Jesus asked, "Where is your faith?" (Lk. 8:24–25, RSV.) In the Marcan account, the disciples asked, "Teacher, are we to drown, for all you care?" Jesus responded, "Have you no faith yet?" (Mk. 4:38, 40, MOFFATT.)

292 *IF FAITH DOES NOT HOLD* The people of Judah became terrified when they learned that Syria was in league with Ephraim against them, but Isaiah warned, "If your faith does not hold, you will never hold out" (Isa. 7:9, MOFFATT).

293 *PREACHING AND PRACTICING* Putting what one preaches into actual practice tests the validity of our faith. When leading the Babylonian exiles back to Jerusalem, Ezra showed the kind of faith upon which high religion is always based: "I was ashamed to ask the king for a guard of cavalry to protect us against the enemy on the road, for we had told the king that 'God's favour is kind to all who seek him' " (Ezra 8:22, MOFFATT).

294 *MISSING THE MARK* To insist on a dichotomy regarding faith and works misses by a wide mark Christ's example and invites inordinate speculation. The Christian equation: faith + works = discipleship. "Some one will say, 'You have faith, I have actions: prove to me your faith apart from corresponding actions and I will prove mine to you by my actions' " (Jas. 2:18, WEYMOUTH).

295 *ACCORDING TO YOUR FAITH* The aging prophet Elisha told Joash to smite the ground with arrows. Three times the king did as Elisha had commanded, and then desisted. The prophet said, "Thou shouldest have smitten five or six times; then hadst thou smitten Syria till thou hadst consumed it: whereas now thou shalt smite Syria but thrice" (2 Kings 13:19). The blessings of God come to the extent of one's faith in the largess of God's bounty. "According to your faith be it unto you" (Matt. 9:29).

FASTING

296 *ISAIAH'S COUNSEL*   Fasting, or any religious discipline, may become perfunctory and devoid of true meaning and unproductive of spiritual growth. Listen as Isaiah counsels: "Is not this my chosen fast, the Lord, the Eternal, asks, to loosen all that fetters men unfairly, and to relax its grip, to free poor debtors from their bonds, and break what binds them? It is to share your food with hungry men, and take the homeless to your home, to clothe the naked when you see them, and never turn from any fellow-creature. Then shall light dawn for you, with healing for your wounds" (Isa. 58:6–8, MOFFATT).

297 *NOT LIKE PLAY ACTORS*   The negative character of the common practice of fasting is the result of a misunderstanding of what fasting is and what spiritual benefits may be derived. Listen to Jesus' prescription: "When you fast, don't look like those miserable play actors! For they deliberately disfigure their faces so that people may see that they are fasting. . . . No, when you fast, brush your hair and wash your face so that nobody knows that you are fasting—let it be a secret between you and your Father" (Matt. 6:16–18, PHILLIPS).

FATHER

298 *LEGACY OF EVIL*   The wicked Manasseh bequeathed to his son Amon a legacy of evil. "And [Amon] did that which was evil in the sight of the Lord, as his father Manasseh did. And he walked in all the way that his father walked in, and served the idols that his father served, and worshipped them: and he forsook the Lord God of his fathers, and walked not in the way of the Lord" (2 Kings 21:20–22).

299 *DEAL GENTLY WITH ABSALOM*   David's love for his rebellious son Absalom did not slacken even after their respective forces readied for battle. The hour of reconciliation having passed, David nonetheless said to his leaders, "Deal gently for my sake with the young man, even with Absalom" (2 Sam. 18:5).

300 *A FATHER'S PATTERN*   David's sin against Bath-sheba made it morally impossible for him to reprimand his son Amnon when he sinned against Tamar (2 Sam. 13: 1–20). Seldom is the instruction of a father as persuasive as the manner in which he lives. Paul's injunction is particularly appropriate for fathers: "In all things shewing thyself a pattern" (Tit. 2:7).

301 *JOSEPH OF NAZARETH*   Joseph of Nazareth is mentioned only in a cursory fashion in the Gospels, yet so great was his loving care and concern that Jesus always thought of God as "father." Jesus spoke from an experience nurtured within the home when he asked, "What father among you, if his son asks for a fish, will instead of a fish give him a serpent; or if he asks for an egg, will give him a scorpion?" (Lk. 11:11–12, RSV).

302 *ABRAHAM'S CHILDREN*   "Like father, like son" is, like most proverbs, only partially true. Many a devout father is shamed by a wastrel son. To those who claimed, "Abraham is our father," Jesus responded, "If you were Abraham's children, you would do what Abraham did" (Jn. 8:39, RSV).

303 *NOT AN INDULGENT FATHER*   Although God loved Israel with a particular love, he was not an indulgent father. He did not wink at the people's follies nor turn his face from their sins. "Whom the Lord loveth he chasteneth" (Heb. 12:6). "You alone, of all men, have I cared for; therefore I will punish you for all your misdeeds" (Amos 3:2, MOFFATT). Discipline is an evidence of God's loving concern.

304 *GOD'S DISCIPLINES*   Through his prophet Nathan, the Lord said to David, "I will be his father, and he shall be my son. If he commit iniquity, I will chasten him with the rod of men, and with the stripes of the children of men" (2 Sam. 7:14). God expresses his fatherly love by imposing such disciplines as will make a man recognize divine demands.

FEAR ✓

305 *DO NOT BE AFRAID*   When great armies had come against Jehoshaphat, Jahaziel said, "Thus saith the Lord unto you, Be not afraid nor dismayed by reason of this great multitude; for the battle is not yours, but God's. . . . Ye shall not need to fight in this battle: set yourselves, stand ye still, and see the salvation of the Lord with you" (2 Chron. 20:15, 17). Little Judah had an invincible Ally. "To them that have no might he increaseth strength" (Isa. 40:29).

306 *THE LORD HATH DELIVERED*   When Gideon and his army marched against the Midianites, Gideon was apprehensive lest the superiority of the enemy would be too great. So the Lord bade Gideon to enter stealthily into the enemy camp and "thou shalt hear what they say; and afterward shall thine hands be strengthened to go down unto the host." Within the camp of the Midianites Gideon heard two men speaking. The one related a strange dream and the second interpreted it as meaning that God would deliver unto Gideon the Midian armies. His fears now gone, Gideon returned to his men and said, "Arise; for the Lord hath delivered into your hand the host of Midian." (Judg. 7:11, 15.) If we investigated those situations which we most fear, many of the troubles we anticipate would vanish.

307 *UNREASONABLE WORRIES*   By making a man more receptive to counsel and reasonably cautious, fear may bring beneficial results; but many of our fears lead us to ill-advised and foolish actions, and most of the things we fear do not happen. "David said to himself, 'I shall be killed by Saul some day'" (1 Sam. 27:1, MOFFATT). But he wasn't.

308 *HE RAN FOR HIS LIFE*   After the slaying of the four hundred priests of Baal, Jezebel threatened Elijah, and the prophet, who had fearlessly stood for the Lord on Mount Carmel, "in terror rose and ran for his life" (1 Kings 19:3, MOFFATT).

309 *GOD SHALL FIGHT FOR YOU*   The unexplored and the untried fill our hearts with apprehension and misgivings. The fears of the Israelites as they stood at the threshold of the land of promise are understandable, for the reports had indeed been ominous: "The people is greater and taller than we; the cities are great and walled up to heaven; and moreover we have seen the sons of the Anakims there." But Moses replied with a conviction born of experience: "Dread not, neither be afraid of them. The Lord your God which goeth before you, he shall fight for you, according to all that he did for you in Egypt before your eyes." (Deut. 1: 28–30.)

310 *THE SEA WAS NO MORE*   The fathomless, unpredictable, and mysterious sea was to the Hebrews a source of alarm and fear. The seer of Patmos spoke of the day when the fear of deep waters would be wiped away: "I saw a new heaven and a new earth; for the first heaven and the first earth had passed away, and the sea was no more" (Rev. 21:1, RSV).

311 *HE FEARED THE PEOPLE*   Saul disobeyed the orders of Samuel when he permitted his soldiers to take spoils from the Amalekites. In response to Samuel's criticisms, Saul confessed his guilt and said that the voices of the people had prevailed over the voice of God: "I have sinned: for I have transgressed the commandment of the Lord, and thy words: because I feared the people, and obeyed their voice" (1 Sam. 15:24).

312 *FEARFUL DECISION*   Pilate was of a mind to release Jesus, but his decision was finally determined on the basis of expediency and fear concerning the loss of his position, for the people had shouted, "If you let him go you are no friend of Caesar's. Any would-be king is disloyal to Caesar" (Jn. 19:12, RIEU).

FELLOWSHIP

313 *KINDRED MINDS*   Paul became distressed and discouraged when opposition to him in Corinth reached a crescendo, but in a vision the Lord encouraged him, saying, "Do not be afraid . . . for I myself am with you . . . [and] there are many in this city who belong to me" (Acts 18:9–10, PHILLIPS). Paul was strengthened not only by the remembrance that the Lord was at his side but also by the realization that in Corinth there was a fellowship of kindred minds.

314 *FAR—AND DEAR*   "I wish you could understand how deep is my anxiety for you, and for those at Laodicea, and for all who have never met me" (Col. 2:1, PHILLIPS). The concern of the Christian is not alone for those who are near and dear but also for those who are far—and dear. To those Christian brethren with whom we have not even a nodding acquaintance we send our dedicated offerings and our children as missionaries.

315 *WE NEED FELLOWSHIP*   Solitary Christians are the most hard pressed. We need the encouragement and instruction of the fellowship. "Epaphras, who is one of yourselves . . . always wrestling on your behalf in his prayers, that you may stand firm— Christians of ripe character and of clear conviction as to everything which is God's will" (Col. 4:12, WEYMOUTH).

316 *TWO BY TWO*   "The Lord commissioned seventy other disciples, and sent them off in twos as advance parties into every town and district where he intended to go" (Lk. 10:1, PHILLIPS). The coterie of the Twelve was insufficient for the task; others were called to prepare for Christ's coming. Note that in these labors each was to be accompanied by a companion. The task assigned long ago continues. We, too, "go before the face of the Lord to prepare his ways" (Lk. 1:76).

FINALITY

317 *THE DIE IS CAST*   "Pilate answered, What I have written I have written" (Jn. 19:22). And so it is also that every word we speak, every deed done, and every good ministry accomplished is cast irretrievably into the vortex of time and eternity.

FORGETFULNESS

318 *THE PAST IS PAST*   After Joseph had been sold into slavery by his brethren, separated from his dearly-beloved father, viciously and unjustly accused by Potiphar's sensual wife, and cast into prison for two years, Joseph gained favor with the Pharaoh and was raised to an undreamed-of position of authority in a strange land. The name which was given to the first-born son of Joseph and Asenath, daughter of the high priest at On, acknowledges his faith that by God's grace the past may be forgotten. Joseph explained the child's name—Manasseh: "God . . . hath made me forget all my toil, and all [of the unhappiness associated with] my father's house" (Gen. 41:51).

319 *MEMORIAL STONES*   After the children of Israel had passed over the Jordan, Joshua set up twelve memorial stones, one for each of the tribes, as a memorial lest future generations forget the Lord's deliverance. (Josh. 4:1–9.)

320 *FORGOTTEN COVENANTS*   Hard pressed by trouble or fearful in sickness, we sometimes make covenants with God which are readily dismissed or forgotten when health and fortune return. Besieged by the Babylonians, Hebrew masters sought God's favor by freeing all slaves; but after the crisis had passed, the masters again imposed bondage on their brethren. (Jer. 34:8–16.)

321 *HIS WORK REMAINED*   A city was spared from an attack by a great king because of the counsel of a poor wise man, "yet no one remembered that poor man" (Eccl. 9:15, RSV). Does it really matter that he was forgotten if through him some worthy achievement was accomplished?

FORGIVENESS

322 *THE ENTHUSIASTIC SINNER*   Jesus interpreted the love and forgiveness of God by telling of two men whose debts were written off the books. The one who had owed more loved more ardently his benefactor. In like manner, the sinner whose sins are more numerous will respond more enthusiastically to God's forgiveness. (Lk. 7:41–43.)

323 *JESUS UNDERSTOOD*   When Jesus entered the home of Simon the Pharisee, a woman who had an unsavory reputation

followed him and began to anoint his feet with soothing oil. Simon
was amazed that Jesus did not recognize her as being the kind of
woman she was; but Jesus, whose mind probed the depths of human
experience, understood the woman's regret for her misspent life,
and he both forgave her and bade her leave in peace. (Lk. 7:36–50.)

324 PARTIAL RECONCILIATION   Joab engineered a com-
promised reconciliation between David and Absalom by which
Absalom was permitted to return to Jerusalem, but David said,
"Let him turn to his own house, and let him not see my face"
(2 Sam. 14:24). David could not bring himself to a point of full forgiveness nor to the standard of our Lord: "Forgive us our debts, as
we forgive our debtors" (Matt. 6:12).

325 KEEPING ACCOUNTS   Thank God that he does not
keep an account book of our sins! Nor should we keep accounts of
those who have wronged us. "Peter approached him with the question, 'Master, how many times can my brother wrong me and I
must forgive him? Would seven times be enough?'" (Matt. 18:21,
PHILLIPS). Jesus suggested seventy times seven. Four hundred and
ninety times? No, times without number, if need be, even as God
forgives without reckoning statistically.

326 FATHER AND SONS   Immediately after revealing his
identity to his brothers, Joseph asked a question which had long
been foremost in his thoughts: "I am Joseph; doth my father yet
live?" (Gen. 45:3). Only after having forgiven his brothers was he
able to inquire concerning his beloved father.

327 THE DOORS HE OPENED   The Christians in Jerusalem
were understandably suspicious of Paul, who had so actively worked
to eradicate their faith. Paul might well have been denied accept-
ance into their fellowship had not Barnabas spoken strongly in his
behalf. Barnabas' willingness to forgive and to recognize Paul's
genuine conversion opened doors which twenty centuries have
failed to close. (Acts 9:26–27.)

328 SECOND CHANCE   Remembering that John Mark had
deserted him at Pamphylia, Paul refused to give him a second

chance. But Barnabas was of a different mind, and he accepted Mark as a companion in his mission to Cyprus. (Acts 15:37–39.)

FREEDOM

329 *BARTERED BIRTHRIGHTS* "Thus lightly did Esau value his birthright" (Gen. 25:34, AT). To be sure, Esau was famished. At that moment the claims of the flesh transcended life's deeper, richer values. And we—would we barter our birthrights of free worship, liberty, and constitutional guarantees for safety, security, and glib promises of privilege? "The spirit indeed is willing, but the flesh is weak" (Matt. 26:41).

330 *TANTALIZING OFFERS* The emissary of King Sennacherib tantalized the Judeans with an offer of good things in exchange for their freedom: "Make your peace with me, surrender to me, and then you can eat the fruit of your vine and your fig-tree and drink from your own water-supply, until I come to deport you to a land like your own land, a land of corn and wine, a land of bread and vineyards" (Isa. 36:16–17, MOFFATT).

331 *THOSE WHO APPRECIATE FREEDOM* After a confinement of thirty-seven years in a Babylonian prison, Jehoiachin, king of Judah, was released and "put off his prison garments" (Jer. 52:33, RSV). Does anyone so greatly appreciate freedom as he to whom it has long been denied?

332 *DISCIPLINES OF FREEDOM* A striking lesson for persons who in our day consider too lightly the disciplines which freedom entails is found in the wilderness sojourn of the children of Israel. Overwhelmed by the prospect of their dying at the hands of Pharoah's advancing armies, they cried unto Moses, "Because there were no graves in Egypt, hast thou taken us away to die in the wilderness? wherefore hast thou dealt thus with us, to carry us forth out of Egypt? Is not this the word that we did tell thee in Egypt, saying, Let us alone, that we may serve the Egyptians? For it had been better for us to serve the Egyptians, than that we should die in the wilderness" (Ex. 14:11–12).

333 *SAMUEL'S WARNINGS*   Samuel enumerated the dangers
of a monarchy, but "the people refused to obey the voice of Samuel;
and they said, Nay; but we will have a king over us; that we may
also be like all the nations; and that our king may judge us, and
go out before us, and fight our battles" (1 Sam. 8:19–20). Many of
Samuel's warnings are still valid, but there are some people who
prefer the arbitrary rule of an absolute leader to the disciplines
which democracy imposes.

334 *I WAS FREE-BORN*   After having been chastised and
bound with thongs, Paul appealed to the centurion, saying, "Is it
lawful for you to scourge a man that is a Roman, and uncon-
demned?" The chief captain, who was called in, said, "With a great
sum obtained I this freedom," and Paul, speaking words which still
thrill the hearts of all who cherish their civic privileges, replied,
"But I was free born." (Acts 22:25, 28.)

FRIENDSHIP

335 *LINKED HEARTS*   Wholesome human relations are
based on mutual trust, and friendship thrives only when hearts and
hands are honorably linked. Jehu "greeted [Jehonadab] and said to
him, 'Is your heart true to my heart as mine is to yours?' And
Jehonadab answered, 'It is.' Jehu said, 'If it is, give me your hand.'
So he gave him his hand" (2 Kings 10:15, RSV).

336 *THE ONE HE LOVED*   When David became convinced
that Saul was seeking to destroy him, "Jonathan, Saul's son, went
away to David at Horesha and encouraged him from God" (1 Sam.
23:16, MOFFATT). One of the truly exemplary friends in all spiritual
and secular literature, Jonathan subordinated himself and even
his personal safety to the best interest of the one he loved.

337 *UNDERGIRDING OUR EFFORTS*   Before initiating a
missionary endeavor in Spain, Paul sought the encouragement and
support of trusted friends. "I have been longing for many years
to visit you on my way to Spain; for I hope to see you as I travel
through, and to be sent there with your support after having en-

joyed your company for a while" (Rom. 15:23, NEB). We need always to know that there are those who are undergirding our efforts.

338 *THE COMING OF TITUS*   Discouraged and downhearted—"afflicted at every turn—fighting without and fear within" —Paul was cheered by the arrival of a trusted friend: "But God, who comforts the downcast, comforted us by the coming of Titus" (2 Cor. 7:5–6, RSV).

339 *HE BRACED ME UP*   Paul was richly blessed in his friendships. Of one of his friends, Onesiphorus, he wrote, "Many a time he braced me up" (2 Tim. 1:16, MOFFATT).

340 *INSTRUMENT OF HEALING*   When friends were unable to carry a paralyzed man through the crowd outside of a house in which Jesus was teaching, they mounted the roof, removed a portion of the roofing materials, and lowered the sick man so that Jesus might heal him. (Lk. 5:18–20.) The faith of the invalid's friends was the instrument of healing.

341 *FRIEND OF GOD*   No more splendid or inspiring word is written concerning Moses than that "the Lord spake unto Moses face to face, as a man speaketh unto his friend" (Ex. 33:11). No relationship exceeds that friendship which God offers to his unworthy and undeserving children.

342 *STRANGE FRIENDS*   Jesus has not only been the tie binding men together in Christian love, but also the cord holding those who oppose him. "On that day Herod and Pilate became firm friends, though previously they had been at daggers drawn" (Lk. 23:12, PHILLIPS).

FUTURE

343 *FEAR NOT*   The unknown future and the unknown country toward which Jacob journeyed filled his mind understandably with forebodings and apprehension. Yet his spirit was shored up by the promise of divine companionship: "I am . . . the God of thy father: fear not to go down into Egypt" (Gen. 46:3).

344 *FUTURE COMMITMENTS*   On Mount Sinai the Lord promised Moses that divine blessings would always attend the labors of a consecrated people. God pointed to the past as evidence of future commitments. "Ye have seen what I did unto the Egyptians, and how I bare you on eagles' wings, and brought you unto myself. Now therefore, if ye will obey my voice indeed, and keep my covenant, then ye shall be a peculiar treasure unto me above all people: for all the earth is mine" (Ex. 19:4–5).

345 *GO FORWARD*   At the Red Sea, the children of Israel complained to Moses who replied, "Fear ye not, stand still, and see the salvation of the Lord," but the Lord replied, "Speak unto the children of Israel, that they go forward" (Ex. 14:13, 15). As we wait upon the Lord we are given divine counsel concerning our next step.

346 *FUTURE GLORY*   The Lord urged Jerusalem to prepare for her future glory: "Widen the place for your tent, spare not your canvas, stretch it out; lengthen your ropes, drive in your tent-pegs" (Isa. 54:2, MOFFATT).

347 *INVESTMENT IN THE FUTURE*   At the time when his people were being taken into exile, Jeremiah purchased the field at Anathoth and so expressed his confidence that the land of their fathers would one day be returned to the rightful heirs. (Jer. 32: 6–15.)

348 *IF IT IS GOD'S WILL*   The future is robed in the garments of mystery and uncertainty. "Just a moment, now, you who say: 'We are going to such-and-such a city today or tomorrow. We shall stay there a year doing business and make a profit'! How do you know what will happen even tomorrow? What, after all, is your life? It is like a puff of smoke visible for a little while and then dissolving into thin air. Your remarks should be prefaced with, 'If it is the Lord's will, we shall still be alive and shall do so-and-so' " (Jas. 4:13–15, PHILLIPS). Of one thing only may we be certain—that the love of God embraces our lives in all circumstances.

349 *THE GOOD ROAD*   The old ways, mapped by the Almighty and blazed by men of faith and vision, offer bright prospects for spiritual journeying. "Stand at the cross-road . . . and look for the old path, ask for the good road and take it, so shall you be safe and prosper" (Jer. 6:16, MOFFATT).

350 *TO WHOM THE FUTURE BELONGS*   Although their sojourning in the wilderness had been accompanied by wondrous signs and blessings betokening God's guidance, many of the children of Israel doubted that they should ever claim Canaan as their home. God said concerning them, "Surely they shall not see the land which I sware unto their fathers, neither shall any of them that provoked me see it" (Num. 14:23). The future always belongs to men who "draw near with a true heart in full assurance of faith" (Heb. 10:22).

GENEROSITY

351 *DISINTERESTED GENEROSITY*   When Abraham's servant reached the well near Nahor, Rebekah offered to draw water to quench his thirst. This was a perfunctory courtesy which her people customarily extended to strangers. But the girl's largeness of heart exceeded social requirements. "I will give thy camels drink also" (Gen. 24:14). True benevolence is measured by such actions of disinterested generosity.

352 *HIS HEART WAS HUMBLED*   After Saul realized that David had spared his life on the hill of Hachilah, the king said, "Blessed be you, my son David! You will do many things and will succeed in them" (1 Sam. 26:25, RSV). So the hard heart of Saul was humbled, at least momentarily, by David's generous spirit.

353 *AT THE KING'S TABLE*   The wide angle of David's generous heart repaid Jonathan's kindness by befriending his lame son, Mephibosheth. "He did eat continually at the king's table; and was lame on both his feet" (2 Sam. 9:13). Incomparably richer is our privilege of sitting at the table of the Lord in a fellowship sealed by the love of Jesus Christ.

354 *CHALLENGING STANDARD*   The generosity of the Macedonian Christians represents a challenging standard for Christians of every generation: "They have shown themselves lavishly

open-handed. Going to the limit of their resources . . . and even beyond that limit, they begged us most insistently, and on their own
initiative, to be allowed to share in this generous service to their
fellow-Christians" (2 Cor. 8:2–4, NEB).

355 *THE ONE THING MISSED*   When a ruler asked Jesus
how he might claim eternal life, the Master first ascertained that
he had met the minimal requirements of the law and then, saying,
"There is still one thing you have missed" (Lk. 18:22, PHILLIPS) or
"There is still one thing left for you to do" (RIEU), Jesus challenged
him with the requirement of higher law to bestow with sacrificial
generosity his wealth upon the less fortunate.

356 *GOD'S GENEROSITY*   Freedom belongs equally to those
descended from the earliest settlers and those who recently acquired
citizenship. The church ministers alike to lifelong members and to
him who joined last week. God's generosity is not reckoned by a
clock or a calendar. Jesus told of a farmer who employed men to
work in his vineyard at the first, third, sixth, ninth, and eleventh
hours. At day's end he paid each the same wages. This seemed
preposterously unjust to those who had borne the daylong burden
and naturally they cried, "Unfair!" But the farmer had paid each
according to his contract, and his generosity in nowise shortchanged
those who had labored since dawn. (Matt. 20:1–15.)

GOD

357 *TO SEE GOD'S FACE*   Moses craved the privilege of looking upon that which eye hath not seen—the face of God. "Moses
said, 'Ah, let me see thy majesty!'" (Ex. 33:18, MOFFATT). Of the
righteous it has been written that "they shall walk, O Lord, in the
light of thy countenance" (Ps. 89:15).

358 *STILL SMALL VOICE*   At Mount Horeb the Lord revealed himself to Elijah, not in the fierceness of a wind storm, nor
in the might of an earthquake, nor in the ravagings of a fire, but in
the whisperings of a "still small voice" (1 Kings 19:12).

359 *LIFE'S CENTRAL FACT*   God is the central fact in our
existence; apart from him nothing much matters. "The universe

owes its origin to Him, was created by Him, and has its aim and purpose in Him" (Rom. 11:36, WEYMOUTH).

360 *NONE LIKE HIM*   When Shadrach, Meshach, and Abednego had been delivered from the burning fiery furnace, Nebuchadnezzar, who understood and appreciated power, decreed that no one should speak against their God, for, he said, "There is no other god who is able to deliver in this way" (Dan. 3:29, RSV).

361 *TO THOSE WHO LISTEN*   "Then the Eternal bade Moses give the Israelites this message: 'You have seen for yourselves that I have been talking to you out of heaven' " (Ex. 20:22, MOFFATT). God is not our silent partner; he communicates to all who have the wit and wisdom to listen to his voice speaking through the world he has created, through the lives of men who love him, through conscience, through his Word, and supremely through his Son.

362 *HALF-BAKED*   "Ephraim is a cake not turned" (Hos. 7:8). To leave God out of life's equation is to be half-baked: secular, but not spiritual; body, and no soul; a week without Sunday; a community without a church; a home without an altar; faith without works; works without consecration; life, but no promise of eternal life. "Thou art weighed in the balances, and art found wanting" (Dan. 5:27).

363 *NO SUBSTITUTES*   "They chose new gods" (Judg. 5:8). Catastrophic consequences attend a people who substitute strange gods for the Eternal. No pinch hitter can replace the Lord, and invariably the truth holds firm that if we do not reverence God we become godless.

364 *DON'T CONSULT GHOSTS*   Isaiah has a word for those who turn to fortunetellers and other prognosticators of superstitious lore: "When they tell you to consult mediums and ghosts that cheep and gibber in low murmurs, ask them if a nation should not rather consult its God. Say, 'Why consult the dead on behalf of the living? Consult the Message and the Counsel of God!' " (Isa. 8:19–20, MOFFATT).

365 *THE DIVINE POTTER*   Jeremiah watched the potter at work with his wheel, "and whenever any vessel he was making got spoiled in his hands, he re-moulded it to please himself, till he was satisfied" (Jer. 18:4, MOFFATT). This became for the prophet a picture of the divine Potter who reworks human clay according to his will and purpose.

366 *THE LORD IS ABLE*   After the prophet said that God would punish Amaziah of Judah for hiring mercenaries to fight for him, "Amaziah said to the man of God, But what shall we do for the hundred talents which I have given to the army of Israel? And the man of God answered, The Lord is able to give thee much more than this" (2 Chron. 25:9).

367 *A PLACE NEARBY*   "Behold, there is a place by me where you shall stand upon the rock" (Ex. 33:21, RSV). The Lord's words to Moses are an invitation to all of his children who pray, "Cast me not away from thy presence" (Ps. 51:11).

368 *HE WAS GOD'S CHOICE*   Gideon considered himself to be a poor choice to lead God's people: "Oh my Lord, wherewith shall I save Israel? behold my family is poor in Manasseh, and I am the least in my father's house." But the Lord assured him, saying, "Surely I will be with thee, and thou shalt smite the Midianites as one man." (Judg. 6:15–16.)

369 *CALLED FROM THE PLOW*   God calls his servants from every walk of life. When Elijah cast his mantle upon him, Elisha was plowing behind twelve yoke of oxen. (1 Kings 19:19.)

370 *BRING ANOTHER WITH YOU*   When God calls us, he expects us to become those through whom others in turn are called. "The Lord called Moses to the top of the mountain, and Moses went up. . . . And the Lord said to him, 'Go down, and come up bringing Aaron with you" (Ex. 19:20, 24, RSV).

371 *UNDER ORDERS*   When Amaziah accused Amos of treason and bade him take his prophecies elsewhere, Amos said, "I am no prophet, nor a prophet's son; but I am a herdsman, and a dresser of sycamore trees, and the Lord took me from following the flock, and the Lord said unto me, 'Go, prophesy to my people Israel' " (Amos 7:14–15, RSV). The quarrel with Amaziah was not of Amos' choosing. Amos was a man under orders, and he could neither close his ears to God's directives nor refrain from speaking the truth despite the consequences.

372 HOW GOD PROVIDES   Elisha told the widow of a member of his prophetic circle, whose creditor demanded that her children become his slaves, that she should borrow vessels into which she should pour oil from the single jar in her house. The oil continued to flow as long as there were other vessels at hand, and she was thereby enabled to pay what she owed. (2 Kings 4:1–7.) In like manner God provides to the limit of our faith.

373 THE FOURTH FIGURE   After Shadrach, Meshach, and Abednego had been cast into the burning fiery furnace for refusing to worship Nebuchadnezzar's golden image, the king was alarmed that not only were the three unharmed but also that with them was a fourth figure who in appearance was "like a son of the gods" (Dan. 3:25, RSV). The Psalmist said, "[The Lord] shall give his angels charge over thee, to keep thee in all thy ways" (Ps. 91:11). Christ said, "I am not alone, for the Father is with me" (Jn. 16:32).

374 BUNDLE OF THE LIVING   Abigail said to David, "The life of my lord shall be bound in the bundle of the living in the care of the Lord your God" (1 Sam. 25:29, RSV). Few figures in the Bible more picturesquely identify God's protection of his human children. As a person ties together loose corners that a treasure may not be lost, so God gathers up that which is precious to him.

375 CLAIMING GOD'S BLESSINGS   Only by doing those things which are consistent with God's will may we claim his blessings. "When ye spread forth your hands, I will hide mine eyes from you: yea, when ye make many prayers, I will not hear" (Isa. 1:15).

376 THE WORD IS NIGH   That man has at hand the capacity of knowing and accomplishing the will of God was emphasized by Moses: "This commandment . . . is not hidden from thee, neither is it far off. It is not in heaven, that thou shouldest say, Who shall go up for us to heaven, and bring it unto us, that we may hear it, and do it? Neither is it beyond the sea, that thou shouldest say, Who shall go over the sea for us, and bring it unto us, that we may hear it, and do it? But the word is very nigh unto thee, in thy mouth, and in thy heart, that thou mayest do it" (Deut. 30: 11–14).

377 *DIVINE GEOGRAPHY*   Believing that the Lord was a God of the hills only, the Syrians proposed fighting the Israelites on the plains. Then a man of God said to Ahab, "Because the Syrians have said, The Lord is God of the hills, but he is not God of the valleys, therefore will I deliver all this great multitude into thine hand, and ye shall know that I am the Lord" (1 Kings 20:28). The mentality of the Syrians who limited the geography of God's sovereignty is not unlike those of our day who conceive of God as Lord of the Sabbath but not of weekdays or as God of a particular race or nation but not of all mankind.

378 *TALKING BACK TO GOD*   Paul argued for God's absolute sovereignty in these words: "Who are you, sir, to answer God back? Can the pot speak to the potter and say, 'Why did you make me like this?' Surely the potter can do what he likes with the clay" (Rom. 9:20–21, NEB).

379 *THE GODS WHO LEFT*   The words of Isaiah are an authentic echo of spiritual truth: "O thou Eternal, our own God, others have been ruling us; but thine authority alone to-day we own. These lords are dead and gone, ghosts that return no more" (Isa. 26:13–14, MOFFATT).

380 *BLANK CIPHERS*   Isaiah affirmed the sovereignty of God in these unforgettable words: "Lo! the nations are like a drop from a bucket, like fine dust in the scales are they counted. . . . All the nations are as nothing before him, blank ciphers he counts them" (Isa. 40:15, 17, AT).

381 *THE BARED ARM*   "All nations have seen the Eternal bare his sacred arm for action, and all ends of the earth shall see how our God gains the victory" (Isa. 52:10, MOFFATT). In wonders beyond reckoning God demonstrates both his power and his love to those who have the wit and wisdom to see and understand. "O Lord God of hosts, who is a strong Lord like unto thee?" (Ps. 89:8).

GOSPEL

382 *REMEMBER MY FETTERS*   Paul closed his letter to the Colossians with the words, "Remember my fetters" (Col. 4:18, RSV). He did not complain because of the chains which bound him; rather he hoped others would remember that he considered the gospel to be worthy of any price which was required.

383 *IF THE BUGLE SOUND*   The gospel needs to be so articulated that none will be confused or misled. Paul urged the need for a profitable interpretation of tongues, for, he said, "If the bugle does not sound a clear call, who will prepare for battle?" (1 Cor. 14:8, GOODSPEED).

GUIDANCE

384 *THE HAND THAT GUIDES*   "And the Lord went before them by day in a pillar of a cloud, to lead them the way; and by night in a pillar of fire, to give them light; to go by day and night" (Ex. 13:21). Even as our spiritual ancestors were guided by God, so are we not without God's guiding hand as found in the Bible, the triumphant church, and the enlightened conscience.

385 *A HEAVENLY LIGHT*   On the road to Damascus, a light not of this world blinded Paul, and he was transformed from a Christ-hater to a Christ-lover. The future, about which Paul had had such certain plans, now seemed foreboding. "Trembling and astonished [Paul] said, Lord, what wilt thou have me to do? The Lord said unto him, Arise, and go into the city, and it shall be told thee what thou must do" (Acts 9:6). Henceforth, he would be guided by invisible hands and would move forward according to divine orders.

386 *THE BROOK DRIED UP*   That upon which we depend for security and peace does not last forever, but God's guidance

never comes to an end. The Lord told Elijah to dwell by the Brook
Cherith where "thou shalt drink of the brook." There he found
respite, but "it came to pass after a while, that the brook dried up."
(1 Kings 17:4, 7.) When the waters ceased, God led Elijah to a
widow whose cruse of oil needed no replenishment.

387 *THE WHISPERING VOICE*   "When you swerve to right
or left, you hear a Voice behind you whispering, 'This is the way,
walk here' " (Isa. 30:21, MOFFATT). When we are attentive, God will
direct through love to obedience. "Shew me thy ways, O Lord; teach
me thy paths" (Ps. 25:4).

388 *STAR-LED LIVES*   "Now the star, which they had seen in
the east, went in front of them as they traveled" (Matt. 2:9, PHIL-
LIPS). Star-led lives are divinely guided even in life's darkest hours,
and they come at last—for God "made the stars also" (Gen. 1:16)—
even unto him who is the bright and morning star.

389 *FALSE GUIDES*   Habakkuk taunted makers of idols who
expected to be guided by that which their own skill had designed
and carved. "Woe to him who prays a wooden thing to 'waken,'
bids a dumb stone 'rise'! Can that give any guidance, cased in gold
and silver as it lies, no breath of life within? What use is it to
carve an image, to mould an image—a false guide?" (Hab. 2:18–19,
MOFFATT).

390 *THE LORD ANSWERED NOT*   Encamped at Gilboa opposite the army of the Philistines, Saul "was afraid, and his heart
greatly trembled." He sought divine guidance, but "the Lord answered him not, neither by dreams, nor by Urim, nor by prophets."
In desperation Saul then turned from true religion and sought
guidance from a medium at Endor. The tragedy of Saul's loss of
contact with God was heightened by the fact that he himself had
previously outlawed all mediums from his kingdom. (1 Sam. 28:5–6.)

GUILT

391 *FURTIVE GLANCES*   When Moses killed an Egyptian
who had beaten a Hebrew, he who later was to mediate the com-

mandment, "Thou shalt not kill" (Ex. 20:13), knew that he did wrong. Only after he had "looked this way and that way" (Ex. 2:12) to determine that no one was watching did he slay the Egyptian.

392 CLOUDED MINDS   Many years after they had sold Joseph into slavery, his brothers' minds were still clouded by guilt. Every difficulty made them fearful and every trouble seemed to them to be a mark of condemnation of their sin. "And they said one to another, We are verily guilty concerning our brother, in that we saw the anguish of his soul, when he besought us, and we would not hear; therefore is this distress come upon us" (Gen. 42:21).

393 THEY COULD NOT BLUSH   Greater than sin is such callousness as makes a man feel no shame. Of the religious leaders of his day, Jeremiah asked, "Are they ashamed at their abominable deeds?" And he answered his own question: "Not they! They know not how to blush." (Jer. 6:15, MOFFATT.)

394 THE PENALTY THEY DRAG   Sins which have mastered lives are described imaginatively by Isaiah: "Woe to those who draw guilt on themselves by stout ungodliness, as with a rope, and drag the penalty of sin upon them, harnessing themselves to it!" (Isa. 5:18, MOFFATT).

395 GUILT BY ASSOCIATION   The raising of Lazarus was so obviously an indication of Jesus' power that "the chief priests laid plans to put Lazarus also to death; because by reason of him more and more of the Jews were believing on Jesus" (Jn. 12:10–11, TORREY). Biblical and subsequent history shows that the enemies of Jesus believe in guilt by association. "I saw the souls of them that were beheaded for the witness of Jesus, and for the word of God [but] they lived and reigned with Christ a thousand years" (Rev. 20:4).

HAND

396 INTO THE HANDS OF GOD   In anguish David said, "I am in a terrible difficulty . . . let me fall into the hands of the

Eternal (for his mercies are many), not into the hands of men"
(1 Chron. 21:13, MOFFATT). David sought the protection of the
gentle hands which had from clay fashioned his life, the strong
hands which cradle "the soul of every living thing" (Job 12:10), and
the loving hands to which the Psalmist and our Lord committed
their spirits (Ps. 31:5; Lk. 23:46).

397 *THE LONG REACH*   Almost as though his words were
charged with incredulous astonishment by their disbelief, the Lord
asked the exiles, "Is my hand shortened, that it cannot redeem?"
(Isa. 50:2, RSV). Too short? "The hand of our God is upon all them
for good that seek him" (Ezra 8:22). His hand reached to a manger
in Bethlehem and reaches in blessing according to our sorest need.

398 *THE HAND STRETCHED TO ME*   "Then I looked,
and there was a hand stretched out to me" (Ezek. 2:9, MOFFATT).
The hand that offered the prophet a scroll extends to us all that is
needful for the welfare of body and spirit.

399 *BEHOLD MY HANDS*   The Lord promised that he would
always remember the children of Israel: "Yet will I not forget thee.
Behold, I have graven thee upon the palms of my hands" (Isa.
49:15–16). Can we forget the love of One who said, "Behold my
hands" (Lk. 24:39)?

400 *THEY KNEW HIM!*   The Stranger in the home at Emmaus was known, not apparently by the words he spoke, but by
the manner in which he broke bread. "Their eyes opened wide and
they knew him!" (Lk. 24:31, PHILLIPS). Had they seen his nail-
scarred hands or was it the way those sensitive hands with reverent
gratitude broke the bread as in a divine blessing upon the morsel?

HARDHEARTEDNESS

401 *THE CALLOUS BROTHERS*   The hardheartedness of
Joseph's brothers is to be found not so much in their contriving to
kill him or to assign him to a lifelong slavery as in the callousness
with which they whetted their appetites while he remained in the

pit. "They . . . cast him into a pit. . . . And they sat down to eat bread" (Gen. 37:24–25).

402 *PITY FOR THE GOURD*   After the Ninevites had listened attentively to Jonah's message, the hardhearted missionary went outside the city and waited to see if Nineveh would be spared. The Lord caused a gourd to grow up and shade Jonah. When, however, the gourd withered, Jonah's miseries were compounded. Then the Lord pointed out to Jonah the folly of his prejudice. "Thou hast had pity on the gourd, for the which thou has not laboured, neither madest it grow . . . and should not I spare Nineveh, that great city, wherein are more than sixscore thousand persons that cannot discern between their right hand and their left hand?" (Jon. 4:10–11).

403 *THE KING WHO WORE BLINDERS*   After Haman had urged King Ahasuerus to decree that all Jews be destroyed, Mordecai put on sackcloth and ashes, but he could not enter the king's gate "for no one might enter the king's gate clothed with sackcloth" (Es. 4:2, RSV). Shielded from evidences of discontent and mourning, the king was spared from facing reality.

HEALING

404 *TO WHOM SHALL WE TURN?*   In his old age "Asa's feet became diseased; the disease was very painful, and Asa had recourse to his physicians, not to the Eternal" (2 Chron. 16:12, MOFFATT). How like so many of us! We in our age of science are dependent on men of medicine, but so often God seems unrelated to medical science. Asa was deprived of knowing the words of the great Physician which can never be erased from Christian teaching: "Thy faith hath made thee whole" (Matt. 9:22).

405 *THE WRONG PHYSICIAN*   When Ahaziah tumbled from his roof, he dispatched messengers to ask Baal-zebub concerning his recovery. The messengers were intercepted by Elijah who reprimanded the king for consulting a pagan deity instead of Israel's God. (2 Kings 1:2–8.) Ahaziah was not the last person who in a crisis turned from the true God to seek his fortunes at the hands of false gods and pseudo-prophets.

406 *USEFUL LABOR*   Having been abandoned on the island of Malta, Paul immediately became engaged in the useful labor of healing the sick, apparently without thought concerning his own welfare or whether the people were worthy of his efforts. (Acts 28:8-9.)

407 *THE POWER HE GIVES*   Some people believed that merely by touching Jesus they would be cured of their infirmities. (Lk. 6:19.) That power which was resident in Jesus is even now communicated through those whose lives find their strength in him.

408 *SWEET WATERS*   God provides healing for the bitter experiences of life. In the wilderness of Shur the children of Israel murmured because the drinking water was bitter, and the Lord showed Moses a tree which, when cast into the waters, made them sweet. (Ex. 15:23-25.) "The leaves of the tree were for the healing of the nations" (Rev. 22:2).

409 *THE ACCEPTABLE PUBLICAN*   A false self-evaluation may cause a man to become insensitive to divine healing and unresponsive to the quickening influences of the Spirit. The Pharisee who told God how good he was erected a wall of conceit between himself and the Eternal. The publican who confessed his sins and claimed for himself no self-righteousness returned to his home accepted by God. (Lk. 18:9-14.)

HEARING

410 *WHAT THEY HEARD*   In Gethsemane Jesus poured out his soul in prayer and commitment—and God responded. "A voice came from heaven. . . . The crowd standing by heard it and said that it had thundered" (Jn. 12:28-29, rsv). God spoke, but some heard only a loud noise!

411 *TINGLING EARS*   After the child Samuel had responded to the Lord, "Speak, for thy servant hears," the Lord said, "Behold,

I am about to do a thing in Israel, at which the two ears of every one that hears will tingle" (1 Sam. 3:10–11, RSV). A rare sensation? Not for them who have attuned their hearing to the wonderful words which God speaks.

412 *WORDS THAT DEMORALIZE*   When the emissary of King Sennacherib demonstrated that Judah was no match for the massed armies of Assyria, the Judean leaders, realizing that his words would demoralize the common people, begged, "Pray, speak to your servants in Aramaic . . . do not speak to us in the language of Judah within the hearing of the people who are on the wall" (Isa. 36:11, RSV).

HEAVEN

413 *WINDOWS TOWARD HEAVEN*   "You must put windows in the barge, eighteen inches from the roof" (Gen. 6:16, MOFFATT). Noah's ark was not completely closed in, for through lofty windows the members of the family were able to gaze toward God.

414 *STEPS UNTO HEAVEN*   "He took of the stones of that place, and put them for his pillows, and lay down in that place to sleep" (Gen. 28:11). Away from the comforts of home, Jacob had to make do with that which was available. Yet in that desolate and uncomfortable place he found rest for his troubled mind and, as the hymn says, "steps unto heaven."

HELPFULNESS

415 *STRANGER AND EXILE*   When David had fled from Jerusalem during Absalom's rebellion, Ittai the Gittite came to him with six hundred men. David said, "Wherefore goest thou also with us? . . . Thou art a stranger, and also an exile." Ittai, expressing a concern for righteousness and justice which transcend national boundaries, said, "As the Lord liveth, and as my lord the king liveth, surely in what place my lord the king shall be, whether in death or life, even there also will thy servant be." (2 Sam. 15:19, 21.)

416 *SHE ASKED FOR NO FAVORS*   Elisha was given food and lodging by a wealthy Shunammite woman whose motive was merely to help a man of God. When Elisha inquired what he might do in return, even to speaking a word in her behalf to the king or the commander of the army, she humbly replied, "I am quite safe, among my own kinsmen" (2 Kings 4:13, MOFFATT). Such disinterested generosity was commended by Christ: "It is more blessed to give than to receive" (Acts 20:35).

417 *A CHRISTIAN'S INITIATIVE*   Christ's followers should take the initiative in helping those who are unable to help themselves. A man who had been sick for thirty-eight years said to Jesus, "Sir, I have no man to put me into the pool when the water is troubled, and while I am going another steps down before me" (Jn. 5:7, RSV).

418 *HALLMARK OF DISCIPLESHIP*   Arguing that philanthropy encouraged a weakening of a virile self-reliance, Emerson asked, "Are they *my* poor?" The Christian witness unhesitatingly affirms that the strong must strengthen their weaker brethren. Within the early Christian community mutuality was a hallmark of discipleship, and distribution from a common treasury "was made unto every man according as he had need" (Acts 4:35).

419 *HE FOLLOWED THROUGH*   The good Samaritan did not respond to the tragedy of the man who fell among thieves with an attitude of do-what-you-can-and-leave-the-rest-to-God. Not only did he bandage the victim's wound and take him to a wayside inn, but he also followed through by providing for the man's recovery in hospitable surroundings and promised upon his later return to pay the innkeeper whatever added costs might accrue. (Lk. 10:33–35.)

420 *NO ONE LIKE HIM*   Paul commended his associate Timothy in words which glow even after the passing of many generations: "I have no one like him, for genuine interest in your welfare. . . . You know how he has stood the test, how he has served with me in the gospel, like a son helping his father" (Phil. 2:20, 22, MOFFATT).

HERITAGE

421 *SOURCE OF LIVING WATERS*   Each generation must speak its distinct word and make articulate its own testimony. Yet strength that is needed for stalwart living may be found in the recognition and appreciation of that legacy which an earlier generation surrenders to its successors. When Isaac encamped in the valley of Gerar, he "digged again the wells of water, which they had digged in the days of Abraham his father" (Gen. 26:18). And from the old wells there came forth once more living waters.

422 *A FATHER'S LEGACY*   At Beer-sheba the Lord appeared unto Isaac and said, "I am the God of Abraham thy father: fear not, for I am with thee, and will bless thee, and multiply thy seed for my servant Abraham's sake" (Gen. 26:24). No legacy which Abraham bestowed upon his son surpassed that of a living, holy faith. The sins of the fathers may indeed set their children's teeth on edge, but fathers may also provide a goodly heritage of devotion.

423 *INHERITANCE OF MY FATHERS*   How zealously do we cling to the legacies of faith which have been bequeathed to us? King Ahab, wanting Naboth's vineyard that he might have a vegetable garden close to his house, offered the owner either another parcel of land or money in exchange. But Naboth was adamant: "The Lord forbid, that I should give you the inheritance of my fathers" (1 Kings 21:3, AT).

424 *ONE GENERATION TO ANOTHER*   The interdependence of man is nowhere more evident than in the fact that one generation inherits the blessings of the labors of another. "I have sent you to reap a harvest which you have not labored to make. Other men have labored, but you have reaped the results of their labor" (Jn. 4:38, WILLIAMS).

425 *A WORTHY HERITAGE*   An individual's house of faith is not built on shifting sands when it finds strength in the testimony and experience of a worthy heritage and a valid tradition. "You are a building that rests on the apostles and prophets as its foundation, with Christ Jesus as the corner-stone" (Eph. 2:20, MOFFATT).

HISTORY

426 *GOD IN HISTORY*   Few verses in the Bible declare so emphatically God's determination of the course of history as does Judg. 5:20: "The stars in their courses fought against Sisera."

HOLINESS

427 *PROFANING THAT WHICH IS SACRED*   Belshazzar the Chaldean entertained a thousand guests at a banquet during which toasts were drunk from the golden and silver vessels which Nebuchadnezzar had taken from the temple in Jerusalem. In their drunken revelry they profaned that which is holy, and that night the kingdom collapsed. (Dan. 5.)

428 *HOLY GROUND*   In the least likely place, far from home and among a strange people, Moses came into the presence of God while he was tending sheep. God called "unto him out of the midst of the bush," saying, "Draw not nigh hither: put off thy shoes from off thy feet, for the place whereon thou standest is holy ground." (Ex. 3:4–5.)

HOME

429 *FAMILIAR REMEMBRANCERS*   When Jacob and his family had made their clandestine escape from Laban, Rachel "had stolen the images that were her father's" (Gen. 31:19). Why had she taken her father's household gods? Perhaps for no other reason than that she wished always to have at hand some familiar remembrancers of all that home life had meant to her. Was there nothing in the unrighteous house of Laban that might speak more eloquently of the meaning of home than pagan gods?

430 *NEW FAMILY OF MAN*   "Then the Lord said to Noah, 'Go into the ark, you and all your household' " (Gen. 7:1, RSV). The Lord spared a family that through them a new family of man might be created.

431 *GO TO YOUR FAMILY*   Our primary responsibility as Christians is to witness for our faith to those who are closest to us, even though they sometimes are less receptive than strangers in faraway lands. Jesus said to the healed demoniac of Gadarene, "Go home to your family, and tell them what the Lord has done for you, and how he has shown you mercy" (Mk. 5:19, TORREY).

432 *CHRISTIANS AT HOME*   Dialectic will not usually persuade those whom we love to share our Christian convictions, and argumentation may disrupt the peace and unity of the home. Counseled St. Peter, "You married women should adapt yourselves to your husbands, so that even if they do not obey the Word of God they may be won to God without any word being spoken, simply by seeing the pure and reverent behavior of you, their wives" (1 Pet. 3:1-2, PHILLIPS).

433 *THE INFLUENCES OF HOME*   "When they had performed all things according to the law of the Lord, [Joseph, Mary, and their newly-born Child] returned into Galilee, to their own city Nazareth" (Lk. 2:39). Thereafter, for nearly thirty years Jesus lived in relative obscurity in an ordinary community where he engaged in ordinary occupations. The gentle influences of home and neighborhood are reflected in his teachings wherein all homes and neighborhoods find blessings.

434 *HOME DISCIPLINES*   The spiritual disciplines of a pious home left their mark forever on the life of Jesus. "Now his parents went to Jerusalem every year at the feast of the passover" (Lk. 2:41), and the road they faithfully followed Jesus would one day again take in order to fulfill God's holy purposes.

435 *LEGACY OF FAITH*   Faith as a home legacy was appealed to by Paul when he reminded Timothy of "a faith which was alive in Lois your grandmother and Eunice your mother before you, and which, I am confident, lives in you also" (2 Tim. 1:5, NEB).

436 ETERNAL GUEST   No one has a greater prerogative to enter our homes than the eternal Guest, but he remains without when we refuse to listen for his knock and his voice. "Behold, I stand at the door, and knock: if any man hear my voice, and open the door, I will come in to him, and will sup with him, and he with me" (Rev. 3:20).

437 THE FAMILY ALTAR   Many generations before the building of churches, Christian worship was held in the homes of the believers. Paul sent a letter to Philemon and "to the church that meets in your house" (Phm. 2, MOFFATT). Wherever else worship may be held—and no place is inappropriate for praise and prayer—the family altar is supremely important, for here day by day young and old together seek inspiration, communion with God, and instruction from his Word.

438 AVOIDING FAMILY STRIFE   So great in number became the herds of Abraham and Lot that their retainers began to quarrel concerning grazing lands. Prosperity made family strife inevitable. Abraham, however, forestalled trouble by saying, "Let there be no strife . . . for we be brethren" (Gen. 13:8). Amicable settlements among kinsmen are possible only when the initiative is taken by one who possesses the spirit of Abraham.

439 EMPTY MANSIONS   "Many a mansion is to lie forlorn, splendid and spacious and—empty!" (Isa. 5:9, MOFFATT). A home is not measured by pillared porches and pinnacled roofs but by people who live together in harmony and love.

HOPE

440 DAWN OF HOPE   At no time was life's burden heavier for Jacob than when he exclaimed in anguish, "Joseph is not, and Simeon is not, and ye will take Benjamin away: all these things are against me" (Gen. 42:36). What Jacob did not know was that Joseph, now second only to Pharoah in the government of Egypt, claimed Simeon and Benjamin for love's sake only, and would soon reunite the family of Jacob once more. That darkest hour, when all things seem to contrive to destroy all hope, may mark the dawn of a new and joyous morning.

441 *MINORITY AND MAJORITY REPORTS*   Of the twelve spies who were sent by Moses into Canaan, only Caleb and Joshua returned with favorable estimates. Caleb reported, "Let us go up at once, and possess it; for we are well able to overcome it" (Num. 13:30), and Joshua said, "If the Lord delight in us, then he will bring us into this land, and give it us; a land which floweth with milk and honey" (Num. 14:8). But those who prepared the majority report were discouraging: "We be not able to go up against the people; for they are stronger than we. . . . The land through which we have gone to search it, is a land that eateth up the inhabitants thereof; and all the people that we saw in it are men of a great stature" (Num. 13:31–32). The hopefulness of Caleb and Joshua was a matter not only of temperament but of faith in God's promises also.

442 *DO NOT LOSE HEART*   Having no guide by which to navigate, the crew of the ship which was taking Paul to Rome abandoned hope: "For days on end there was no sign of either sun or stars, a great storm was raging, and our last hopes of coming through alive began to fade." Then Paul spoke words born of his confidence in God's purposes: "Now I urge you not to lose heart. . . . For last night there stood by me an angel of the God whose I am and whom I worship." (Acts 27:20, 22–23, NEB.)

443 *THE HOPE JESUS BRINGS*   When Jesus bade Peter and his associates, who had fished without success all night, to return to their boats, Peter said, "At thy word I will let down the net" (Lk. 5:5). Jesus restores hope to all who confidently believe him.

444 *WHAT HOPE MEANS*   To hope means to anticipate that which has as yet not been realized, and so Paul interprets it: "Hope really means *hope;* for a hope you can see is no hope at all—for why does anyone endure patiently for what he can see?" (Rom. 8:24, BARRETT).

445 *BEYOND DESPAIR*   "If Winter comes, can Spring be far behind?" (Shelley). Beyond the dark night is the dawn; beyond despair, hope. "For lo, the winter is past, the rain is over and gone. The flowers appear on the earth, the time of singing has come, and the voice of the turtledove is heard in our land" (S. of S. 2:11–12, RSV).

446 *CAN THESE BONES LIVE?*   In the valley of dry bones— the battle ground where lie lost hopes and failures—Ezekiel was asked, "Can these bones live?" (Ezek. 37:3). And he prophesied that vanquished hopes might yet become virile, renewed by God's spirit.

HOSPITALITY

447 *YOU ARE WELCOME*   Returning from Bethlehem to Ephraim, a Levite and his traveling companions stopped at Gibeah for the night. "He entered and sat down in the open square of the town, but no one took them into his house to spend the night." There they were noticed by "an old man [who] was coming in from his work in the fields at eventide; he belonged to the highlands of Ephraim, but he was residing in Gibeah (the inhabitants being Benjaminites)." Like the good Samaritan, this man extended hospitality that was denied by the native citizens. "You are welcome . . . all your needs shall be in my charge; only, do not spend the night in the open." (Judg. 19:15–16, 20, MOFFATT.)

448 *ANGELS UNAWARES*   "Be not forgetful to entertain strangers: for thereby some have entertained angels unawares" (Heb. 13:2). When three strangers came to Abraham on the plains of Mamre, he responded instinctively to their need by preparing water for their feet and food for their hunger. Little did the patriarch then know that one of the visitors was the Lord. (Gen. 18:1–8.)

449 *THE RETURNING TIDES*   When Elijah asked a widow in Zarephath to bake a little cake to assuage his hunger, he promised that her hospitality would mean an increase, not a loss, in her portion. "And the barrel of meal wasted not, neither did the cruse of oil fail, according to the word of the Lord, which he spake by Elijah" (1 Kings 17:16). The returning tides always recompense us for the bread which we generously cast upon the waters of human need.

HUMILITY

450 *HUMBLE BEGINNINGS* Samuel called together the tribes of Israel to name a king, but Saul was nowhere to be found. At last he was located among the baggage where he was hiding. (1 Sam. 10:22.) The humility which marked that moment was short-lived. Had he continued to be humble-hearted his reign would have been recorded in a different manner.

451 *WHAT DAVID UNDERSTOOD* While David was flee-ing from Jerusalem during Absalom's rebellion, a Benjaminite named Shimei insulted the king by cursing, throwing dust, and casting stones. When one of David's attendants, Abishai, wanted to kill him, David, who was not without an understanding of his own weaknesses, said in genuine humility, "Behold, my own son seeks my life; how much more now may this Benjaminite! Let him alone, and let him curse; for the Lord has bidden him" (2 Sam. 16:11, RSV).

452 *HE LOST A KINGDOM* Proud Nebuchadnezzar lost his kingdom and "he was driven from men, and did eat grass as oxen, and his body was wet with the dew of heaven." His throne was not restored to him until he was humbled and acknowledged that God's "dominion is an everlasting dominion, and his kingdom is from generation to generation." (Dan. 4:33–34.)

453 *ADVICE FOR SOCIAL CLIMBERS* Jesus warned social climbers that their zeal to acquire the best seats at a dinner party might become a source of real embarrassment, for a host, wishing properly to honor more distinguished guests, might find it necessary to ask them to move. The humble man by taking an obscure place might be asked by the host to be seated in a more prominent chair. (Lk. 14:7–10.)

454 *LORD, IS IT I?*   When Jesus told his disciples that one of them would betray him, each responded, "Lord, is it I?" (Matt. 26:22). Each knew himself to be capable of so foul a deed. Each read well his own weaknesses. None was so certain of himself that he could say, "Lord, is it he?"

HUNGER

455 *INNER HUNGER*   "You shall eat, but not be satisfied, and there shall be hunger in your inward parts" (Mic. 6:14, RSV). To have food that tantalizes but never satisfies, nourishes but not completely, is the lot of millions of God's children today as in past times. Hunger is not of the flesh only but also of the spirit. "Blessed are they which do hunger and thirst after righteousness: for they shall be filled" (Matt. 5:6).

456 *AIM OF THE PAGANS*   Some people eat to live; others live to eat. In the one, food sustains life; in the other, life's meaning is measured in terms of food consumed. Jesus showed the difference between the spiritual and the nonspiritual life by referring to eating and drinking: "Do not be troubled . . . and cry, 'What are we to eat?' or 'what are we to drink?' or 'how are we to be clothed?' (pagans make all that their aim in life) for well your heavenly Father knows you need all that" (Matt. 6:31–32, MOFFATT).

457 *THE PRECIOUS FRAGMENTS*   After Jesus had fed the five thousand, he told his disciples, "Gather up the fragments left over, that nothing may be lost" (Jn. 6:12, RSV). The Master, who did not consider one sheep expendable, even when ninety and nine were safe, did not want to see any evidence of God's prodigality wasted. A people who customarily consigns to trash cans that which would nourish others might well learn from him the value of leftovers.

458 *FATE WORSE THAN DEATH*   The children of Israel complained to Moses, "Would that we had died . . . in the land of Egypt, when we sat by the fleshpots and ate bread to the full" (Ex. 16:3, RSV). Hungry now, they forgot Egyptian serfdom and their longing to be free, and they cried for a fate worse than death.

IDLENESS

459 *AN IDLER'S TRAGEDY* "And it came to pass . . . at the time when kings go forth to battle, that David sent Joab. . . . But David tarried still at Jerusalem" (2 Sam. 11:1). Idleness culminated in tragedy for David, for while the others labored David committed his sin against Bath-sheba.

460 *MINDING EVERYBODY'S BUSINESS* Paul censured members of the church in Thessalonica who were not bearing their share of the work: "Some of your number are idling their time away, minding everybody's business but their own" (2 Thess. 3:11, NEB), or "Some of your number are loafing, busybodies instead of busy" (MOFFATT).

IDOLATRY

461 *BLISTERING SARCASM* The folly of idolatry is satirically described by Isaiah: "The ironsmith fashions it and works it over the coals; he shapes it with hammers, and forges it with his strong arm; he becomes hungry and his strength fails, he drinks no water and is faint. The carpenter stretches a line, he marks it out with a pencil; he fashions it with planes, and marks it with a compass; he shapes it into the figure of a man, with the beauty of a man, to dwell in a house. He cuts down cedars; or he chooses a holm tree or an oak and lets it grow strong among the trees of the forest; he plants a cedar and the rain nourishes it. Then it becomes fuel for a man; he takes a part of it and warms himself, he kindles a fire and bakes bread; also he makes a god and worships it, he makes it a graven image and falls down before it. Half of it he burns in the fire; over the half he eats flesh, he roasts meat and is satisfied; also he warms himself and says, 'Aha, I am warm, I have seen the fire!' And the rest of it he makes into a god, his idol; and falls down to it and worships it; he prays to it and says, 'Deliver me, for thou art my god!' " (Isa. 44:12–17, RSV).

462 *PURSUING FALSE GODS* In his condemnation of Israel, the historian wrote, "They went after false idols, and became

false" (2 Kings 17:15, RSV). Inevitably a man becomes like that
which he admires, respects, and reverences.

463 *THE GODS THEY CHOSE*   When in pain and panic
men return from following after strange and powerless gods, they
deserve only to hear such words as the Lord spoke to the troubled
children of Israel: "Go and cry unto the gods which ye have chosen;
let them deliver you in the time of your tribulation" (Judg. 10:14).

464 *SCARECROWS*   "Idols are like scarecrows in a cucumber
field" (Jer. 10:5, RSV). Completely impotent and devoid of life-giving
strength are all those things to which we give reverence save God
only.

465 *MEANINGLESS SENTIMENTS*   Paul found that Athens
was not devoid of religious sentiments: "His soul was irritated at
the sight of the idols that filled the city" (Acts 17:16, MOFFATT). A
city which cherishes idols of whatever kind or nature soon becomes
"completely idolatrous" (PHILLIPS), and man's finest feelings are reduced to a meaningless religiosity.

466 *TROPHIES OF WAR*   Ahaziah, victorious over the Edomites, returned with the gods of his vanquished foe. These he set up
as his own gods and worshiped. When a prophet reproved him, saying, "Why have you resorted to the gods of a people, which did not
deliver their own people from your hands?" the king turned from
the logic of the prophet's censure and said, "Have we made you a
royal counselor?" (2 Chron. 25:15–16, RSV).

IMMORTALITY

467 *WHAT HOPE FOR MAN?*   "There is hope for a tree that
is felled; it may flourish yet again, the shoots of it need not fail;
though its root decays in the soil, though its stump is dead in the
ground, it may bud at the scent of water, and put out boughs like a
plant. But man dies and departs, man breathes his last—and where
is he?" (Job 14:7–10, MOFFATT). So Job contrasted the new life with
which God clothes nature with the miserable lot of man. Such
despondency is answered by the radiant Christian testimony, "He

which raised up the Lord Jesus shall raise up us also by Jesus" (2 Cor. 4:14).

468 *A CLARION CALL*   A sub-Christian attitude, formed in a generation before Christ's resurrection, asserted, "The fate of the sons of men and the fate of beasts is the same; as one dies, so dies the other. They all have the same breath, and man has no advantage over the beasts" (Eccl. 3:19, RSV). But the clarion words of Christian faith are sounded by him who said, "I give unto them eternal life" (Jn. 10:28).

469 *REFLECTIONS IN A MIRROR*   Our present lives permit only the most vague intimations of immortality, and speculation provides slight comfort. "Now we see only reflections in a mirror which leave us with nothing but riddles to solve, but then we shall see face to face" (1 Cor. 13:12, BARCLAY).

INCARNATION

470 *WORD MADE FLESH*   "But will God in very deed dwell with men on the earth? Behold, the heaven and the heaven of heavens cannot contain thee; how much less this house which I have built!" (2 Chron. 6:18). So prayed Solomon at the dedication of the temple. The question is still spiritually pertinent. The ringing affirmation of Isaiah was this: "I dwell in the high and holy place, with him also that is a contrite and humble spirit" (Isa. 57:15). Christian faith is built upon the words of John: "And the Word was made flesh, and dwelt among us" (Jn. 1:14).

471 *THE DIVINE YES*   Christian certainty is premised on Christ himself: "Jesus Christ . . . was not 'yes and no'—the divine 'yes' has at last sounded in him, for in him is the 'yes' that affirms all the promises of God" (2 Cor. 1:19–20, MOFFATT).

472 *THE OPEN SECRET*   In Christ the mind and purpose of the eternal Father were made crystal clear, and God wore, as it were, his heart on his sleeve that men might not thereafter speculate hopelessly. "So richly has God lavished upon us his grace, granting us complete insight and understanding of the open secret of his will . . . that all things in heaven and earth alike should be gathered up in Christ" (Eph. 1:9–10, MOFFATT).

473 *REVEALER OF TRUTH*   In the incarnation the obscurity of centuries vanished, for Christ is the revealer of divine truth. "To this day whenever Moses is read a veil lies over their minds; but when a man turns to the Lord the veil is removed" (2 Cor. 3:15–16, RSV).

474 *GOD'S SACRIFICIAL LOVE*   At the hour of Jesus' death, "the veil of the temple was rent in twain from the top to the bottom" (Matt. 27:51), symbolically revealing to men of every generation the true character of God's sacrificial love. God was no longer hidden from mortal eyes.

INFLUENCE

475 *THEY THOUGHT HE JESTED*   When Lot warned his family of the judgment which was about to fall upon Sodom, "his sons-in-law thought he was merely jesting" (Gen. 19:14, MOFFATT). What had Lot done or failed to do in word or deed that brought such a lack of influence among those who were closest to him?

476 *CONTAMINATING INFLUENCES*   Moses wanted in his army no weakhearted men whose trepidations might contaminate the hearts of their fellows. "What man is there that is fearful and faint-hearted? let him go and return unto his house, lest his brethren's heart faint as well as his heart" (Deut. 20:8). By the same token, the spirit of faith and good cheer are contagious and permeate the lives of others.

477 *BY FAITH HE SPEAKS*   The body of a dead man was put into the tomb of Elisha, and "as soon as the man touched the bones of Elisha, he revived, and stood on his feet" (2 Kings 13:21, RSV). However differently Bible scholars may interpret this miracle, one truth is apparent: contact with the mind, personality, witness, and words of a godly man always invigorates, inspires, and encourages, for though "he died . . . by his faith he is speaking to us still" (Heb. 11:4, MOFFATT).

478 *NOT BY WORDS ONLY*   The conversation between Jesus and Zacchaeus is not recorded by the Evangelist, but perhaps it was not the words Jesus spoke which transformed the tax collector. In Jesus was seen something that riches and position had not brought to Zacchaeus, and the man of Jericho reacted spontaneously by offering to make amends to all whom he had defrauded. (Lk. 19:8.)

479 *HEALING SHADOWS*   So great were the signs and wonders which the Spirit wrought at the hands of the apostles that the sick were taken into the streets "that at the least he shadow of Peter passing by might overshadow some of them" (Acts 5:15). We live within the lengthening shadows of many good and noble men, and the efficacy of their influence is such as to sustain, counsel, and inspire us.

480 *THE VOICE OF THE MOUNTAINS*   From Mount Sinai came the law, from the height of an unnamed mountain came Christ's sermon concerning spiritual behavior, and from Mount Olivet came love's redeeming sacrifice. "See that you make everything according to the pattern which was shown you on the mountain" (Heb. 8:5, RSV).

INSTRUCTION

481 *GOD'S CLASSROOM*   After Ahaziah had been killed, his mother Athaliah claimed the throne and sought to destroy all legitimate heirs. But Jehoiada the priest and his wife rescued Ahaziah's son Joash and "he remained with them six years, hid in the house of God" (2 Chron. 22:12, RSV). There in the most fitting of situations the child was instructed worthily against the day when he should become king.

482 *A WORTHY EXAMPLE*   Ezra's handling of God's Word is a worthy example for Christian interpreters. He "set his heart upon studying the law of God, upon obeying it, and upon teaching its rules and regulations in Israel" (Ezra 7:10, MOFFATT).

483 *GUIDANCE NEEDED*   Philip asked the Ethiopian eunuch whether he understood the words of Isaiah which he was reading. "How can I, except some man should guide me?" (Acts 8:31). Then as now, Christian education is fundamental to the understanding of God's Word.

484 *UNDERSTANDABLE WORDS*   Urging the need for clarity and understanding in preaching, Paul wrote, "Thank God, I speak in 'tongues' more than any of you; but in church I would rather say five words with my own mind for the instruction of other people than ten thousand words in a 'tongue'" (1 Cor. 14:18–19, MOFFATT).

485 *THANK GOD FOR TEACHERS*   2 Kings 12:2 (RSV) underscores the beneficial consequences of a substantial religious education: "Jehoash did what was right in the eyes of the Lord all his days, because Jehoiada the priest instructed him."

486 *BRING ME UP SAMUEL*   The medium at Endor asked Saul, "Whom shall I bring up unto thee?" Saul replied, "Bring me up Samuel." (1 Sam. 28:11.) In desperation Saul sought the counsel of the prophet whose guidance had brought prosperity. Given the opportunity, many of us would cherish the privilege of sitting once more at the feet of a spiritual instructor whose words had previously girded us for life.

487 *THEY KNEW NOT THE LORD*   Only when children are instructed concerning their spiritual heritage may their minds be girded for continued faithfulness. This is underscored by the following: "The people served the Lord all the days of Joshua, and all the days of the elders that outlived Joshua. . . . And there arose another generation after them, which knew not the Lord, nor yet the works which he had done for Israel" (Judg. 2:7, 10).

488 *SOMETHING WENT WRONG*   Although sons of a devoted servant of God, Hophni and Phinebas "were worthless men; they had no regard for the Lord" (1 Sam. 2:12, RSV). How does one explain impious sons of a devout father? Did Eli neglect the religious instruction of his sons because of the pressures of his ecclesiastical responsibilities? Or did the sons turn from their father's instructions?

489 *DIVINE SCHOOLMASTER*   Man profits most when he learns from his Maker. "Does the plowman keep plowing all the time, is he forever opening and harrowing his ground? Does he not, after leveling its surface, scatter dill, and sow cummin, and put in wheat and barley? . . . For his God instructs and teaches him aright" (Isa. 28:24–26, AT).

490 *TEN O'CLOCK SCHOLARS*   Lackadaisical and ten o'clock scholars prolong interminably their mastery of the elemental lessons in the school of Christ and so are ill-prepared to instruct others. "At a time when you should be teaching others, you need teachers yourselves to repeat to you the ABC of God's revelation" (Heb. 5:12, PHILLIPS).

491 *WANT OF KNOWLEDGE*   "My people are dying for want of knowledge," God declared to the priests in Israel, "and you reject my knowledge" (Hos. 4:6, MOFFATT). The church is a body of believers whose faith is sustained by proper instruction in him who is the Truth. Without this, faith perishes, and all preaching is "as sounding brass, or a tinkling cymbal" (1 Cor. 13:1). "This is life eternal, that they might know thee the only true God, and Jesus Christ, whom thou hast sent" (Jn. 17:3).

INTEGRITY

492 *AN UNPURCHASABLE MAN*   Balak, attempting to persuade Balaam to curse the Israelites, sent this word to him, "I will pay you richly," but Balaam replied, "Though Balak were to give me his very house full of silver and gold, I could not do a single thing beyond what the Eternal my God bids me" (Num. 22:17–18, MOFFATT).

493 *NEITHER PRICE NOR FAVOR*   To a soldier who had seen Absalom hanging from the branches of an oak tree, Joab said, "Thou sawest him, and why didst thou not smite him there to the ground? And I would have given thee ten shekels of silver, and a girdle." Obedient to David's command that none should lay a hand on Absalom, the soldier replied, "Though I should receive a thousand shekels of silver in mine hand, yet would I not put forth mine hand against the king's son." (2 Sam. 18:11–12.) His integrity knew neither price nor favor.

494 *MINORITY OF ONE*   Micaiah was a stubborn and honest minority of one when the four hundred hirelings of Ahab forecast his victory against Ramoth-gilead. Urged by Ahab's messenger to conform, Micaiah declared, "As the Lord liveth, what the Lord saith unto me, that will I speak" (1 Kings 22:14).

495 *IN A FAR COUNTRY*   The true measure of the goodness of a young man is to be found, not when he is within range of his father's watchful eye, but when in a far country he lives according to the virtues which home life instilled in him. Young Joseph in Egypt was distinguished for his moral soundness. His was a genuine and not a simulated integrity. So Potiphar "made him overseer over his house, and all that he had he put into his hand" (Gen. 39:4).

496 *INWARD WORTH*   Integrity before God is a matter, not of an attractive and seemingly spiritual façade, but of a righteous heart. Paul spoke of those "who are proud of externals instead of the inward reality" (2 Cor. 5:12, MOFFATT), or "whose pride is all in outward show and not in inward worth" (NEB), or "are so proud of the outward rather than the inward qualification" (PHILLIPS).

497 *CLEAR EXPLANATIONS*   When Nebuchadnezzar asked him to interpret a dream, Daniel was astonished and alarmed, for the dream meant that the kingdom would be taken from Nebuchadnezzar. (Dan. 4:4–27.) Should Daniel reveal the truth? With integrity Daniel gave a clear explanation. St. Paul counseled, "By manifestation of the truth commending ourselves to every man's conscience in the sight of God" (2 Cor. 4:2).

INTERCESSION

498 *ALWAYS IN MY PRAYERS*   Paul's love for the Roman Christians was no hot-and-cold affair, for he greeted them with these words: "Before God, whom I serve with all my heart in the Gospel of his Son, I assure you that you are always in my prayers" (Rom. 1:9, PHILLIPS).

499 *LINKED IN PRAYER*   Intercessory prayer by which our lives are linked to the needs of others is requested by St. Paul: "Let me have your co-operation in prayer" (2 Cor. 1:11, MOFFATT). So are our lives "bound by gold chains about the feet of God" (Tennyson).

500 *HE WAS NOT ALONE*   Herod cast Peter into prison, but Peter was not alone: "Long and fervent prayer was offered to God by the church on his behalf" (Acts 12:5, WEYMOUTH).

501 *GOD REMEMBERED ABRAHAM*   "And Abraham went early in the morning to the place where he had stood before the Lord" (Gen. 19:27, RSV). As he had prayed in behalf of the inhabitants of the condemned cities of Sodom and Gomorrah (Gen. 18:23–33), he now prayed for his nephew Lot. And "God remembered Abraham" (Gen. 19:29), not because Lot was deserving, but because of Abraham's intercession.

502 *IF THOU WILT FORGIVE*   Moses is a prototype of devoted men who intercede in behalf of sinners. After the children of Israel had fashioned a calf of gold which they worshiped, Moses pleaded with God, saying, "Yet now, if thou wilt forgive their sin—; and if not, blot me, I pray thee, out of thy book which thou hast written" (Ex. 32:32). And it is written of One greater than Moses, "That he might be a merciful and faithful high priest in things pertaining to God, to make reconciliation for the sins of the people" (Heb. 2:17).

503 *BORNE UPON THE HEART*   "And Aaron shall bear the names of the children of Israel in the breastplate of judgment upon his heart, when he goeth in unto the holy place, for a memorial before the Lord continually" (Ex. 28:29). In like manner both pastor and people bear on their hearts the names of others as they approach the throne of grace in intercessory prayer.

JEALOUSY

504 *VICTIM OF JEALOUSY*   Without children of her own, Sarah volunteered that Abraham should father a son and heir by Hagar, her maid. But after Hagar had conceived, Sarah became a victim of the corroding disease of jealousy. Egged on by Hagar's evident condescension toward her childless mistress, the enraged Sarah made Hagar's life unbearable. (Gen. 16:1-6; see also 21:9-11.)

505 *WHAT THE LORD REQUIRES*   The jealousy of Miriam regarding the leadership of Moses is a page from human experience. Miriam, who was unquestionably a remarkably talented person, said, "Hath the Lord indeed spoken only by Moses? hath he not spoken also by us?" (Num. 12:2). Yet the Lord, who singled out Moses above all others, had a worthy work for Miriam also. The Lord has given "to every man according to his several ability" (Matt. 25:15), and requires of each man a willingness to be used where he is most needed.

506 *SAUL'S JEALOUSY*   The military achievements of David made him such a popular hero that the women of Israel sang, "Saul hath slain his thousands, but David his ten thousands." Saul became so enraged with jealousy that he "eyed David from that day and forward." (1 Sam. 18:7, 9.)

507 *OCCASION FOR COMPLAINING*   Certain Chaldeans, jealous because of the rise to favor in the Babylonian court of Shadrach, Meshach, and Abednego, seized upon their loyalty to God as an occasion for complaining to Nebuchadnezzar that they had violated a royal decree in not worshiping the golden image. (Dan. 3:1-12.)

508 *HE MUST GROW GREATER*   Perceiving that Jesus was attracting more followers, the jealously loyal disciples of John the Baptist complained, "Master, look, the man who was with you on the other side of the Jordan, the one you testified to, is now baptizing and everybody is coming to him!" John's response should be that of every Christian pastor: "My happiness is now complete. He must grow greater and greater and I less and less." (Jn. 3:26, 29-30, PHILLIPS.)

JOY

509 *WINDOW-SILL VIEW*   With unbridled enthusiasm David brought the ark into Jerusalem. When "Michal Saul's daughter looked through a window, and saw king David leaping and dancing before the Lord . . . she despised him in her heart." David said, "It was before the Lord, which chose me . . . ruler over the people of the Lord, over Israel: therefore will I play before the Lord." (2 Sam. 6:16, 21.) Michal's objections are similar to those raised by persons who, lacking the zeal of the faithful and knowing religion only from a window sill, are unable to comprehend what it means to "be glad in the Lord, and rejoice, ye righteous: and shout for joy, all ye that are upright in heart" (Ps. 32:11).

510 *ANGELS REJOICE*   Jesus said that angels in heaven rejoice when a sinner repents, and he likened their joy to that of a woman who, having lost one of her ten silver coins, swept her house until it was found and then invited her neighbors to share her celebration. (Lk. 15:8–10.)

511 *ON HIS WAY REJOICING*   After Philip had baptized the Ethiopian eunuch, "the Spirit of the Lord caught away Philip [and] the eunuch saw him no more," but a wonderful change took place in the eunuch's life and "he went on his way rejoicing" (Acts 8:39). "These things have I spoken unto you, that my joy might remain in you, and that your joy might be full" (Jn. 15:11).

512 *BOON AND BLESSING*   That life is a boon and a blessing was long ago enunciated: "For men, I find, there is nothing better than to be happy and enjoy themselves as long as they are alive; it is indeed God's gift to man, that he should eat and drink and be happy as he toils" (Eccl. 3:12–13, MOFFATT).

513 *STRANGERS TO JOY*   Evidences of religious enthusiasm, such as we find among the early Christians, may become a source of criticism and perplexity among the uninitiated. Those who are strangers to the exhilaration and joy of genuine faith are likely to say scornfully, "These men are full of new wine" (Acts 2:13). Yet joyousness is the most natural expression of the faithful. "With unflagging energy, in ardour of spirit, serve the Lord" (Rom. 12:11, NEB).

JUDGMENT

514 *PARABLE OF THE TREES*   God's judgment differs from that of men. At the throne of grace the last shall be first; the neglected will be rescued; and the thirsty, refreshed with a living water. "All the trees of the field shall know that I the Lord have brought down the high tree, have exalted the low tree, have dried up the green tree, and have made the dry tree to flourish" (Ezek. 17:24).

515 *HOUR OF RECKONING*   For every sin there follows inevitably an hour of reckoning. Moses presumed that no man saw him kill the Egyptian who had struck a Hebrew. Perhaps the very man whose life he had saved boasted of Moses' prowess to the others. So widely did Moses' act become noised among his own people that on the following day when he sought reconciliation between two Hebrews they said in effect that one who had blood on his hands was unworthy to judge over them. (Ex. 2:13–14.)

516 *DAVID'S INDIGNATION*   After David had so schemed that the husband of Bath-sheba, Uriah, was killed on the battle-field, the prophet Nathan told the king a story of a rich man who took from a poor man his one little ewe lamb. Without recognizing that the parable concerned him, David flared with indignation and said that the rich man should surely die. (2 Sam. 12:1–6.)

517 *AND IT WAS SO*   After Naboth refused to sell his vine-yard to King Ahab, Jezebel the queen instigated a plot wherein the guileless Naboth was found guilty of a fabricated crime and exe-cuted. But whatever joy Ahab might gain by the destruction of Naboth was short-lived. Elijah relayed to the king the judgment of the Lord: "In the place where dogs licked the blood of Naboth shall dogs lick thy blood, even thine" (1 Kings 21:19). And it was so.

518 *LINE AND PLUMMET*   Through his prophets the Lord brought judgment upon Judah: "I will stretch over Jerusalem the line of Samaria, and the plummet of the house of Ahab: and I will wipe Jerusalem as a man wipeth a dish, wiping it, and turning it upside down" (2 Kings 21:13).

519 *GOD'S PLUMBLINE*   "I will set a plumbline in the midst of my people Israel" (Amos 7:8). The moral universe is meaning-less unless God tests to determine the uprightness of his children and brings "every work into judgment" (Eccl. 12:14).

520 *THE BROKEN JAR*   Dramatically portraying divine judgment, Jeremiah broke a clay jar so that it was beyond repair and then said that in a like manner God will deal with sinful people. (Jer. 19:1–13.)

521 *DARK SECRETS TO LIGHT*   It is the prerogative of God through Jesus Christ, who alone reads the hearts of men, to blame or commend. "The Lord will come to bring dark secrets to the light and to reveal life's inner aims and motives" (1 Cor. 4:5, MOFFATT).

522 *PLANK AND SAWDUST*   In a telling and facetious indictment of censorious persons who are ready always to judge and condemn others but are incapable of properly judging themselves, Jesus asked, "Why do you look at the speck of sawdust in your brother's eye, with never a thought for the great plank in your own? How can you say to your brother, 'My dear brother, let me take the speck out of your eye,' when you are blind to the plank in your own?" (Lk. 6:41–42, NEB).

523 *UNMARKED TOMBS*   The supercilious Pharisees who claimed front seats in the synagogues and desired men to bow and show deference to them in the market place were compared by Jesus to unmarked tombs over which people unwittingly walk. (Lk. 11:43–44.)

524 *SUPERFICIAL JUDGMENT*   High religion is concerned primarily with the transformation of a man's inner nature and only secondarily with his outer fashion and behavior. To those who judged only by superficial standards, Jesus said, "What comes out of a man, that is what profanes the man. For it is from the inside, out of men's minds, that evil plans proceed" (Mk. 7:21–22, JOHNSON).

525 *CROSS-QUESTIONING*   Paul turned from his Corinthian critics to a higher tribunal: "It matters very little to me that you or any human court should cross-question me. . . . I do not even cross-question myself . . . it is the Lord who cross-questions me" (1 Cor. 4:3–4, MOFFATT).

526 *FINAL APPEAL*   Paul culminated his defense before Festus with the declaration, "I appeal unto Caesar" (Acts 25:11), a privilege which any citizen had a right to claim. The Christian's final appeal is not to an earthly potentate only, but to God who "with righteousness [judges] the world, and the people with equity" (Ps. 98:9).

527 *A RIGHT TO LIVE*   "Now also the axe is laid unto the root of the trees: therefore every tree which bringeth not forth good fruit is hewn down, and cast into the fire" (Matt. 3:10). In the economy of both heaven and earth that which is unproductive is expendable and that only is preserved which earns a right to live. "Herein is my Father glorified, that ye bear much fruit" (Jn. 15:8).

JUSTICE

528 *SCALES OF JUSTICE*   Believing himself to have been falsely accused, Job threw himself upon the justice of God and exclaimed, "Let God take scales of justice to my life, and he would own that I am innocent!" (Job 31:6, MOFFATT).

529 *SOWING AND REAPING*   "Sow justice for yourselves, and reap a harvest of God's love" (Hos. 10:12, MOFFATT). "The Lord loveth righteousness" (Ps. 11:7), and those whose lives are divinely oriented receive God's unlimited affection.

530 *THE SHOUTS PREVAILED*   Too often justice is determined, not after reasonable deliberation, but by the ferocity of editorial denunciation and the intemperate outcries of people who seek revenge. The crowd before Pilate "loudly urged their demand that he should be crucified, and their shouts carried the day" (Lk. 23:23, MOFFATT).

531 *GUARANTEE OF JUSTICE*   The tattletale mentality which results in persons not speaking when their forthright testimony is needed makes a sham of civil relations and is unworthy of Christians whose honorable speech may assure that justice is guaranteed. "If any person sins by not giving information when as a witness, either as one who has seen it or knows of it, he hears the oath of adjuration, he must answer for his iniquity" (Lev. 5:1, AT).

532 *CONFRONTED BY ACCUSERS*   To those who brought charges against Paul, Festus explained a principle honored not only in jurisprudence but also by all decent men: "It is not Roman practice to hand over any accused man before he is confronted with his accusers and given an opportunity of answering the charge" (Acts 25:16, NEB).

KINDNESS

533 *EVIDENCES OF KINDNESS*   The survivors of the ship that was to have taken Paul to Rome swam to shore where, according to the chronicler, "the natives showed us unusual kindness, for they kindled a fire and welcomed us all, because it had begun to rain and was cold" (Acts 28:2, RSV). Despite evidences of man's inhumanity to man, there are evidences, too, in ancient and contemporary life of an elemental compassion of man toward his human brethren.

534 *ONE KINDNESS DESERVES ANOTHER*   Having saved the lives of the Israelites who had gone into hostile Jericho to investigate the fortifications, Rahab caused the spies to swear that her kindness would be reciprocated when the city was taken. They said, "We will deal kindly and truly with thee" (Josh. 2:14)—and they kept their promise.

535 *PLEA FOR KINDNESS*   Balaam angrily struck his ass three times, and "the Eternal opened the mouth of the ass, and she asked Balaam, 'What have I done to you, that you have struck me these three times? . . . Am I not your own ass, the ass you have always ridden?" (Num. 22:28, 30, MOFFATT). From that animal which is often considered to be the most foolish came this plea for kindness to all animals.

KINGDOM OF GOD

536 *PRESENT REALITY*   Through the incarnation the Kingdom became a present reality, not a distant dream. "The kingdom of God," Jesus said, "is not coming with signs to be observed; nor will they say, 'Lo, here it is!' or 'There!' for behold, the kingdom of God is in the midst of you" (Lk. 17:21, RSV). NEB translates the last phrase, "The kingdom of God is among you" and in the margin, "The kingdom of God is within your grasp."

537 *DOORS THROWN OPEN*   After the socially desirable begged off, saying that they had other things to do, a householder sent his servant into the streets to fetch less desirable guests to his dinner party. (Lk. 14:16–24.) In like manner, when those who should be expected to enter the Kingdom reject the privilege, the doors are thrown open to publicans and sinners.

538 *FROM ALL DIRECTIONS*   The holy city envisioned by St. John "had twelve gates. . . . On the east three gates; on the north three gates; on the south three gates; and on the west three gates" (Rev. 21:12–13). Does this not suggest symbolically that admittance to Christ's Kingdom is from every direction and by men of whatever color, race, or nation?

LAUGHTER

539 *INCREDULOUS LAUGHTER*   For years on end Abraham had laid before the Lord his petition that a child be born to Sarah his wife. When at long last the Lord said that his prayer would be answered, "Abraham fell upon his face, and laughed, and said in his heart, Shall a child be born unto him that is a hundred years old? and shall Sarah, that is ninety years old, bear?" (Gen. 17:17; see also the laughter of the incredulous Sarah, Gen. 18:9–15).

LAYMEN

540 *CAPABLE ASSISTANTS*   When Moses undertook the detailed responsibilities of ruling the children of Israel, Jethro made the salutary suggestion that able men be selected to assist him. "And Moses chose able men out of all Israel, and made them heads over the people, rulers of thousands, rulers of hundreds, rulers of fifties, and rulers of tens. And they judged the people at all seasons: the hard causes they brought unto Moses, but every small matter they judged themselves." (Ex. 18:25–26.)

541 *ARMS THAT UPHOLD*   Standing on a hill overlooking the army of Joshua, Moses held up his hands as in a benediction. When his arms became tired, "Aaron and Hur stayed up his hands, the one on the one side, and the other on the other side; and his hands were steady until the going down of the sun" (Ex. 17:12). In like manner, faithful laymen uphold the word and witness of their minister, bolstering and encouraging him as he proclaims God's Word and struggles to do what God requires.

542 *THEY RISKED THEIR NECKS*   The achievements of the great-name Christians are dependent on the little-known persons who have supported and sustained them. Paul wrote to the Roman Christians, "Salute Prisca and Aquila, my fellow-workers in Christ Jesus, who have risked their lives for me" (Rom. 16:3-4, MOFFATT), or "who risked their necks for my life" (RSV).

543 *LAY PARTICIPATION*   Worship in our churches usually provides that the minister officiate, but the early church encouraged participation by laymen. "When you meet together, each contributes something—a song of praise, a lesson, a revelation, a 'tongue,' an interpretation? Good, but let everything be for edification" (1 Cor. 14:26, MOFFATT). Would anything add a more beneficial ingredient to our sometimes cold and stuffy worship services than such lay participation?

544 *UNEXPECTED SUPPORT*   After the delivering of his temple sermon, Jeremiah received criticism from the religious leaders and unexpected support from laymen: "The priests and the prophets and all the people laid hold of him, saying, 'You must die! . . . Then the princes and all the people said to the priests and prophets, 'This man does not deserve the sentence of death, for he has spoken to us in the name of the Lord our God" (Jer. 26:8, 16, RSV).

LEADERSHIP

545 *ENSAMPLES TO THE FLOCK*   After the discovery of the ancient book of the law, Josiah called his people together, read the venerated words, and "made a covenant before the Lord, to walk after the Lord and to keep his commandments and his testimonies and his statutes, with all his heart and all his soul, to perform the words of this covenant that were written in this book." Guided by the initiative of their king, "all the people joined in the covenant." (2 Kings 23:3, RSV.) Christian leaders are called upon to "feed the flock of God which is among you, taking the oversight thereof . . . being ensamples to the flock" (1 Pet. 5:2–3).

546 HE LED THEM ASTRAY   After reciting the wicked deeds of Manasseh, the historian culminated his astringent accusations by declaring, "Manasseh made [the children of Israel] go wrong, worse than the very pagans whom the Eternal had destroyed before the Israelites" (2 Kings 21:9, MOFFATT). He compounded his personal sins by leading his people into apostasy.

547 HOW WEARISOME!   Church leadership may be the most engaging and satisfying work in the world, or it may be permitted to degenerate into a treadmill routine and complete ennui. Malachi wrote of halfhearted priests who sighed, "What a weariness it all is!" (Mal. 1:13, MOFFATT).

548 MORAL ANARCHY   When we have no leader who commands our respect and whose authority we recognize, confusion reigns. "In those days there was no king in Israel: every man did that which was right in his own eyes" (Judg. 21:25), or "Everyone did exactly as he pleased" (MOFFATT).

549 DESERVING RESPECT   Having been struck by order of the high priest Ananias, Paul turned wrathfully toward the official and said, "God shall strike you, you whitewashed wall!" Reminded that he was reviling God's high priest, Paul replied, "I did not know, brethren, that he was high priest." (Acts 23:3, 5, RSV.) Paul's enigmatic words may suggest that he was unaware of the position Ananias held, which is unlikely. Did he rather mean that a leader possesses authority, not by virtue of appointment only, but because his actions warrant respect and esteem?

550 CUPIDITY AND GULLIBILITY   "The chief priests stirred up the mob to demand the release of Barabbas" (Mk. 15:11, BARCLAY). The cupidity of the priests and the gullibility of the crowd—false leaders and the too-easily led—combined in this unconscionable crime.

551 *ONE MAN STANDS FORTH*   After Demetrius and other silversmiths, saying that the Christians were bringing the goddess Diana into disrepute, had caused great confusion in Ephesus, an unnamed official stood forth and successfully persuaded the mob that they should take their grievances to a legally-established assembly (Acts 19:35–41). And the appeal to law, not violence, prevailed.

552 *THE KING'S PRAYER*   At the beginning of his reign Solomon expressed a humility of spirit which with the passing years became a diminished thing: "O Lord my God, thou hast made thy servant king instead of David my father: and I am but a little child: I know not how to go out or come in" (1 Kings 3:7).

553 *THE LORD'S ANOINTED*   While seeking to destroy David, Saul happened to enter a cave where David was hiding. David's followers urged him to kill Saul, but David said, "The Lord forbid that I should do this thing unto my master, the Lord's anointed, to stretch forth mine hand against him, seeing he is the anointed of the Lord" (1 Sam. 24:6). David recognized that a certain respect is due even to a vindictive and wrong-minded ruler.

554 *VINDICATED LEADERSHIP*   Korah and others rebelled against the leadership of Moses and Aaron and said, "Ye take too much upon you, seeing all the congregation are holy, every one of them, and the Lord is among them: wherefore then lift ye up yourselves above the congregation of the Lord?" (Num. 16:3). Had their accusations of superior authority and highhandedness been well-founded—and apparently they were not—it was right for them to raise voices in protestation. Leaders of both church and state sometimes become arbitrary self-seekers. Moses vindicated his leadership by proposing a test to determine which leaders God desired.

LIFE

555 *TAKE A LITTLE HONEY*   As his sons departed on a second journey into Egypt to purchase corn, Jacob made a gracious suggestion: "Take some of the choice fruits of the land in your bags, and carry down to the man a present, a little balm and a little honey, gum, myrrh, pistachio nuts, and almonds" (Gen. 43:11, RSV). In our journey through life we, too, would do well to carry a little balm and a little honey!

556 *OURS FOR THE ASKING*   Many of the best things in life may be ours for the asking—or for the accepting. Many of those things which are rightly ours we do not claim. "The king of Israel said to his officers, 'Are you aware that Ramoth-gilead belongs to us? Yet here we sit still, instead of taking it over from the king of Aram!'" (1 Kings 22:3, MOFFATT).

557 *A COBWEB WIPED AWAY*   Our brief lives—threescore years and ten or, perhaps, fourscore, according both to the Psalmist and also normative human experience—are too quickly gone to be squandered recklessly or wasted frivolously, for "our life is over like a sigh" (Ps. 90:9, MOFFATT), or "our years are like a cobweb wiped away" (AT), or are spent "as a tale that is told."

558 *PAGEANT OF TRIUMPH*   The Christian's journey through life is one of victory: "Wherever I go, thank God, he makes my life a constant pageant of triumph in Christ" (2 Cor. 2:14, MOFFATT).

559 *LIFE'S PIONEER*   In our spiritual pilgrimage we are followers of Christ. As Christians we are called to "run our appointed course with steadiness, our eyes fixed upon Jesus as the pioneer and the perfection of faith" (Heb. 12:1-2, MOFFATT), or "the perfect leader and example of faith" (WILLIAMS), or "the source and goal of our faith" (PHILLIPS), or "the Leader and the Source of our faith [giving the first incentive for our belief] and . . . also its Finisher, [bringing it to maturity and perfection]" (AMNT).

560 *RADIANT LIVING*   "And when Aaron and all the children of Israel saw Moses, behold, the skin of his face shown" (Ex. 34:30). To enter through prayer into the very presence of God enlightens one's heart and makes radiant one's life. Christians should "shine." Without such a glow something is missing which none except God can supply.

561 *GLOW OR CINDER?* A new life in Christ begins with an inner glow, but that glow, if not properly tended, may become little more than a burnt-out cinder. "Surely you can't be so idiotic as to think that a man begins his spiritual life in the Spirit and then completes it by reverting to outward observances? Has all your painful experience brought you nowhere? I simply cannot believe it of you!" (Gal. 3:3–4, PHILLIPS).

562 *BY THESE MEN LIVE* After recovering from sickness, King Hezekiah spoke of the experiences which all men must face— pain, suffering, weariness, sleeplessness, and death—and said, "O Lord, by these things men live" (Isa. 38:16). Through the least desirable experiences we often come to a fuller understanding and appreciation of life's fundamental meanings.

LIGHT

563 *HEAVENLY LIGHT* To King Agrippa Paul spoke of his conversion on the road leading to Damascus in these words: "At midday, O king, I saw on the way a light from heaven, brighter than the sun, shining round me" (Acts 26:13, RSV). The path of Christians is illumined by a heavenly light "that shineth more and more unto the perfect day" (Prov. 4:18).

564 *LIMITED LIGHT* The self-sufficient man can offer no other guidance than his ingenuity makes possible. "All you who kindle a fire, who set brands alight! Walk by the light of your fire, and by the brands which you have kindled!" (Isa. 50:11, RSV).

565 *SHADOWS ARE BANISHED* "I am searching Jerusalem with a lamp, to punish careless men, living at ease, who think the Eternal never does anything" (Zeph. 1:12, MOFFATT). All shadows are banished by God's light, and no man's heart will remain unexposed.

566 *INEXTINGUISHABLE LIGHT* "The lamp of God has not yet gone out" (1 Sam. 3:3, AT). The hope of man lies in this light which, though at times it flickers and grows dim in our hearts, will not fail. In this "light shall we see light" (Ps. 36:9).

567 *BATHED IN RADIANCE*   On the night of Christ's birth
"the glory of the Lord shone round about [the shepherds]" (Lk.
2:9). In like manner our lives are bathed in the radiance of heaven.
David affirmed, "The Lord will lighten my darkness" (2 Sam. 22:29),
and Paul wrote, "God, who commanded the light to shine out of
darkness, hath shined in our hearts" (2 Cor. 4:6).

568 *LIGHT IN THE HOME*   The ninth plague brought upon
the people of Egypt a darkness so great that the people "saw
not one another, neither rose any from his place for three days."
But the historian showed a vivid contrast between the shrouded
Egyptians and "the children of Israel [who] had light in their
dwellings." (Ex. 10:23.) The Light of the world sheds his light not
only in the homes where Christians dwell but also in their minds
and hearts.

LOVE

569 *TESTIMONY OF DEVOTION*   Expressions of affection
vary according to an individual's temperament and devotion. When
Naomi said good-by to her daughters-in-law, both wept and "Orpah
kissed her mother in law; but Ruth clave unto her" (Ruth 1:14).

570 *THE MAN SHE LOVED*   Learning that his daughter
Michal loved David, Saul, who was jealous of David's popularity,
said, "I will give him her, that she may be a snare to him, and that
the hand of the Philistines may be against him" (1 Sam. 18:21). But
Michal did not become a party to her father's intrigues and was
able to protect the man she loved.

571 *THE FLEETING YEARS*   Few words concerning loving
fidelity in biblical and secular literature exceed in beauty and
meaning those which speak of Jacob's affection for Rachel: "And
Jacob served seven years for Rachel; and they seemed unto him but
a few days, for the love he had to her" (Gen. 29:20).

572 *TO WOO HER BACK*   The concubine of an unnamed
Levite of Ephraim "in a fit of anger left him for her father's home

at Bethlehem in Judah, where she stayed some time, indeed four months." Then and now misunderstandings drive wedges into domestic relations. The Levite, perhaps after having first admitted to himself his blame, sought reconciliation. "Her husband then went after her to woo her back." (Judg. 19:2–3, MOFFATT.) The RSV reads, "Then her husband arose and went after her, to speak kindly to her." The man and wife renewed a courtship which should not have been permitted to become cold and casual.

573 PERVERTED SYMBOL   The perfidy of Judas was compounded when he betrayed Jesus by using an age-long symbol of affection: " 'Rabbi!' he said—and kissed Him as a lover would" (Mk. 14:45, BARCLAY).

574 LIKE A MORNING CLOUD   True love is nurtured by faithfulness and fidelity. Hosea despaired of the inconstant love shown by the two kingdoms: "Ephraim, what can I do with you? Judah, what can I do with you? This love of yours is like a morning cloud, like dew that soon will disappear" (Hos. 6:4, MOFFATT).

575 LOVE A PREREQUISITE   Brotherly love is prerequisite to wholehearted worship of God: "If thou bring thy gift to the altar, and there rememberest that thy brother hath aught against thee; leave there thy gift before the altar, and go thy way; first be reconciled to thy brother, and then come and offer thy gift" (Matt. 5:23–24).

576 QUIET ELOQUENCE   Eschewing the pomposity of empty boasting, Christian love speaks in accents of quiet eloquence and unaffected simplicity. "Love makes no parade" (1 Cor. 13:4, MOFFATT).

577 DIMENSIONS OF LOVE   Paul invited the Ephesians to learn the dimensions of Christian love: "May you be so fixed and founded in love that you can grasp with all the saints what is the meaning of 'the Breadth,' 'the Length,' 'the Depth,' and 'the Height,' by knowing the love of Christ which surpasses all knowledge!" (Eph. 3:18–19, MOFFATT).

578 *SPRING OF OUR ACTIONS*   What is the wellspring of Christian living? "The very spring of our actions is the love of Christ" (2 Cor. 5:14, PHILLIPS), or "It is Christ's love that controls me" (GOODSPEED), or "The love of Christ leaves us no choice" (NEB).

579 *INCREDIBLE LOVE*   No honor we may claim equals that of being God's sons, but it is a distinction bestowed in love and not gained by worthiness or effort. "Consider the incredible love that the Father has shown us in allowing us to be called 'children of God'—and that is not just what we are called, but what we *are*" (1 Jn. 3:1, PHILLIPS).

580 *NONE BEYOND GOD'S LOVE*   In the economy of God no human being is beyond God's loving concern. "Are not five sparrows sold for two pennies?" Jesus asked. "And not one of them is forgotten before God. . . . You are of more value than many sparrows." (Lk. 12:6–7, RSV.)

LOYALTY

581 *PROVEN LOYALTIES*   "When Daniel knew that the writing was signed . . . his windows being open in his chamber toward Jerusalem, he kneeled . . . and prayed, and gave thanks before his God, as he did aforetime" (Dan. 6:10). In a strange country, Daniel was no stranger to God and his heart continued to be oriented toward the city of his fathers. That man is truly safe who maintains proven loyalties in any circumstance.

582 *FIDDLER'S TUNE*   After the kings of Judah and Israel had linked their forces to recapture Ramoth-gilead, Jehoshapat wished to consult the Lord and so Ahab called together four hundred prophets. When the king of Judah indicated dissatisfaction, Ahab admitted, "There is yet one man, Micaiah . . . but I hate him; for he doth not prophesy good concerning me, but evil" (1 Kings 22:8). One true prophet, however, is more reliable than four hundred time-servers whose loyalty is to the man who calls the fiddler's tune.

583 *WE SERVE THE LORD*   A challenge of compelling relevance for men who vacillate between loyalty to God or to strange gods was given by Joshua: "Choose you this day whom ye will serve; whether the gods which your fathers served that were on the other side of the flood, or the gods of the Amorites, in whose land ye dwell: but as for me and my house, we will serve the Lord" (Josh. 24:15).

584 *SUPREME LOYALTY*   Joseph's rejection of the many advances of Potiphar's wife reflected both the moral disciplines of his upbringing and also his loyalty to his Egyptian master. But a supreme loyalty determined his conduct and buttressed him against the enticements of sinners: "How then can I do this great wickedness, and sin against God?" (Gen. 39:9).

585 *GOD'S LOYALTY TO MAN*   The Psalmist glories, not in man's loyalty to God, but in God's loyalty to him, for it is this which empowers and sustains man's feeble efforts to respond worthily: "So shall I praise thee on the lute for loyalty to me, my God" (Ps. 71:22, MOFFATT).

586 *FOR PETER ONLY?*   "And immediately the cock crew" (Matt. 26:74). For Peter only? Our vaunted protestations of loyalty and our affirmations and resolutions—how soon they become diminished things. And the cock's crowing reminds us of what we might have been and what we might have done. Peter, at any rate, did not forever weep bitterly; he rose on steppingstones of his dead self to higher things.

587 *CONTRADICTED LOYALTIES*   Christians whose lives contradict the loyalties which their lips profess may become, as Moses warned his people, "an astonishment, a proverb, and a byword, among all nations whither the Lord shall lead thee" (Deut. 28:37).

588 *INSTABILITY AT EVERY TURN*   Spiritual schizophrenia results when a man attempts to serve both God and mammon. "The life of a man of divided loyalty will reveal instability at every turn" (Jas. 1:8, PHILLIPS).

MAN

589 *HUMAN VARIATIONS*   "The voice is Jacob's voice, but the hands are the hands of Esau" (Gen. 27:22). No two men are identical. Jacob and Esau represent human variations, not only physically, but as regards also temperament, manner, and attitude. Of the many appealing attributes of human nature, none is more appealing than that each man is unique.

590 *IDENTITY WITH HUMANITY*   "He who is joined with all the living has hope" (Eccl. 9:4, RSV). The promise of abundant life belongs to him who identifies himself with humanity and "connects up" with the human race.

591 *THE WIDE HEART*   God "hath set the world in their heart" (Eccl. 3:11). "He has put eternity into man's mind" (RSV). The mind and heart of man are capable of an expansiveness unlike that known to any other living creature. Man may embrace the lives and situations of all human beings, and even within his mortal circumstance he may know something of the wonders and marvels of that divine life which is bound neither by time nor by space.

592 *OF DIVINE ORIGIN*   In Luke's genealogy, Jesus is identified as "being the son (as was supposed) of Joseph . . . the son of Adam, the son of God" (Lk. 3:23, 38, RSV). His lineage, like that of every member in the family of man, culminated in a divine origin.

MATURITY

593 *SPIRITUAL MATURITY*   "And there arose not a prophet since in Israel like unto Moses, whom the Lord knew face to face" (Deut. 34:10). This eulogy was not won in a day. Moses had turned from God, hurled excuses when God issued orders, doubted and disobeyed God. Far from perfect, he did nonetheless achieve spiritual maturity and enjoyed an intimacy with the Eternal such as few men have known.

594 *DIET OF MILK*   Paul discerned the spiritual immaturity of the Corinthian Christians: "I fed you with milk, not solid food; for you were not ready for it" (1 Cor. 3:2, RSV). The wise pastor knows what spiritual nourishment his people are prepared to receive.

MIRACLE

595 *DIVINE SIMPLICITY*   God's miracles are often wrought in simple and quiet ways. Elisha sent word to Naaman that he would be healed of his leprosy if he washed seven times in the Jordan, but "Naaman was enraged and left, and he said, 'Here I have been saying to myself, "He will surely come out and stand and call on the name of the Lord his God, and wave his hand toward the place and cure the leper" ' " (2 Kings 5:11, AT). The spectacle of a Cecil B. De Mille scenario is foreign to the ways of the Lord.

596 *THE GREATEST MIRACLE*   When on Mount Carmel "the fire of the Lord fell . . . all the people . . . fell on their faces: and they said, The Lord, he is the God; the Lord, he is the God" (1 Kings 18:38-39). Wondrous miracles persuade men to believe, and yet the greatest miracle was that in such a generation there should have been a prophet like Elijah.

597 *SHOW ME A SIGN*   When called by the Lord to lead Israel, Gideon said, "If now I have found grace in thy sight, then shew me a sign that thou talkest with me" (Judg. 6:17). Paul offered a more substantial basis for knowing and doing: "We walk by faith, not by sight" (2 Cor. 5:7).

598 *WANTED: A MIRACLE*   Loving Jesus for secondary reasons—because we may thereby claim benefits we don't deserve or for what he can do for us—echoes the attitude of Herod who "was greatly delighted to see Jesus" for "he had long wanted to see him, because he had heard about him, and also because he hoped to see him perform some miracle" (Lk. 23:8, MOFFATT).

599 *KEYS FOR THE GATES*   Herod cast Peter into prison, but God delivered him. Peter and the angel of the Lord "came to the iron gate [which] opened to them of its own accord" (Acts 12:10, RSV). Just as miraculous is the opening by the keys of love and trust of the iron gates of hate, distrust, and misunderstanding between men and nations.

600 *THEY PRAISED GOD*   A blind man, having inquired concerning the commotion on the Jericho road, was told that Jesus was passing by. When he cried aloud to Jesus, the people told him to be silent; but Jesus, sensing the man's need, restored his sight. The miracle was such that the people, who had tried to hush up the blind man, joined in praising God. (Lk. 18:35–43.)

MONEY

601 *PARTRIDGE EGGS*   The man who appropriates or in devious ways claims for himself that which belongs to another does a double wrong, for he not only deprives himself of the pleasure of gleaning where he has sown but also robs another of the harvest which should have been the reward of his labors. "Like a partridge hatching eggs it never laid, so is the man who makes money unfairly" (Jer. 17:11, MOFFATT).

602 *LET ME BUY IT!*   By sorcery Simon had bewitched the Samaritans into believing him to be a person possessing remarkable powers, but his luster was dimmed by the manifestation of the Spirit's power through the apostles. He offered Peter money that he too might be able to perform similar wonders. Peter rebuked him, saying, "Thy money perish with thee, because thou hast thought that the gift of God may be purchased with money. Thou hast neither part nor lot in this matter: for thy heart is not right in the sight of God" (Acts 8:20–21).

603 *FAVORS FOR A PRICE*   Although charged with the administration of justice, Felix offered favors for a price, even to the releasing of prisoners. The historian says that "he nursed a secret hope that Paul would pay him money—which is why Paul was frequently summoned to come and talk with him" (Acts 24:26, PHILLIPS).

604 *WHAT MONEY CANNOT BUY*   Thoreau said, "Money is not required to buy one necessity of the soul." Then what is? At the Beautiful Gate, a man born lame mechanically stretched his hands toward Peter and John and besought them to give him alms. Peter said, "Silver and gold have I none; but such as I have give I thee: In the name of Jesus Christ of Nazareth rise up and walk" (Acts 3:6). In his newly found strength the man leaped to his feet and entered the temple where he praised God for that which the money he solicited could never have guaranteed.

605 *NO PRICE TAGS*   Some things are unpurchasable and God's miracles do not bear price tags. Elisha, having expressly refused gifts in exchange for Naaman's healing, asked Gehazi, who had surreptitiously acquired gratuities from Naaman, "Is it a time to accept money, and garments, and olive orchards and vineyards, and sheep, and oxen, and menservants and maidservants?" (2 Kings 5:26, AT).

MOTHER

606 *THE LAD'S ROBE*   Although Hannah joyously surrendered her son Samuel to the Lord, she continued to love him as only a mother can. "His mother used to make him a little robe, which she brought to him year by year when she came up with her husband to offer the yearly sacrifice" (1 Sam. 2:19, MOFFATT).

607 *A MOTHER'S VIGIL*   When the Gibeonites, having hanged the two sons of Rizpah, refused to permit a proper burial but rather required that the bodies should be exposed to bird and beast, the mother began a summer-long vigil near the remains of those she loved. (2 Sam. 21:10–14.)

608 *THE LONG WAIT*   The destruction of Sisera brought great joy to Israel, but not every heart was made glad. No one who reads the chronicle can remain insensitive to the anguish which blackened a mother's heart: "The mother of Sisera looked out at a window, and cried through the lattice, Why is his chariot so long in coming? why tarry the wheels of his chariot?" (Judg. 5:28).

609 *POSITION OF HONOR*   The honor which Solomon bestowed upon his mother Bath-sheba is deserved by every good mother: "The king rose up to meet her, and bowed himself unto her, and sat down on his throne, and caused a seat to be set for the king's mother, and she sat on his right hand" (1 Kings 2:19).

610 *WICKED COUNSELOR*   Concerning Ahaziah, who ruled one year in Jerusalem, the historian wrote, "He also walked in the ways of the house of Ahab: for his mother was his counselor in doing wickedly" (2 Chron. 22:3, RSV). Athaliah, like her mother Jezebel, represents the antithesis of all that the word "mother" connotes to those who cherish memories of one about whom he may say, "Strength and honour are her clothing. . . . She openeth her mouth with wisdom; and in her tongue is the law of kindness. She looketh well to the ways of her household" (Prov. 31:25–27).

MUSIC

611 *SOLACE IN MUSIC*   Overwhelmed and distracted by the responsibilities of his office and his loss of God's favor, Saul found solace only in music. "Whenever the evil spirit from God overpowered Saul, David would take the lyre and play music, till Saul breathed freely; then all would be well, and the evil spirit would depart from him" (1 Sam. 16:23, MOFFATT).

612 *WHEN THE MINSTREL PLAYED*   "Music has charms to soothe a savage breast" (Congreve). Elisha became angry when the kings of Judah, Israel, and Edom sought his counsel concerning their struggle against Moab. Then he called for a minstrel, "and it came to pass, when the minstrel played, that the hand of the Lord came upon him" (2 Kings 3:15).

613 *THE BATTLE WON BY SONG*   Outnumbered and ill-prepared to do battle against their enemies, the Judahites turned to God and Jehoshaphat their king appointed singers to praise God. "And when they began to sing and praise, the Lord set an ambush against the men of Ammon, Moab, and Mount Seir, who had come against Judah, so that they were routed" (2 Chron. 20:22, RSV).

614 *LYRICAL WITNESS*   After Paul had healed a mentally sick girl, her masters who had exploited her supposed powers of divination charged Paul and his companion Silas with disturbing the peace. The magistrates ordered them beaten and thrust into prison. But the hearts of the prisoners were undaunted and "at midnight Paul and Silas prayed, and sang praises unto God." An unlikely place indeed for worship! But "the other prisoners heard them." (Acts 16:25.) Even in such an unpretentious situation their message was proclaimed to attentive ears, and their influence and witness penetrated the stone walls.

NATION

615 *MEASURING JERUSALEM*   "Whither goest thou?" Zechariah asked an angel who held a measuring line in his hand. "To measure Jerusalem, to see what is the breadth thereof, and what is the length thereof." (Zech. 2:2.) What are the spiritual dimensions of our nation, our communities—our hearts?

616 *THE LORD'S CONTROVERSY*   God took Israel to task for her infidelities. Can we read these words without realizing similar complaints he would level against us and our nation? "The Lord hath a controversy with the inhabitants of the land, because there is no truth, nor mercy, nor knowledge of God in the land" (Hos. 4:1).

617 *RIGHTS AS CITIZENS*   Citizenship is a treasure that no man should despise. When on one occasion Paul and Silas had been beaten and cast into prison, they protested that as Roman citizens they had been treated unjustly. And the magistrates, recognizing their rights as citizens, relented. (Acts 16:36–39.)

618 *THE LIGHTS OF HOME*   During the purging of all Edomites by Joab, the child Hadad was taken to Egypt where he became a favorite of Pharaoh who gave him both food and lodging and also his sister-in-law as a wife. When at last word came that both David and Joab had died, Hadad desired to return to his homeland. "Let me depart, that I may go to mine own country," he said to Pharaoh, who replied, "But what hast thou lacked with me, that, behold, thou seekest to go to thine own country?" "Nothing," replied Hadad, "howbeit let me go in any wise." (1 Kings 11:21–22.)

619 *IN THEIR STEPS*   Erecting monuments and setting aside special days on which to honor a nation's heroes represent insufficient commemorations. "Go ahead then, and finish off what your ancestors tried to do!" (Matt. 23:32, PHILLIPS).

620 *CONTINUAL REMINDER*   "And Moses took the bones of Joseph with him" (Ex. 13:19). As the children of Israel moved toward their promised land, the precious burden was a continual reminder of those heroes whose memory inspires and challenges.

621 *ILLUSIONS*   A word from Isaiah speaks soberly to men who would surrender the future security and safety of the nation to push-button devices and foreign alliances: "The Egyptians are men, and not God; and their horses are flesh, and not spirit" (Isa. 31:3, RSV).

622 *NATION WITHOUT A LEADER*   Basic to good government is responsible leadership. "In those days . . . there was no king in Israel" (Judg. 19:1). The text is from a story of unmitigated sordidness—that which a strong king might well have prevented.

623 *SOLOMON'S PRAYER*   Few prayers by a nation's leader are more appropriate and propitious of good government than that of Solomon: "Give . . . thy servant an understanding heart to judge thy people, that I may discern between good and bad: for who is able to judge this thy so great a people?" (1 Kings 3:9).

NATURE

624 *NATURE'S WITNESS*   Nature proclaims its Creator. "The heavens declare the glory of God; and the firmament sheweth his handiwork" (Ps. 19:1). Job called upon nature's witness: "Ask the very beasts, and they will teach you; ask the wild birds—they will tell you; crawling creatures will instruct you, fish in the sea will inform you: for which of them all knows not that this is the

Eternal's way, in whose control lies every living soul, and the whole life of man" (Job 12:7–10, MOFFATT).

625 *THE GARDENER*   On Easter morning Mary did not recognize Jesus—"supposing him to be the gardener" (Jn. 20:15). Her mistake is not without meaning, for he indeed is Lord of life and cultivator of our appreciation of all things beautiful. Seldom does he seem closer than when we walk with him in spots of natural beauty.

NEGLECT

626 *ALTAR FIRES*   Lest we neglect the altars of the church, home, and heart, our spiritual ancestors wisely counseled, "Fire must be kept burning always on the altar; it must never be allowed to go out" (Lev. 6:13, MOFFATT).

627 *POOR BARGAINERS*   The Lord charged Israel with two evils: "They have forsaken me, the reservoir of fresh water, and hewn out cisterns for themselves, leaky cisterns that cannot hold any water!" (Jer. 2:13, MOFFATT). Poor bargainers, they exchanged fresh for foul water and so made their lives stagnant.

628 *ALL YE THAT PASS BY*   Jeremiah sounded a clarion to spiritual-minded men lest they neglect the call both of God and of other men: "Is it nothing to you, all ye that pass by?" (Lam. 1:12), or "And you who pass by, look, look all of you and see" (MOFFATT).

NEIGHBOR

629 *WHAT WILL THE NEIGHBORS SAY?*   For years beyond number Abraham and Sarah had bombarded heaven with their petitions that the birth of a son crown their marriage. Yet when God graciously responded to their need, Sarah dampened their joy by her extreme sensitivity to what her neighbors might say. "God has made me a laughing-stock; everyone that hears of it will laugh at me" (Gen. 21:6, AT).

630 BEREFT OF NEIGHBORS   Covetous persons "who join house to house, who add field to field, until there is no more room" condemn themselves to misery, for they "are made to dwell alone," bereft of neighbors (Isa. 5:8, rsv).

631 BORROWED AXES   As a member of Elisha's prophetic guild was cutting timber near the Jordan, "the head of the axe fell into the water." The man was doubly concerned: "Alas, my master! . . . it was borrowed." (2 Kings 6:5, moffatt.) The prophet miraculously retrieved that which a neighbor had generously loaned.

632 FRIENDLY BRANCHES   In his final blessing upon his sons, Jacob said, "Joseph is a fruitful bough, a fruitful bough by a spring, his branches run over the wall" (Gen. 49:22, rsv). Can we imagine a more suggestive idea of neighborliness than that of fruit boughs extending beyond fences?

633 MORE THAN KIN   For a lawyer, who had with punctiliousness kept the command to love one's neighbor as oneself, the word "neighbor" meant anyone who belonged to the house of Israel. Jesus told him of a good Samaritan who outdistanced even Jews in his loving-kindness toward a man in trouble. (Lk. 10:25–28.) Within the mind of Jesus "neighbor" meant not one's kith and kin but all humanity.

634 WHAT TO EXPECT   Paul suggested the most likely alternative to the wisdom of loving one's neighbor as yourself: "If you go on fighting one another, tooth and nail, all you can expect is mutual destruction" (Gal. 5:15, neb).

OBEDIENCE

635 ESCAPE FROM GOD   To disobey God is to alienate oneself from the Eternal. When God commissioned him to go to Nineveh and preach there, Jonah left immediately for a far country that he might escape from the Lord's entreaties and disciplines. (Jon. 1:2–3.)

636 SAUL'S OBLIGATION   Samuel, who considered Saul's attack upon the Amalekites to be inadequate, reprimanded the king, saying, "When thou wast little in thine own sight, wast thou not made the head of the tribes of Israel, and the Lord anointed thee king over Israel? . . . Wherefore then didst thou not obey the voice of the Lord?" (1 Sam. 15:17, 19). Saul's obligation to obey God was more important because he was king, and his disobedience had far-reaching consequences.

637 *HIS NAME IS JOHN*   The neighbor women, crowding about Elizabeth and Zecharias after the birth of their first child, suggested that the baby should be given his father's name. But Zecharias remembered that the Lord had chosen another name, and obedient to God he wrote on his tablet, "His name is John" (Lk. 1:63).

638 *BLIND OBEDIENCE*   Rebekah exacted obedience from her son Jacob. "Now therefore, my son, obey my voice according to that which I command thee" (Gen. 27:8). And forthwith she instructed him concerning the way by which he should beguile his father and snatch away his brother's blessing. Blind obedience, even toward a parent, is not always virtuous.

OBLIGATION

639 *UNIVERSAL OBLIGATION*   Christ's Kingdom embraces humanity, for he said, "Go ye therefore, and teach all nations" (Matt. 28:19). Paul's response was according to such latitude: "I feel myself under a sort of universal obligation, I owe something to all men, from cultured Greek to ignorant savage" (Rom. 1:14, PHILLIPS), or "Both to Greeks and to barbarians (to the cultured and to the uncultured), both to the wise and the foolish I have an obligation to discharge and a duty to perform and a debt to pay" (AMNT).

640 *GREATER REQUIREMENTS*   Jesus condemned Pharisees who were so punctilious in their observance of the law that they even tithed such kitchen-garden commodities as mint, rue, and herbs, but disregarded the requirements of justice and the love of God. (Lk. 11:42.)

OBSTACLE

641 *SENT TO HINDER HIM*   As Balaam journeyed to Moab
"the angel of the Lord . . . stood in a narrow place, where was no
way to turn either to the right hand or to the left." It is well for
him who is attentive to the obstructions by which God would lead
our steps, whether he speaks through his Word, his Son, the counsel
of saintly men, the voice of conscience—or an angel. To Balaam the
angel said, "Here am I, sent to hinder you, at the sight of your
headlong ways." (Num. 22:26; v. 32, MOFFATT).

642 *BLOCKED CHANNELS*   Before Saul engaged in combat
with the Philistines, a priest advised him to seek God's guidance,
but when Saul asked God if he should move against the Philistines,
God "answered him not that day" (1 Sam. 14:37). Sin had blocked
the channels of communication.

643 *PATHWAY OF OBSTACLES*   "Any man of Israel who
takes his idols to his very heart . . . is bent upon the sin that trips
him up" (Ezek. 14:4, MOFFATT). The sins we covet bring our un-
doing. The sinner walks along a pathway filled with obstacles.

644 *THE DOOR WAS CLOSED*   "When they reached the
frontier of Mysia, they were about to enter Bithynia, but the Spirit
of Jesus would not permit this" (Acts 16:7, WEYMOUTH). Paul and
his companions may have considered Bithynia a fertile and promis-
ing field for evangelism, but depending upon Christ for directions,
they followed those paths along which he guided them.

645 *STUMBLING BLOCKS*   After urging the Corinthian
Christians to avoid placing stumbling blocks in the paths of others,
Paul took a stand that was consistent with his words: "Such is my
own rule, to satisfy all men in all points, aiming not at my own
advantage but at the advantage of the greater number—at their salvation" (1 Cor. 10:33, MOFFATT).

646 *HIS COMING IMPEDED*   When his enemies were about
to pelt him with stones, "Jesus hid himself" (Jn. 8:59), or "Jesus
concealed himself" (MOFFATT). But what of those times when we

most need him and cannot find him? Does he deliberately turn from us? Is it not rather that we have permitted impediments to obstruct his coming into our hearts?

OFFERING

647 *THEY CONTRIBUTED MIRRORS* The Israelites contributed according to their means to the construction of the tabernacle. Some of the women offered that which held more than ordinary value for them: Bezaleel, the craftsman, "made the laver of bronze, and its base of bronze, out of the mirrors of the serving-women who served at the door of the tent of meeting" (Ex. 38:8, AT).

648 *MAN'S TRUSTEESHIP* After the people had enthusiastically given to the building of God's house, David dedicated the gifts in a radiant recognition of God's ownership and man's trusteeship. "Yet who am I, what is my people, that we should be able to offer such freewill offerings? All gifts come from thee, and we only give thee what is thine. . . . O thou Eternal, our God, all these . . . come from thine own hand and are all thine own" (1 Chron. 29:14, 16, MOFFATT).

649 *CHEERFUL GIVERS* "Let everyone give as his heart tells him, neither grudgingly nor under compulsion, for God loves the man who gives cheerfully" (2 Cor. 9:7, PHILLIPS). When David called upon his people to support the building of God's house, both king and people responded enthusiastically: "The people rejoiced at this, at this freewill offering, contributed without grudging to the Eternal, and David the king was . . . overjoyed" (1 Chron. 29:9, MOFFATT).

650 *TWO SMALL COINS* True generosity is not rightly determined by the size of a gift, for even a substantial donation by a rich man may make no dent in his possessions or his heart. Jesus commended the poor widow by saying that her two small coins represented more than any other offering: "From what they could well spare they have all of them contributed to the offerings, but she in her need has thrown in all she had to live on" (Lk. 21:4, WEYMOUTH).

651 *UNBLEMISHED SACRIFICES*   The Lord instructed Moses that all animals offered as sacrifices should be without blemish. (Lev. 22:20–22.) In like manner, our offerings should be free from such shoddy practices as the surrender only of a niggardly residue or self-seeking by appealing to the praises of our fellow worshipers. Rather, we are to "offer the sacrifices of righteousness" (Ps. 4:5).

652 *NOT WRUNG OUT OF YOU*   Pastors who plead for money for worthy causes may take comfort in the fact that Paul found it necessary to make similar pleas: "I want it to be forthcoming as a generous gift, not as money wrung out of you" (2 Cor. 9:5, MOFFATT).

653 *STRANGE FIRE*   The strange and unholy fire which Nadab and Abihu, Aaron's sons, offered to the Lord consumed them. (Lev. 10:1–3.) No one can now explain what inadequacy or irreverence this offering represented, but we do know that theirs were not "spiritual sacrifices, acceptable to God" (1 Pet. 2:5) and that they did not worship "in spirit and in truth" (Jn. 4:24).

654 *MORE THAN ENOUGH*   No Budget Sunday appeal could culminate in a more heart-warming response than that which followed Moses' invitation that the children of Israel bring "free offerings" for the building of the tabernacle: "And they spake unto Moses, saying, The people bring much more than enough for the service of the work, which the Lord commanded to make. And Moses gave commandment, and they caused it to be proclaimed throughout the camp, saying, Let neither man nor woman make any more work for the offering of the sanctuary" (Ex. 36:5–6).

655 *THOSE WHO CHEAT GOD*   The Lord accused his people, saying, "You are cheating me." The accusation seemed preposterous. They asked how they had done such a thing, and the Lord replied, "By your tithes and offerings." (Mal. 3:8, MOFFATT.)

OPINION

656 *LIMPING BETWEEN OPINIONS*   Elijah challenged the children of Israel at Mount Carmel, "How long will you go limping with two different opinions? If the Lord is God, follow him; but if Baal, then follow him" (1 Kings 18:21, RSV). The people were unresponsive to his plea.

657 CHANGE OF MIND   The willingness to alter one's opinion is a distinguishing and corrective characteristic of men. When a viper fastened itself to the hand of Paul, the Maltese natives said, "The man must be a murderer; he may have escaped from the sea, but divine justice has not let him live," but after he shook off the viper without incident, "they changed their minds and now said, 'He is a god.' " (Acts 28:4, 6, NEB.)

658 DIFFERENCES THAT MATTER   Differences of opinion may mean that seeds of disharmony are being sown or that new truth is being stoutly defended. Festus reported to Herod Agrippa concerning a mighty important point of disagreement: "They quarrelled with [Paul] about certain matters connected with their own religion, and about one Jesus who had died, but—so Paul persistently maintained—is now alive" (Acts 25:19, WEYMOUTH).

659 OBSESSION FOR NOVELTIES   Paul captivated the minds of the Athenian philosophers, not because they sought divine truth, but rather because "all the Athenians . . . had an obsession for any novelty and would spend their whole time talking about or listening to anything new" (Acts 17:21, PHILLIPS). The words of eternal life are not according to the latest fad or fashion, but are to be found in the old, old Story.

660 TRUSTED OPINION   Knowledgeable concerning the requirements of the Spirit and having read aright God's Word, a pastor, after the manner of Paul, is obligated and privileged to speak positively concerning matters about which the New Testament does not offer explicit injunctions. "I have no orders from the Lord for unmarried women, but I will give you the opinion of one whom you can trust, after all the Lord's mercy to him" (1 Cor. 7:25, MOFFATT).

661 THE PEOPLE WERE DIVIDED   The Jews at Iconium so "stirred up the Gentiles and poisoned their minds against the brethren" that "the people of the city were divided; some sided with the Jews, and some with the apostles" (Acts 14:2, 4, RSV). Jesus said, "I have not come to bring peace, but a sword" (Matt. 10:34, RSV). Even in our communities the word of life separates men of faith from unbelievers.

OPPORTUNITY

662 *UNDER ADVERSE CIRCUMSTANCES*   Undaunted by his opponents, Paul would not permit adversity to destroy opportunity. "I am staying on for the present at Ephesus till Pentecost, for I have wide opportunities here for active service—and there are many to thwart me" (1 Cor. 16:8–9, MOFFATT).

663 *CAPERNAUM RECEIVES HIM*   Jesus' reception in Nazareth was disheartening and discouraging. "All in the synagogue were filled with wrath. And they rose up and put him out of the city." When one door is closed, God always opens another. "Passing through the midst of them [Jesus] went away" to Capernaum where he was received by a people who "were astonished at his teaching, for his word was with authority." (Lk. 4:28–29, 30, 32, RSV.)

664 *TO SEE FOR HIMSELF*   Zacchaeus had heard about Jesus, but the testimony of others did not satisfy him. So when Jesus passed through Jericho, Zacchaeus, who was too short to see above the heads of the people, cast aside the amenities which his social position required, and climbed a sycamore tree that he might see Jesus for himself. (Lk. 19:1–4.)

PARENTHOOD

665 *GOD'S CHARGE*   What the Lord said concerning Abraham reflects a responsibility which he gives to every parent: "I have chosen him that he may charge his sons and his household after him to follow the directions of the Eternal by doing what is good and right" (Gen. 18:19, MOFFATT).

666 *LET HIM COME AGAIN*   Before the birth of Samson, a messenger of God told the wife of Manoah the kind of training her child should receive. Manoah then offered a prayer which is worthy of emulation by all parents: "O my Lord, let the man of God which thou didst send come again unto us, and teach us what we shall do unto the child that shall be born" (Judg. 13:8).

667 *SOBERING EXPERIENCE*   "And to Seth . . . was born a son . . . then began men to call upon the name of the Lord" (Gen. 4:26). Parenthood is both a joyous and a sobering experience. To train children in the way they should go parents often become especially sensitive to their dependence upon the "one God and Father of all, who is above all, and through all, and in you all" (Eph. 4:6).

668 *SPIRITUAL INSTRUCTION*   The responsibility of parents to instruct children in their spiritual heritage is illustrated in these words: "And it shall come to pass, when your children shall say unto you, What mean ye by this service? that ye shall say, It is the sacrifice of the Lord's passover" (Ex. 12:26–27).

669 *THEY BROUGHT THEIR CHILDREN*   Christian parents covet for their little ones the touch of the Master's hand. "Then people began to bring babies to him so that he could put his hands on them" (Lk. 18:15, PHILLIPS).

670 *WHO IS TO BLAME?*   "And she, being put forward and prompted by her mother, said, Give me the head of John the Baptist right here on a platter" (Matt. 14:8, AMNT). A parent's responsibility and privilege of guiding children into wholesome living is perverted by those parents who use their children for devious and self-seeking purposes. "Master, who did sin, this man, or his parents?" (Jn. 9:2). Or who is more to blame—parental delinquents or juvenile delinquents?

PARTICIPATION

671 *HE SAT WITH THEM*   Too often we donate money to help unfortunate people, or we send others to help them, or we content ourselves merely by remembering them in our prayers. The prophet did not look upon the Babylonian exiles from afar, but he shared their miseries. "Then I came to them of the captivity at Tel-abib, that dwelt by the river of Chebar, and I sat where they sat, and remained there . . . among them seven days" (Ezek. 3:15).

672 SPECTATOR OR PARTICIPANT?   The men of Israel were filled with consternation because of the Philistine champion, Goliath. Into their midst came the shepherd boy, David, asking questions. David's elder brother, Eliab, was angry that David should meddle in the affairs of men. "Why have you come here? . . . Whom did you leave in charge of that poor flock in the open country? I know your forwardness and your self-will; you came to see the battle!" David replied, "I merely asked a question." (1 Sam. 17:28–29, MOFFATT.) But there was a remarkable difference between the brothers: the eldest son of Jesse was confounded by Goliath and the boy David was determined to do what lay within his power. The one was a spectator and the other a participant; the one concerned with the problem and the other with the answer.

PAST

673 FATAL REGRET   The family of Lot, providentially rescued from the doomed cities of Sodom and Gomorrah, were advised not to turn back toward the life they had known. "But his wife looked back from behind him, and she became a pillar of salt" (Gen. 19:26). Did she for a fleeting moment wistfully yearn for her hearth and home, her companions of other days? Her erstwhile regret was fatal. "No man, having put his hand to the plough, and looking back, is fit for the kingdom of God" (Lk. 9:62).

674 CHERISHED MEMORIES   Old men, who remembered the first temple, "wept with a loud voice" when they saw the foundation of the post-exilic structure, but those who had never beheld God's house "shouted aloud for joy" (Ezra 3:12). Some wondered why "the former days were better than these" (Eccl. 7:10); others were "reaching forth unto those things which are before" (Phil. 3:13). Better a sanctuary for the present hour than cherished memories of that which served well our fathers.

675 *LEARNING FROM THE PAST*   One of the tragedies of human life is that we so seldom seem capable or willing to learn from past experiences. "There is no remembrance of former things; neither shall there be any remembrance of things that are to come with those that shall come after" (Eccl. 1:11).

PASTOR

676 *WHERE KINGS ENTER*   The Lord told Jeremiah to proclaim the divine word "in the Benjamin Gate, by which the kings of Judah enter and by which they go out, and in all the gates of Jerusalem" (Jer. 17:19, RSV). Here is a bona fide word for pastors who remain in their ivory towers—or in their elevated pulpits—and eschew the streets and highways where needy men hunger for guidance and inspiration.

677 *ASSAYER AND TESTER*   The privilege and responsibility of all spiritual leaders is found in the Lord's words to Jeremiah: "I have made you an assayer and tester among my people" (Jer. 6:27, RSV).

678 *DIVINE SANCTION*   Neither academic degrees, ordination, nor clerical garb offers assurance that a pastor speaks with divine sanction. Paul said, "Make full proof of your ministry" (2 Tim. 4:5). Jeremiah said, "The prophets are but windbags; the Word is not in them!" (Jer. 5:13, MOFFATT).

679 *SCORN FOR THE FORTHRIGHT*   Micah's trenchant preaching was too directly aimed to please some in his audience. "Stop it," one man interrupted, "such harping is not prophecy; no shameful fate can e'er o'ertake the house of Jacob." A preacher who offers only comforting words seldom wins the scorn of sinners, but to preach fearlessly will inevitably make indignant those who do not want the waters stirred. Micah hurled back his answer: "The prophet for such folk would be some empty fellow and a liar, who promised to prophesy of wine and spirits!" (Mic. 2:6, 11, MOFFATT.)

680 *NOT I, BUT CHRIST*   There is mighty little room in the gospel ministry for luxurious self-commendation, whatever compliments seem in order because of a pastor's eloquence, splendid phrase-making, purple rhetoric, or impassioned peroration. "He who glories is to glory in this, that he has insight into me, that he knows I am the Eternal, dealing in kindness, justice, and goodness upon earth—for these are my delight" (Jer. 9:24, MOFFATT). "Not I, but Christ" (Gal. 2:20).

681 *DILUTED JUDGMENT*   Jeremiah's stinging condemnation of false prophets applies to contemporary pastors who dilute God's fearsome judgment: "Never listen to what the prophets say; they fill you up with idle hopes, they tell you fancies of their own, not anything the Eternal says; 'All will be well,' they repeat, to people who scorn what the Eternal says; 'No harm will come to you,' they tell the folk who follow their own stubborn minds" (Jer. 23:16–17, MOFFATT).

682 *RESPONSIBILITY OF PASTORS*   No responsibility of a pastor surpasses that of leading his people to the heavenly throne, praying in their behalf, and making them sensitive to the spiritual possibilities of a life of close communion with God. Samuel said, "Assemble all Israel at Mizpeh that I may intercede on your behalf with the Lord" (1 Sam. 7:5, AT).

683 *THEY WILL NOT OBEY*   Entranced and attentive, the people gathered about Ezekiel, but "they heed you as they would a love-song beautifully rendered and well-played—they hear your words, but they will not obey them" (Ezek. 33:32, MOFFATT).

PATIENCE

684 *THAT WHICH IS NEEDED*   A property owner was determined to uproot a tree which bore no fruit and occupied valuable space, but the gardener begged for the opportunity to give the tree proper care. "If it bears fruit next year, well and good; but if not, you may cut it down" (Lk. 13:9, RSV). Patience is often essential to bring children to maturity, to bring seed to flower, or—as in the context of this story—to bring sinners to repentance.

685 *A CHRISTIAN DISCIPLINE*   Patient waiting is a discipline required of Christians. Some serve on far-flung battle lines;

others must remain until some unknown though propitious moment. Jesus told his disciples, "Wait patiently in the City until you are clothed with power from on high" (Lk. 24:49, WEYMOUTH).

686 *WAITING FOR DAY*   Having drifted fourteen days on the Sea of Adria, the sailors aboard the ship which was taking Paul to Rome, "fearing that [the ship] might be cast ashore on a rugged coast . . . dropped four anchors from the stern and prayed for daylight to come" (Acts 27:29, NEB). Such are the circumstances in many a life when, having done what is possible, a man has no alternative except to pray and be patient.

PEACE

687 *THE WAY OF PEACE*   In his relations with Abimelech the Philistine, Isaac chose the way of peace, preferring to remove his flocks to Beer-sheba rather than to arouse enmity. No doubt Abimelech was amazed and wondered why Isaac would not rise belligerently to a contest of arms. But Abimelech was subsequently persuaded by Isaac's example of good will and approached him with an offer to negotiate a covenant. "And they departed from him in peace." (Gen. 26:31.)

688 *DON'T ROCK THE BOAT*   Ahab called Elijah a "troubler of Israel" (1 Kings 18:17, RSV). Modern Christians who have developed the fine art of not rocking the boat ought not to forget that the prophets neither took nor prescribed sedatives and that our Lord said, "I came not to send peace, but a sword" (Matt. 10:34).

PERMANENCE

689 *THE PASSING VISION*   "And just as they were starting to leave Him, Peter said to Jesus, 'Master, it is good for us to be here. Let us put up three tents, one for you, one for Moses, and one for Elijah'—although he did not know what he was saying" (Lk. 9:33, WILLIAMS). Peter did not know that even such an overawing experience as the Transfiguration could not be clung to permanently. The vision would pass, but the inspiration remains.

PERSEVERANCE

690 *STORMING HEAVEN'S GATES*   After knocking on a
neighbor's door late at night and asking for bread to set before an
unexpected traveler, an unprepared host received a blunt retort
that it was too late to be bothered. But his need was great, and he
continued to plague the neighbor until at last he reluctantly ac-
ceded. (Lk. 11:5–10.) Perseverance is essential for the accomplish-
ment of many things, and a man should persistently storm heaven's
gate with his prayers and petitions.

691 *THE WIDOW'S PETITION*   Jesus illustrated the need
for persistence in prayer by telling of a widow who, because she continually petitioned a dishonest judge, finally won attention for her
claim. (Lk. 18:1–8.) How much more readily will a just God respond
to those who persevere in prayer!

PERSPECTIVE

692 *POINT OF VIEW*   Here is a sobering word for those who
are intoxicated by novelty and claim for their generation a unique
point of view, attitude, or artifact: "Men may say of something,
'Ah, this is new!'—but it existed long before our time" (Eccl. 1:10,
MOFFATT).

693 *GOD'S COIGN OF VANTAGE*   When Peter remonstrated
against Jesus' prediction of his passion, Jesus said, "You look at
things from man's point of view and not from God's" (Matt. 16:23,
PHILLIPS), or "You think as men think, not as God thinks" (NEB).

PLAN

694 *PATTERN OF SALVATION*   To a people who had been
conquered by the Philistines, Samuel offered battle plans which will
also shore up our strength for successful spiritual warfare: "If you
are returning to the Lord with all your heart, then put away the
foreign gods and the Ashtaroth from among you, and direct your

heart to the Lord, and serve him only, and he will deliver you out of the hand of the Philistines" (1 Sam. 7:3, rsv).

695 *HE CHARTS OUR WAY*   The Lord gave this assurance to the exiles: "I know the plans I have for you . . . plans for welfare and not for evil, to give you a future and a hope" (Jer. 29:11, rsv). Those who love God are within the circumference of a divine love which charts the paths we must take. "In all thy ways acknowledge him, and he shall direct thy paths" (Prov. 3:6).

696 *CONTRARY PLANS*   Having already determined to flee to Egypt, the commanders of the Jewish forces asked Jeremiah to tell them what the Lord wished them to do. But when the prophet conveyed to them God's will, which was contrary to their plans, they challenged Jeremiah's integrity, saying, "You are telling a lie" (Jer. 43:2, rsv).

697 *IMMEDIATE PLANNING*   In a nocturnal vision, a man of Macedonia petitioned Paul to "come over into Macedonia, and help us" (Acts 16:9). Paul, neither distrusting nor doubting the vision, made immediate plans to depart.

POPULARITY

698 *HE STOLE THEIR HEARTS*   Absalom, who rode in splendor in a chariot and promised synthetic justice to the people, "stole the hearts of the men of Israel" (2 Sam. 15:6). The spectacle and the glib promise have often been used by politicians to win elections from more competent leaders.

699 *UNPOPULAR WORDS*   The stern words of Amos made him unpopular. Amaziah the priest, who wanted to leave well enough alone, charged the prophet with treason and informed Jeroboam, "Amos hath conspired against thee in the midst of the house of Israel." What he said made the people restive and encouraged revolution. "The land is not able to bear all his words." (Amos 7:10.) The priest urged the prophet to flee to Judah and never return to Bethel. By one means or another we strive to silence those who speak the truth boldly, but the welfare of a community depends upon those who have prophetic fearlessness. Such people are the living conscience of society.

700 *PRICE OF POPULARITY*   Popularity often exacts a fearful price. "Then Pilate, anxious to appease the mob, set Barabbas free for them" (Mk. 15:15, RIEU), or "Pilate wished to please the mob, and he released Barabbas for them" (BARCLAY). Ultimately, Pilate satisfied neither his conscience nor the howling people, and the popularity he sought was, as history shows, short-lived.

701 *THE PRAISE THEY CHERISHED*   To believe in Christ secretly is not to believe at all. Playing it safe by keeping mum lest one be held in contempt by his nonbelieving associates is to play fast and loose with one's spiritual welfare. "Among the chief rulers also many believed on him; but because of the Pharisees they did not confess him, lest they should be put out of the synagogue: for they loved the praise of men more than the praise of God" (Jn. 12:42–43).

PRAYER

702 *EXPECTANT PRAYER*   Convinced that God would an-swer his prayer for rain, Elijah made his petition with expectancy and persistency: "And Elijah went up to the top of Carmel; and he bowed down upon the earth. . . . And he said to his servant, 'Go up now, look toward the sea.' And he went up and looked, and said, 'There is nothing.' And he said, 'Go again seven times.' And at the seventh time he said, 'Behold, a little cloud like a man's hand is rising out of the sea' " (1 Kings 18:42–44, RSV).

703 *ANSWER TO HIS PRAYER*   "And Isaac went out to meditate in the field at the eventide: and he lifted up his eyes, and saw, and, behold, the camels were coming" (Gen. 24:63). What thoughts were in his mind? What prayers on his lips? Was he ap-prehensive? He arose from a posture appropriate to one who faces an unknown future and beheld the answer to his prayers—Rebekah.

704 *PETER CONTINUED KNOCKING*   Delivered miracu-lously from prison, Peter went to the home of Mary, the mother of

John Mark, where his friends were praying for him. Rhoda answered his knock on the door, but in her excitement she neglected to let him in before she told the good news to the others. At first they refused to believe that their prayers had been answered, and it was only after "Peter continued knocking" (Acts 12:16) that they were convinced. Jesus said, "If ye abide in me, and my words abide in you, ye shall ask what ye will, and it shall be done unto you" (Jn. 15:7).

705 *THY WILL BE DONE*   Our prayers should be tempered with the words that God's will be done, lest we seek that which God does not consider to be for our good. "And he gave them their request; but sent leanness into their soul" (Ps. 106:15), or "He let them have what they desired, then—made them loathe it!" (MOFFATT).

706 *REINFORCED PRAYERS*   When the Hebrews attempted to rebuild the walls of Jerusalem, their labors were frustrated by their enemies who were equally determined that the walls not rise again. "And we prayed to our God, and set a guard as a protection against them day and night" (Neh. 4:9, RSV). Their prayers were reinforced—as prayers should be—by their doing that which lay within their power.

707 *HALFHEARTED PETITIONS*   The Lord denounced Ephraim, saying, "They never put their heart into their prayers, but howl away for corn and wine beside their altars" (Hos. 7:14, MOFFATT). Theirs were halfhearted petitions which sought to move the arm of God without being moved themselves. They begged for physical necessities but did not surrender their lives to the will of God.

708 *THE SHAKING OF THINGS*   "More things are wrought by prayer than this world dreams of" (Tennyson). To pray listlessly and unexpectantly brings inconsequential results. After the friends of Peter and John joined in prayer, "the place was shaken where they were assembled together" (Acts 4:31). Fervent and righteous prayer upsets the normal equilibrium, transforms our motives, and disrupts—as in a mighty shaking—the character of our lives.

709 *A PRIVATE AFFAIR* Meaningful prayer is a private affair between a petitioner and his God. "When you wish to pray, enter your private room and when you have shut your door pray to your Father who dwells in secret" (Matt. 6:6, RIEU).

710 *PRAYING ON STRAIGHT STREET* The Lord told Ananias that he would recognize Paul at the street called Straight, for "he is praying at this very moment" (Acts 9:11, MOFFATT). Even as Paul prayed for divine guidance, his petition was being answered.

711 *EARLY PRAYERS* Elkanah and Hannah were constant in their prayers that the Lord might give them a child. "And they rose up in the morning early, and worshipped before the Lord" (1 Sam. 1:19).

712 *VIGILS THAT SUSTAIN* Jesus' strength in body and purpose was sustained by his prayer vigils. "When he had sent the multitudes away, he went up into a mount apart to pray: and when the evening was come, he was there alone" (Matt. 14:23).

PREJUDICE

713 *LEAVEN OF MISERY* After Mordecai had refused to show him the respect he claimed, Haman lamented to his friends that although he was rich in possessions, children, and honors at court, "Yet all this availeth me nothing, so long as I see Mordecai the Jew sitting at the king's gate" (Es. 5:13). The little lump of prejudice became the leaven in his loaf of misery.

714 LEX TALIONIS Pleading earnestly in behalf of the Jews, Esther exclaimed, "How can I endure to see the evil that shall come upon my people? or how can I endure to see the destruction of my kindred?" Yet given permission to oppress their oppressors, the Jews with fanatical zeal excoriated the Gentiles. "The Jews smote all their enemies with the stroke of the sword, and slaughter, and destruction, and did what they would unto those that hated them." (Es. 8:6; 9:5.) This story sharpens our understanding of the fact that prejudice is a two-edged sword. Not *lex talionis* but a higher principle is needed to obliterate prejudice:

"There is no difference between the Jew and the Greek: for the same Lord over all is rich unto all that call upon him" (Rom. 10:12).

715 *JONAH'S ANGER*   Jonah's prejudice against the Ninevites was so great that when, in obedience to God's word, both king and commoner repented of their sins, Jonah was exceedingly displeased and angered. (Jon. 3:4–4:1.)

PREPARATION

716 *PATIENT PREPARATION*   An alluring short cut may not be the route God has chosen for us. "And it came to pass, when Pharaoh had let the people go, that God led them not through the way of the land of the Philistines, although that was near" (Ex. 13:17). The goals we seek are not reached in a night's travel. Our road may be, as for the people of old, the labyrinthian way of patient preparation.

717 *HE ABUNDANTLY PREPARED*   Unable to construct the temple, which was his lifelong ambition, David worked enthusiastically so that another might successfully reap where he had sown. "And David said, Solomon my son is young and tender, and the house that is to be builded for the Lord must be exceeding magnifical . . . I will therefore now make preparation for it. So David prepared abundantly before his death" (1 Chron. 22:5).

718 *ARABIAN SOJOURN*   After his conversion on the Damascus road, Paul "went into Arabia. . . . Then after three years . . . went up to Jerusalem" (Gal. 1:17–18). Before launching his new work, Paul went into the desert to contemplate the deeper meanings of his experience and by prayer and study to prepare himself.

719 *DRY LAMPS*   To be prepared is half of faith's victory. The young women who had not anticipated the need for sufficient oil for their lamps were denied the pleasure of the wedding party. When their supply ran low, "the foolish ones said to the sensible ones, 'Please give us some of your oil—our lamps are going out!' 'Oh, no,' returned the sensible ones, 'there might not be enough for all of us' " (Matt. 25:8–9, PHILLIPS).

720 *IF HE HAD KNOWN*   Failure to anticipate the return of the Son of man was likened by Jesus to an unwary landlord: "If the householder had known at what hour the thief was coming, he would have been awake and would not have left his house to be broken into" (Lk. 12:39, RSV).

721 *HIS HEART MADE READY*   The initial appearance of Saul in the story of the early church was an accessory, if not a participant, in the stoning of Stephen where he "gave silent assent to his execution" (Acts 8:1, PHILLIPS). Yet Stephen's testimony was pervasive and kindled in Saul a restiveness which prepared his heart and mind for the Spirit's invasion.

PRIDE

722 *HOUSE OF MIRRORS*   The man who continually commends himself lives in a house of mirrors. He is, as someone has said, a self-made man who worships his maker. Or, to change the figure, he is all wrapped up in himself and makes a mighty small package. Paul spoke of such persons: "All they are doing . . . is to measure themselves by their own standards or by comparisons within their own circle, and that doesn't make for accurate estimation, you may be sure" (2 Cor. 10:12, PHILLIPS).

723 *SEE WHAT I HAVE!*   Made proud by the arrival of Babylonian emissaries, Hezekiah flung wide the doors of his kingdom and vainly paraded his treasures, showing "them all the house of his precious things, the silver, and the gold, and the spices, and the precious ointment, and all the house of his armour, and all that was found in his treasures: there was nothing in his house, nor in all his dominion, that Hezekiah shewed them not." Isaiah rebuked him, "Behold, the days come, that all that is in thine house . . . shall be carried unto Babylon: nothing shall be left, saith the Lord." (2 Kings 20:13, 17.)

724 *I AM A GOD*   Ezekiel's condemnation of Tyre is apropos for any nation—or individual—which, proud in its wealth and achievements, boasts of a sufficiency that cancels its debt to God. "Your heart is proud, and you have said, 'I am a god, I sit in the seat of the gods, in the heart of the seas,' yet you are but a man, and no god, though you consider yourself as wise as a god" (Ezek. 28:2, RSV).

725 *AN UNHEEDED WARNING*   Nebuchadnezzar turned from Daniel's warning that he "break off your sins by practicing righteousness, and your iniquities by showing mercy to the oppressed." A year later the king, standing on his palace roof, declared proudly, "Is not this great Babylon, which I have built by my mighty power as a royal residence and for the glory of my majesty?" No sooner had he made the boast than a voice from heaven said, "O King Nebuchadnezzar, to you it is spoken: The kingdom has departed from you." (Dan. 4:27, 30–31, RSV.)

726 A PRIORI *BOASTING*   Ahab's message to Ben-hadad, the Syrian king who arrayed a mighty army against Samaria, is wise counsel for any braggadocio: "The man who is arming had better not boast like the man who is unarming" (1 Kings 20:11, MOFFATT).

727 *THE PATHS OF GLORY*   The king of Babylon boasted, "I will ascend into heaven, I will exalt my throne above the stars of God . . . I will ascend above the heights of the clouds; I will be like the most High" (Isa. 14:13–14), but he too was carried at last to his tomb.

728 *CASUALTIES OF CLEVERNESS*   Isaiah's words, spoken to Babylon, apply to any nation or individual who becomes unduly proud of his ingenuity or cleverness: "It was your own magic craft and cunning that misled you, till you thought to yourself 'I am supreme' " (Isa. 47:10, MOFFATT).

729 *THE LAST WORD*   Isaiah promised that the Lord would speak the last word to the arrogant and boastful king of Assyria who declared, "My strong hand did it all, my clever strategy; I shifted the boundaries of nations, I plundered their treasuries, I reduced them to ashes, and felled their folk like a bullock; the wealth of nations, I rifled it all, like the nest of a bird, I ransacked the wide world as a man who gathers eggs, till not a wing fluttered, none dared cheep or chirp" (Isa. 10:13–14, MOFFATT).

730 *NOT BY MIGHT*   The Lord told Gideon to reduce considerably the number of his warriors lest by overwhelming their enemies by massed armies the people might conclude that the victory belonged to them and not to God. (Judg. 7:2–3.)

731 *ZION'S HAUGHTY DAUGHTERS*   Isaiah condemned the haughty daughters of Zion who "walk with outstretched necks, glancing wantonly with their eyes, mincing along as they go, tinkling with their feet" (Isa. 3:16, RSV), who give themselves to vanity rather than to a becoming modesty.

732 *THE SNOB IN THE TEMPLE*   The Pharisee who in the temple recited the manner in which he had adhered to his religious obligations is not unlike the religious snob of our day who, proud of his self-righteousness, isolates himself from common clay. (Lk. 18:9–14.)

733 *THE LUXURY OF PRIDE*   Alien to Pauline Christianity is the luxury of boastfulness and pride in mental agility or prowess: "Who singles you out, my brother? What do you possess that has not been given you? And if it was given you, why do you boast as if it had been gained, not given?" (1 Cor. 4:7, MOFFATT).

PROMISE

734 *THEY SHALL FLOURISH*   God's promise to the penitent children of Israel glows with a lively hope for all who turn to him: "They shall return and dwell beneath my shadow, they shall flourish as a garden; they shall blossom as the vine, their fragrance shall be like the wine of Lebanon" (Hos. 14:7, RSV).

735 *I WILL BE WITH YOU*   When God called Moses, who was tending the flocks on Mount Horeb, Moses complained that he lacked the wherewithal to stand up to Pharaoh. But God promised, "I will be with you. And here is your proof that I myself have sent you: when you have brought the people out of Egypt, they shall worship God on this very hill" (Ex. 3:12, MOFFATT).

736 *THE YEARS OF THE LOCUSTS*   To a penitent people, who are responsive to his judgments, God promises a reprieve and restoration: "I will restore to you the years that the locust hath eaten" (Joel 2:25).

PURPOSE

737 *THE FORGOTTEN PITCHER*   She had come to draw water, but found instead him who is the living water. In her haste to report to her neighbors, she "left her pitcher" (Jn. 4:28, WILLIAMS). When we become followers of Jesus, many of our first purposes become secondary and many things must be left behind.

738 *THE MASTER'S MISSION*   The neighbors of Zacchaeus, blind to the inclusive love of God, criticized Jesus when he entered the home of the notorious tax collector. "Now he has gone to stay with a real sinner" (Lk. 19:7, PHILLIPS). They failed to realize that the Master's mission was to claim for God those who by censorious human standards seem unworthy.

739 *CHALLENGING MOTIVATION*   Othniel accepted Caleb's offer of the hand of his daughter Achsah in marriage to the warrior who captured Debir. (Josh. 15:16–17.) Given a challenging motivation, many men accomplish feats which might otherwise be impossible.

740 *THE SET FACE*   Having set his face resolutely toward Jerusalem, Jesus dispatched James and John to a Samaritan village to arrange for a night's lodging; but when the villagers refused to help, the disciples spitefully asked, "Lord, may we call down fire from heaven to burn them up?" (Lk. 9:54, NEB). Jesus reproved them, for his mind could not be turned from major purposes by trivial irritations.

741 *TO ROME AT LAST*   "And so we came to Rome" (Acts 28:14, RSV). The Book of Acts seems to suggest the inevitability of Paul's arriving at Rome, the seat of empire and what may have seemed to him to be the scene of his execution. To appeal to Caesar had been his choice, and he may well have believed that his words would reverberate—as indeed they did—to the far reaches of the Roman world. "Neither count I my life dear unto myself," he had said, "so that I might finish my course with joy, and the ministry, which I have received of the Lord Jesus, to testify the gospel of the grace of God" (Acts 20:24).

RECONCILIATION

742 FEEDING THE ENEMY   When the Syrians attempted to capture Elisha, who had been keeping the king of Israel informed of their battle plans, Elisha prayed that they might be made blind. This having happened, the king of Israel urged that they be killed, but Elisha, in a memorable example of reconciliation, said that the enemy should first be fed and then permitted to leave peacefully. The result? "The Syrians came no more on raids into the land of Israel" (2 Kings 6:23, rsv).

743 LAMB AND LION   Early American folk artists frequently painted pictures of the peaceable kingdom in which all of the animals of the forest dwell together. Their text was from Isaiah: "The wolf also shall dwell with the lamb, and the leopard shall lie down with the kid; and the calf and the young lion and the fatling together; and a little child shall lead them" (Isa. 11:6). To men of the twentieth century is this a far-fetched fantasy? A reconciliation among men of diverse backgrounds, temperaments, and conditions is no longer merely desirable; it is a necessity for survival. We must give our hearts to the endeavor "to keep the unity of the Spirit in the bond of peace" (Eph. 4:3).

744 NO OTHER ESCAPE   After Amnon had sinned against Tamar, he "hated her exceedingly; so that the hatred wherewith he hated her was greater than the love wherewith he had loved her" (2 Sam. 13:15). By pushing Tamar from his sight, Amnon may have hoped that the memory of his guilt would not continue to plague him. But when a man is convicted by his own conscience, no escape is possible save reconciliation between himself and God and his fellow man which forgiveness makes possible.

745 MET BY ANGELS   Years after his estrangement from Esau, Jacob turned once more toward his home and hoped that old wounds would have healed. The path he took was that of reconciliation. Jacob went on his way and the angels of God met him; and when Jacob saw them he said, 'This is God's army!' " (Gen. 32:1-2, RSV).

746 *DIVINE RECONCILER* "O that there were an umpire between us, that he might lay his hand upon both of us" (Job 9:33, AT). Christ, the reconciler, is the umpire Job sought, and he shows us the way to justice through love.

REJECTION

747 *THEY KEPT MOCKING* God's magnanimity is contrasted with human perversity in the chronicler's summing up of Judah. "The Lord, the God of their fathers, sent persistently to them by his messengers, because he had compassion on his people and on his dwelling place; but they kept mocking the messengers of God, despising his words, and scoffing at his prophets, till the wrath of the Lord rose against his people, till there was no remedy" (2 Chron. 36:15-16, RSV).

748 *THE MAN GOD REJECTED* Prophet and king came to a parting of their ways after Saul disobeyed Samuel's orders by taking spoils from the Amalekites. Samuel said, "I will not return with thee: for thou hast rejected the word of the Lord, and the Lord hath rejected thee from being king over Israel." As Samuel turned to leave, Saul, realizing that God's favor would depart from him when the prophet was gone, "laid hold upon the skirt of his mantle, and rent it." (1 Sam. 15:26-27.)

RELIGION

749 *WORK OF THE SERVANT* Too easily prone to discouragement and ready to capitulate before the day is over, church leaders need to remember the mission and promise of the Servant of the Lord: "Loyally shall he set forth true religion, he shall not be broken nor grow dim, till he has settled true religion upon earth, till far lands long for his instruction" (Isa. 42:3-4, MOFFATT).

750 *WHAT THEY WANTED TO HEAR*   Isaiah condemned the children of Judah who, urging their prophets to offer only chocolate-coated words, said, "Prophecy not to us what is right; speak to us smooth things, prophecy illusions, leave the way, turn aside from the path, let us hear no more of the Holy One of Israel" (Isa. 30:10–11, RSV).

751 *MARGIN OF SAFETY*   Paul perceived that the Athenians were a very religious people who had erected altars to many gods; and lest they incur the displeasure of some unhonored deity, they even set up an altar "To an unknown god" (Acts 17:23, MOFFATT). For many, God continues to be unknown and unclaimed.

752 *SHORT BED AND NARROW BLANKET*   Describing defective religions of his day, Isaiah said facetiously, "The bed is shorter than that a man can stretch himself on it: and the covering narrower than that he can wrap himself in it" (Isa. 28:20).

753 *RELIGION BY ROTE*   The stupidity of a religion which is fashioned according to the movements of the lips and not according to the heart is characterized in this manner by Isaiah: "This people draw near me with their mouth . . . honouring me with their lips, while their hearts are far remote . . . their religion is a mockery, a mere tradition learned by rote" (Isa. 29:13, MOFFATT).

REMEMBRANCE

754 *LOOK TO THE ROCK*   Spiritual competence comes with the remembrance of our spiritual origin. "Look to the rock from which you were hewn, and to the quarry from which you were digged" (Isa. 51:1, RSV). We are children of Adam, whom God fashioned in his image; of Christ, who called us to be his disciples; of the Pilgrim Fathers, who looked for a country whose maker and builder is God.

755 *NAILS DRIVEN HOME*   "A wise man's words are like goads, and his collected sayings are like nails driven home; they put the mind of one man into many a life" (Eccl. 12:11, MOFFATT). Of Jesus it is written, "And they remembered his words" (Lk. 24:8), and his remembered words have enriched the lives of unnumbered multitudes.

756 *WHAT THE BUTLER FORGOT*   After interpreting the dream of Pharaoh's butler, Joseph said, "Think on me when it shall be well with thee, and shew kindness, I pray thee, unto me, and make mention of me unto Pharaoh, and bring me out of this house. . . . Yet did not the chief butler remember Joseph, but forgat him" (Gen. 40:14, 23).

757 *HE KNEW NOT JOSEPH*   There was a day when the Hebrew people, through the good offices of Joseph, were guests of Pharaoh. But after the passing of many generations "there arose up a new king over Egypt, which knew not Joseph" (Ex. 1:8). Unless the flame of remembrance is continually kindled, men soon forget those who have served their nation.

758 *MEMORIAL DAY*   "This day shall be unto you for a memorial; and ye shall keep it a feast to the Lord throughout your generations; ye shall keep it a feast by an ordinance for ever" (Ex. 12:14). These words tell of the observance by which men would ever remember the Passover. All high and holy days serve to remind us of ways by which God has blessed mankind. Remembrance nourishes the spirit so that past blessings may be harbingers of future devotion.

759 *A FRINGE FOR REMEMBRANCE*   God told the children of Israel to "make . . . fringes in the borders of their garments . . . and . . . put upon the fringe of the borders a ribband of blue" (Num. 15:38) that they might remember the commandments of the Lord and do them. Whatever device may encourage remembrance —a motto for the wall, a jewel to be worn, or a scripture verse written upon the heart—is worthwhile if it shores up our remembrance of God's promises and blessings. "I stir up your pure minds by way of remembrance" (2 Pet. 3:1).

760 *REMEMBRANCE OF THINGS PAST*   After the Philistines had been subdued, "Samuel took a stone, and set it between Mizpeh and Shen, and called the name of it Eben-ezer, saying, Hitherto hath the Lord helped us" (1 Sam. 7:12). He wanted the children of Israel to be reminded of God's blessings in the past. Whatever the future may hold for us, we are sustained by the remembrance of past blessings.

761 *WHAT MARY REMEMBERED*   "Mary kept all these things, and pondered them in her heart" (Lk. 2:19). What a wonderful experience to think about and to remember! And her remembrance would make her strong on that day when a sword would pierce her soul.

RENEWAL

762 *SPIRITUAL THERAPY*   Recognizing that David had spared his life, Saul exclaimed, "I have sinned . . . I have played the fool" (1 Sam. 26:21). For the moment, Saul's heart, darkened by jealousy and hatred, was enlightened. Such a confession is the spiritual therapy which brings the promise of spiritual cleansing and renewal.

763 *REKINDLED PLEDGES*   "The Lord made not this covenant with our fathers, but with us, even us, who are all of us here alive this day" (Deut. 5:3). Moses recognized the need of men of each succeeding generation to renew their spiritual vows. The faith of our fathers was inspiring and propitious, but it is not sufficient for a later people who must rekindle ancient pledges within their own hearts.

764 *RENEWED DEVOTION*   "God said to Jacob, 'Arise, go up to Bethel . . . and make there an altar to the God who appeared to you when you fled from your brother Esau' " (Gen. 35:1, RSV). By renewing earlier devotion and dedication we rekindle the flame on the altars where we have known and communed with God.

765 *BACK TO THE UPPER ROOM*   Our spiriual experience is often deepened when we return to those places and scenes associated with commitment and resolution. "On entering the city they went to the upper room where they were in the habit of meeting" (Acts 1:13, MOFFATT). There they had shared the Master's last supper, and there the disciples renewed their fellowship and sense of mission.

766 *THE GAZE THAT HEALS*   "And the Lord turned, and looked upon Peter. And Peter remembered . . ." (Lk. 22:61). The eyes of Christ discern the innermost secrets of the heart, depths known to none other. In his gaze is healing and restoration, for then, if ever, we respond to his confidence in our discipleship.

767 *RENEWED MINDS*   There is hope for weary and exhausted minds. Renewal and refreshment are possible and also a recreation of worn hopes and frazzled dreams. "Be transformed by the entire renewal of your minds, so that you may learn by experience what God's will is—that will which is good and beautiful and perfect" (Rom. 12:2, WEYMOUTH).

REPENTANCE

768 *THIS TIME HE WENT*   "And the word of the Lord came unto Jonah the second time. . . . So Jonah arose, and went unto Nineveh" (Jon. 3:1, 3). After a benevolent and forgiving God had given Jonah a second chance, the erstwhile reluctant missionary, now chastened and repentant, accepted God's directives. The measure of a penitent's sincerity is according to his willingness to rectify his former mistakes.

REPUTATION

769 *BETTER THAN RICHES*   "A good name is rather to be chosen than great riches" (Prov. 22:1). Boaz said to Ruth, "It hath fully been shewed me, all that thou hast done unto thy mother in law since the death of thine husband: and how thou hast left thy father and thy mother, and the land of thy nativity, and art come unto a people which thou knewest not heretofore" (Ruth 2:11).

770 *HE WON A NAME*   By his successful engagements against the Philistines, the Moabites, the Syrians, and others, "David won a name for himself" (2 Sam. 8:13, RSV), but enduring reputations are won also by those who are builders of peace and architects of reconciliation.

771 *NO REGRETS*   What others shall say about us after we are dead is largely determined by what we are and what we do. Jehoram was unfaithful in life and unheralded in death. "He was thirty-two years old when he began to reign, and he reigned eight years in Jerusalem; and he departed with no one's regret" (2 Chron. 21:20, RSV).

772 *SYNONYMOUS WITH CHARITY*   When the disciple Tabitha (Dorcas) died at Joppa, her friends recalled her good works and acts of charity and showed Peter "the coats and garments which Dorcas made, while she was with them" (Acts 9:39). An ordinary individual who applied her talents to the commonplace task of hemstitching, she "gave so generously of herself to others that her name today, almost two thousand years later, is synonymous with acts of charity [and] out of this first work of hers grew the Dorcas Sewing Societies, now world-wide" (Edith Deen).

773 *ONLY A REPUTATION*   How many individuals or churches are identified by reputations which are no longer really applicable? John wrote to the church at Sardis, "I know what you have done, that you have a reputation for being alive, but that in fact you are dead. Now wake up! Strengthen what you still have before it dies!" (Rev. 3:1–2, PHILLIPS).

RESPONSIBILITY

774 *FOCUS ON SELF*   A prophet approached Ahab, who was hard pressed by the Syrian king Ben-hadad, and said, "Thus says the Lord, Have you seen all this great multitude? Behold, I will give it into your hand this day; and you shall know that I am the Lord." Ahab asked, "Who shall begin the battle?" Narrowing the focus of responsibility, the prophet replied, "You." (1 Kings 20:13–14, RSV.)

775 *FOR SUCH A TIME AS THIS*   Urged by Haman, Ahasuerus permitted the destruction of all Jews, even though, unbeknown to him, Queen Esther was herself Jewish. Adorned in sackcloth and ashes, Mordecai sent word to Esther, saying, "Think not with thyself that thou shalt escape in the king's house, more than all the Jews. For if thou altogether holdest thy peace at this time, then shall there enlargement and deliverance arise to the Jews from another place; but thou and thy father's house shall be destroyed: and who knoweth whether thou art come to the kingdom for such a time as this?" (Es. 4:13–14).

776 *THOSE WHO REMAINED*   David called upon his men to gird on their swords, "and there went up after David about four hundred men, while two hundred remained with the baggage" (1 Sam. 25:13, AT). Not every man can be a front-line hero. Some must maintain the home base where their responsibilities are equally essential for victory.

777 *SPIRITUAL ROLANDS*   The church, which is indebted to vanguard Christians who have built highways of faith that reach to the ends of the earth, is no less indebted to rearguard Christians, the Rolands of the faith who have done faithfully the less-appealing tasks assigned to them. To Titus, the trail blazer Paul wrote, "I left you behind in Crete in order to finish putting things right" (Tit. 1:5, MOFFATT).

778 *THE PEOPLE DID IT*   Moses angrily upbraided Aaron for permitting the people to dance about the golden calf. Aaron discounted his responsibility, claiming that the people, after all, were inclined to mischievousness. He had done no more than to cast their golden trinkets into the fire—and "there came out this calf" (Ex. 32:24, RSV).

779 *NOT I!*   Refusing to accept responsibility for his sin, Adam protested, "The woman whom thou gavest to be with me, she gave me fruit of the tree, and I ate." And in like manner Eve, too, attempted to free herself, saying, "The serpent beguiled me, and I ate." (Gen. 3:12–13, RSV). Spiritual healing requires that a man confess, "Father, I have sinned against heaven and before you" (Lk. 15:18, RSV).

780 *UNFINISHED WORK*   Felix reneged in his responsibilities toward his prisoner Paul, and his unfinished work fell to his successor Festus, who explained to King Agrippa, "There is a certain man left in bonds by Felix" (Acts 25:14).

781 *COMPLETELY UNMOVED*   The proconsul of Achaia, Gallio, rejected responsibility when the Jews attacked Paul; and when Sosthenes, a follower of Paul, was beaten, Gallio "paid no attention" (Acts 18:17, RSV), was "quite unconcerned" (NEB), remained completely unmoved" (PHILLIPS).

782 *IT IS YOUR AFFAIR*   Shrugging off the responsibility which his position required him to accept, Pilate "took some water and washed his hands in the presence of the crowd, saying, 'I am innocent of this good man's blood. It is your affair!' " (Matt. 27:24, MOFFATT).

783 *INSPIRING MOMENT*   After the shepherds had visited the baby Jesus, they "returned [to their flocks], glorifying and praising God for all the things that they had heard and seen" (Lk. 2:20). The radiant hour now past, they took up again their old responsibilities; but their moment in Bethlehem, like an hour of worship, became, as it were, the leaven of life.

784 *BEYOND BETHANY*   "He led them forth, until they were near Bethany; then . . . he parted from them" (Lk. 24:50–51, TORREY). Every life comes at last to Bethany, where, apprenticeship having been completed, a man must assume the responsibilities of the work in which he has been trained.

RESPONSIVENESS

785 *I AM PERSUADED*   Jeremiah's receptiveness to the will of God is told in words which have not diminished through long centuries: "Eternal One, thou didst persuade me, and I let myself be persuaded!" (Jer. 20:7, MOFFATT).

786 *OPEN HEARTS*   Paul solicits the mutual and openhearted trust which is the hallmark of the Christian community: "O Corinthians, I am keeping nothing back from you; my *heart is wide open* for you. . . . Open your hearts wide to me" (2 Cor. 6:11, 13, MOFFATT).

787 *JESUS SAW HIM* After he climbed a sycamore tree, Zacchaeus not only saw Jesus, but Jesus also saw him. Knowing that his position as a tax collector had isolated him socially, Jesus was quick to recognize that Zacchaeus did not wish always to be isolated from God. So Jesus called to him and said he wished to talk things over. (Lk. 19:5.)

788 *NOTHING GOOD IS LOST* "God is ever bringing back what disappears" (Eccl. 3:15, MOFFATT). Nothing that is worthy is expendable, and what one man casts aside is picked up by responsive persons. That which is good and true, though trodden underfoot, rises once more.

789 *WHOLEHEARTED RESPONSE* When Jesus told his disciples how difficult it is for the wealthy to enter God's Kingdom, the disciples, who naturally thought that God favors those whom common men consider to be privileged, wondered what chance they could conceivably expect. Peter no doubt spoke for his colleagues when he said, "Lo, we have left all, and followed thee" (Lk. 18:28). More than that God asks of no man, for judgment is based, not on the quantity of a man's benevolences, but on the quality and wholeheartedness of his response.

790 *WOULD THEY RESPOND?* A rich man, who had scorned the beggar Lazarus, died and in hell he pleaded with Abraham to send the beggar to warn his five brothers of the wrath to come; but Abraham doubted that their hard hearts would be responsive. (Lk. 16:27–31.)

791 *NO MORE THAN WORDS* For spiritually unresponsive persons the vision of Isaiah was "no more than words in a sealed scroll. When men place it in the hands of a scholar, asking him to read it, he answers, 'I cannot; the scroll is sealed.' When it is handed to an illiterate person, to be read, he answers, 'But I cannot read' " (Isa. 29:11–12, MOFFATT).

792 *WITH HASTE* "When the angels went away . . . the shepherds said to one another, 'Let us go' " and "they went with haste" (Lk. 2:15–16, RSV). No questioning, no doubting, and no hesitating! When God speaks, no other response is worthy.

RESURRECTION

793 *GOOD MORNING!*   To the women who had come to anoint his body on the first Easter, Jesus said, "Good morning!" (Matt. 28:9, GOODSPEED). Is there a more appropriate resurrection greeting? The night of fear and apprehension having passed, Easter marked the morning of hope, victory, and life eternal.

794 *STORY'S END*   "But they fled out of the tomb, for they were seized with terror and beside themselves. They said nothing to anyone, for they were afraid of—" (Mk. 16:8, MOFFATT). So ends, according to Professor Moffatt and other biblical scholars, the authentic text of the second gospel. What if, however, the story of Jesus had in fact concluded in this way? A picture of frightened women only—

795 *THEY TURNED THEIR BACKS*   Those who in love sought to embalm the body of their beloved Master found the sepulcher empty. "They turned their backs on the tomb and went and told all this to the eleven and the others who were with them" (Lk. 24:9, PHILLIPS). Christians worship not before a sealed tomb, but, turning their backs, they face the newness of resurrection life.

796 *NOT AMONG THE DEAD*   "Why search among the dead for one who lives?" (Lk. 24:5, NEB). Perennial significance is attached to this question, for the living Christ is to be found neither in the tomb in Joseph's garden nor in some of the time-hallowed but substantially meaningless confessions of earlier generations. The Pioneer of life calls us from his advance position to know him in the new adventures he invites us to share.

797 *I AM GOING FISHING*   Confronted on Easter by the stupendous fact of Christ's resurrection, many people nonetheless return to their homes as though nothing much had happened. Even after Peter had seen the risen Lord, he seemed ready enough to return to the way of life he had known before he met Christ: "I am going fishing" (Jn. 21:3, RSV).

RETRIBUTION

798 *DIVINE COMPENSATION*   Although the beggar Lazarus could claim only the crumbs which fell from the rich man's table, in the next world, according to a divine compensation, he rested securely on Abraham's bosom; and the rich man, who had hardly given him passing notice, was later to beseech Lazarus to touch his tongue with cool water. (Lk. 16:20–25).

799 *POETIC JUSTICE*   "So they hanged Haman on the gallows that he had prepard for Mordecai" (Es. 7:10). A most satisfying example of poetic justice. Retribution is variously expressed in God's Word: "Their sword shall enter their own heart" (Ps. 37:15); "Whoso diggeth a pit shall fall therein" (Prov. 26:27); "They have sown the wind, and they shall reap the whirlwind" (Hos. 8:7); "Whatsoever a man soweth, that shall he also reap" (Gal. 6:7).

800 *IRONY*   Although 1 Sam. 31 records that Saul took his own life, the first chapter of 2 Sam. introduces an Amalekite who claimed that he inflicted the mortal wound. The Amalekite may have hoped thereby to claim preferential treatment from David. Ironically, however, David ordered him slain for having taken the life of the Lord's anointed. (2 Sam. 1:1–16.)

REVENGE

801 *GOD'S GREATER PURPOSES*   Their father having died, the sons of Jacob feared that Joseph would now seek revenge for their having sold him into slavery. Years before Joseph might have welcomed such an opportunity, but his forgiving spirit reflected his understanding of the greater purposes of the Eternal. "Ye thought evil against me," Joseph said, "but God meant it unto good, to bring to pass, as it is this day, to save much people alive" (Gen. 50:20).

802 *A WOMAN'S REVENGE*   Elijah knew well the tides of exultation and depression. One day he triumphantly defied four hundred priests of Baal on Mount Carmel, and the next day, threatened by the revengeful Jezebel and lamenting for himself, he fled "a day's journey into the wilderness" (1 Kings 19:4).

803 *A PROPHET RETALIATES*   When small boys, too young perhaps to know better, taunted Elisha for being baldheaded, the prophet, who by God's grace should have known better, retaliated vindictively by using his God-given power to set bears upon the youngsters. (2 Kings 2:23–24.)

804 *GRIM SATISFACTION*   The satisfaction which vindictive men require often brings destruction to both victors and victims. Samson's prayer of bitter revenge—"O Lord God, remember me, I pray thee, and strengthen me, I pray thee, only this once, O God, that I may be avenged upon the Philistines for one of my two eyes" (Judg. 16:28, RSV)—was answered, but the brick and mortar which crushed his enemies destroyed him also.

805 *A PLEA FOR DESTRUCTION*   Angered because Mordecai would not show a befitting deference to him, Haman retaliated against all Jews and petitioned King Ahasuerus, saying, "There is a certain people scattered abroad and dispersed among the peoples in all the provinces of your kingdom; their laws are different from those of every other people, and they do not keep the king's laws, so that it is not for the king's profit to tolerate them. If it please the king, let it be decreed that they be destroyed" (Es. 3:8–9, RSV).

REWARD

806 *YET I WILL REJOICE*   God should be loved for his own sake and not thereby to glean benefits, rewards, or protection. "Though the fig tree do not blossom, nor fruit be on the vines, the produce of the olive fail and the fields yield no food, the flock be cut off from the fold and there be no herd in the stalls, yet I will rejoice in the Lord, I will joy in the God of my salvation" (Hab. 3:17–18, RSV).

807 *ALWAYS TOGETHER*   We can surely sympathize with the elder brother of the prodigal who said to their father, "Look at all the years I have been serving you!" He felt his loyal faithfulness should be rewarded. Like James and John, long-serving Christians feel that God should honor them above all others, but the father's reply indicates a reward which makes anything else seem pale: "My son, you and I are always together." (Lk. 15:29, 31, MOFFATT.)

808 *NOT FOR SALE* Perplexed by the words which a strange hand had written on the wall, Belshazzar promised Daniel that if he interpreted the message he would be clothed in scarlet. Daniel replied, "Let thy gifts be to thyself, and give thy rewards to another; yet I will read the writing unto the king, and make known to him the interpretation" (Dan. 5:17). Although the understanding which God had given to Daniel was not for sale, he willingly became God's interpreter.

809 *EVERY MAN'S PRICE* "Doth Job fear God for nought?" (Job 1:9). A perfectly natural question for Satan to ask God. We say that every man has his price. We ask what's in it for me. To reverence God without soliciting favors seemed inconceivable to Satan. Yet St. Paul said, "For me to live is Christ, and to die is gain" (Phil. 1:21).

810 *THE TRUE REWARD* Concerning Hezekiah, the most devout king of Judah, the historian wrote, "And every work that he undertook in the service of the house of God and in accordance with the law and the commandments, seeking his God, he did with all his heart, and prospered." Surely the rewards for such devotion ought to be beyond reckoning, but the verse immediately following reads, "After these things and these acts of faithfulness Sennacherib king of Assyria came and invaded Judah and encamped against the fortified cities, thinking to win them for himself." (2 Chron. 31:21–32:1, RSV.) The true reward of pious living is not peace and quiet content but rather an empowering of a man to meet the pressures of unexpected trouble.

811 *ABOVE RICHES* After the prophet from Judah had restored Jeroboam's paralyzed hand, the king said, "Come home with me, and refresh thyself, and I will give thee a reward." But the prophet, whose work was accomplished without fear or favor, replied, "If thou wilt give me half thine house, I will not go in with

thee, neither will I eat bread nor drink water in this place."
(1 Kings 13:7-8.)

RIDICULE

812 *DOES YOUR GOD SLEEP?*   On Mount Carmel Elijah
scorned the priests of Baal by suggesting the impotence of their
god: "Cry aloud: for he is a god; either he is talking, or he is pursuing, or he is in a journey, or peradventure he sleepeth, and must
be awakened" (1 Kings 18:27).

813 *BITING WORDS*   Having learned that Judah's king had
removed all shrines and altars, the emissary of King Sennacherib
taunted the Judeans: "Do you think that mere words are strategy
and power for war? On whom do you now rely? . . . If you say to
me, 'We rely on the Lord our God,' is it not he whose high places
and altars Hezekiah has removed?" (Isa. 36:5, 7, RSV).

814 *NOTHING LIKE THIS BEFORE*   Hezekiah sought to
restore the confidence and unity of his people by calling them to
Jerusalem to celebrate the Passover, but many of those to whom
the king's message was taken ridiculed the idea. Yet there were those
who humbled themselves and went, for "the hand of God was also
upon Judah to give them one heart to do what the king and the
princes commanded by the word of the Lord. . . . So there was great
joy in Jerusalem, for since the time of Solomon . . . there had been
nothing like this in Jerusalem" (2 Chron. 30:12, 26, RSV).

815 *FOX ON THE WALL*   Angered and indignant because
the Jews were building a wall around Jerusalem, Sanballat resorted
to ridicule. "What are these feeble Jews doing? Will they restore
things? Will they sacrifice? Will they finish up in a day? Will they
revive the stones out of the heaps of rubbish, and burned ones at
that?" Tobiah added further derision: "Yes, what they are building
—if a fox goes up on it he will break down their stone wall!" (Neh.
4:2-3, RSV.)

816 *WHO HIT YOU?*   Grown men playing blindman's buff!
Such is the scene portrayed in Christ's passion when "they blind-

folded him and asked him, 'Now, prophet, guess who hit you that time!' " (Lk. 22:64, PHILLIPS). Horseplay in an hour above all others fraught with eternal meanings! But is there substantial difference between those mockers and the nominal Christians who today fiddle while evil overrides the hopes of man?

RIGHTEOUSNESS

817 *LIFE OF RIGHTEOUSNESS*   "And Samuel said unto all Israel. . . . I am old and grayheaded . . . and I have walked before you from my childhood unto this day" (1 Sam. 12:1–2). Like the pages of an open book, the life of a righteous man, whose consecration in youth is confirmed in his latter days, may be seen by all.

818 *YEAST OF RIGHTEOUSNESS*   Like the contagion of a smile, righteous behavior permeates a situation and brings healing and strength. Who can measure correctly the influence of goodness or the contamination of evil? "The kingdom of Heaven is like yeast, taken by a woman and put into three measures of flour until the whole lot has risen" (Matt. 13:33, PHILLIPS).

819 *REQUIREMENT AND CONSEQUENCE*   When tax collectors, seeking baptism at the hands of John the Baptist, asked concerning requirements, he responded, "Collect no more than is appointed you" (Lk. 3:13, RSV). Righteous behavior is both a requirement of and an expected consequence of baptism.

820 *NEITHER POOR NOR RICH*   Unable to find a righteous man on the streets of Jerusalem, Jeremiah explained to the Lord that the people "are the poor . . . mere ignorant folk, who never learned the rules of the Eternal or the religion of their God." He proposed that he then look among those in "the upper classes . . . for they have learned the rules of the Eternal, and the religion of their God." (Jer. 5:4–5, MOFFATT.) But even among them he could find none who possessed integrity and an honest mind.

821 *UNSATIATED HUNGER*   Isaiah characterized the unrighteous man "as a hungry man [who] dreams he is eating and wakens still hungry, as a thirsty man [who] dreams he is drinking and wakens still faint with his craving" (Isa. 29:8, MOFFATT).

822 *UNBEARABLE GOODNESS*   Jesus told his accusers that they were seeking to kill him because "my word makes no headway among you!" (Jn. 8:37, MOFFATT). Challenged by claims they were unwilling to meet, Jesus' opponents wished to do away with him. Their pattern of behavior persists, for we, too, wish to destroy him whose goodness is unbearable and whose example deflates our egos and embarrasses our counterfeit goodness.

823 *PETER CAPITULATES*   To do that which is right because it is right, irrespective of the pressures and persuasions of others, represents a position which is difficult to maintain. Speaking of Peter's capitulation to conservative demands, Paul wrote, "Until the arrival of some of James's companions, he, Peter, was in the habit of eating his meals with the Gentiles. After they came, however, he withdrew and ate separately from the Gentiles—out of sheer fear of what the Jews might think" (Gal. 2:12, PHILLIPS).

824 *THESE ARE THE UNRIGHTEOUS*   The letter of Jude describes selfish and unrighteous men through a series of vigorous figures: "They are like clouds driven up by the wind, but they bring no rain. They are like trees with the leaves of autumn but without a single fruit—they are doubly dead, for they have no roots either. They are like raging waves of the sea, producing only the spume of their own shameful deeds. They are like stars which follow no orbit, and their proper place is the everlasting blackness of the regions beyond the light" (Jude 12–13, PHILLIPS).

825 *DECEPTIVE PHRASES*   Jeremiah in his remarkable temple sermon called for righteous living, not the repetition of pious words or "deceptive" phrases such as "This is the temple of the Lord, the temple of the Lord, the temple of the Lord" (Jer. 7:4, RSV).

RUTHLESSNESS

826 *NOTHING IS SACRED*   Ruthless men despise even that which represents humanity's supreme achievements. "Thine enemies bawled inside thy house . . . they smashed the doors down with their axes, like woodmen felling trees, then broke up all the carved work there with hatchet and with hammer" (Ps. 74:4–6, MOFFATT).

827 *LYNCH MOB*   The detractors of Stephen, unmoved by the eloquent simplicity and sincerity of his defense, "cried out with a loud voice, and stopped their ears, and ran upon him with one accord" (Acts 7:57). Having closed tightly their minds, their wrath kindled a violence which transformed them into an illegal lynch mob.

SACRIFICE

828 *THEY RISKED THEIR LIVES*   David at the cave of Adullam longed for water from the well in Bethlehem which was surrounded by the Philistines. Three of his loyal men made a dangerous passage through the enemy's fortifications and returned with a vessel of water. But David, realizing the self-sacrifice involved, poured out the water as an offering to the Lord and said, "Far be it from me, O Lord, that I should do this. Shall I drink the blood of the men who went at the risk of their lives?" (2 Sam. 23:17, RSV). For the many sacrifices which have secured our blessings, only a humble gratitude seems appropriate.

829 *SACRIFICES OF FLESH*   Perfunctory worship, which amounts to little more than a treadmill ritual, neither generates righteous living nor solicits God's response. Micah wrote of those who made sacrifices of flesh but not of the heart. "Wherewith shall I come before the Lord, and bow myself before the high God? . . . Will the Lord be pleased with thousands of rams, or with ten thousands of rivers of oil?" No, something more is needed. "He hath shewed thee, O man, what is good; and what doth the Lord require of thee, but to do justly, and to love mercy, and to walk humbly with thy God?" (Mic. 6:6—8.)

830 *IMPERFECT SACRIFICES*   To the priests who offered imperfect sacrifices—animals which were blind, lame, and sick—to the Lord, Malachi said, "Present that to your governor; will he be pleased with you or show you favor?" (Mal. 1:8, RSV). God is delighted with first fruits, not leftovers. The words of Paul stand as a judgment upon our halfhearted devotion: "I beseech you therefore, brethren, by the mercies of God, that ye present your bodies a living sacrifice, holy, acceptable unto God, which is your reasonable service" (Rom. 12:1).

831 *TO OBEY AND TO HEARKEN*   Spoils taken by Saul from the Amalekites in disobedience to the directives of Samuel were to be offered, Saul said, as a sacrifice to the Lord in Gilgal. But Samuel, probing the depths of true religion, said, "Hath the Lord as great delight in burnt offerings and sacrifices, as in obeying the voice of the Lord? Behold, to obey is better than sacrifice, and to hearken than the fat of rams" (1 Sam. 15:22).

SEARCH

832 *UNREWARDING SEARCH*   The Lord dispatched Jeremiah on a search that would prove futile. "Run to and fro through the streets of Jerusalm, look and take note! Search her squares to see if you can find a man, one who does justice and seeks truth" (Jer. 5:1, RSV). How rewarding would such an investigation in our neighborhoods and homes prove to be?

833 *SEARCH WITH CARE*   "When you get there, search for this little child with the utmost care. And when you have found him, come back and tell me—so that I may go and worship him too" (Matt. 2:8, PHILLIPS). To all appearances Herod shared the quest of the wise men, but appearances are deceiving, and Herod hoped, not to worship, but to destroy.

834 *INCOMPARABLE QUEST*   The joy of the spiritual quest is incomparable. "Happy are they who, nerved by thee, set out on pilgrimage!" (Ps. 84:5, MOFFATT), or "Oh the happiness of the man whose strength is in Thee! Pilgrimage is in their heart!" (LESLIE).

SELF-INTEREST

835 *NOT IN MY TIME*   When Isaiah foretold the dreadful consequences of the Babylonian captivity, Hezekiah sighed with relief. " 'Very good,' said Hezekiah; 'it is the word of the Eternal you utter!' (thinking to himself that there would be no trouble or change at least so long as he was alive)" (2 Kings 20:19, MOFFATT), or "At least there will be peace and security in my time" (Isa. 39:8, AT).

836 *NOT JUST YET*　　In his plea for support for the rebuilding of the temple, Haggai asked a question which is perennially relevant: "Is it a time for you yourselves to dwell in your paneled houses, while this house lies in ruins?" (Hag. 1:4, RSV). Perhaps the people had said that as soon as they got roofs over their own heads they would attend to God's house!

837 *SELF-CENTERED TALK*　　The conversation of the disciples as they journeyed toward Capernaum concerned which of them was the greatest. "What were you arguing about on the road?" Jesus asked. "They said nothing." (Mk. 9:33–34, MOFFATT.) Ashamed that their talk was so self-centered, they would not admit to One who was so transparently selfless that their minds were still oriented to themselves.

838 *ASHES ON THE TONGUE*　　A man who could boast, "Richer and richer I grew, more than any before me in Jerusalem. . . . Nothing I coveted did I refuse myself" (Eccl. 2:9–10, MOFFATT), concluded that a self-engrossed and self-centered life brings only ashes on the tongue. The only enduring satisfactions life offers are dividends from the investment of time and talent in human need and godly purpose.

839 *BEFITTING HONOR*　　Ahasuerus asked Haman what honors would be commensurable for one who had served well the king. Thinking the honors were to be his, Haman enumerated many befitting honors. But the proud Haman unwittingly stipulated honors which the king bestowed upon his mortal enemy Mordecai. (Es. 6:1–11.)

840 *NO SURETY*　　The self-centered aggrandizement of the rich man who built larger barns so that he might hoard his abundant harvest is not without modern parallels (Lk. 12:16–21), but, as Jesus said, material possessions offer no surety against death.

841 *HIS REAL MOTIVE*　　After Mary had anointed the feet of Jesus with costly perfume, Judas remonstrated and said that it should have been sold and the profit given to the poor. His suggestion sounds reasonable, even commendable, but it was a disguise for self-interest: "Not that he cared for the poor; he said this because he was a thief, and because he carried the money-box and pilfered what was put in" (Jn. 12:6, MOFFATT).

842 *A MATTER OF OBLIGATION*   A perfunctory exchange of dinner invitations makes socializing a matter of obligation and self-interest. Rather, Jesus said, invite to your home those who have no way of returning your beneficence. "When you give a party, ask the poor, the crippled, the lame, and the blind; and so find happiness" (Lk. 14:13–14, NEB).

SELFISHNESS

843 *WE DO NOT WELL*   During a devastating siege of Samaria by the Syrians, four lepers reasoned that their lot could not be worse even if they surrendered to the enemy. When they entered the Syrian camp they found no inhabitants. Concerned primarily with their own misfortunes, they hurriedly gathered silver, gold, and other things which the fleeing Syrians had left behind. Then, sensing their interdependence with others who were suffering, they said to one another, "We do not well: this day is a day of good tidings, and we hold our peace . . . now therefore come, that we may go and tell the king's household" (2 Kings 7:9).

844 *LOT'S CHOICE*   Abraham generously offered Lot a choice between the land of Canaan and the lush Jordan valley which was like "the garden of the Lord." Lot grasped the more fertile grazing lands and pitched his tent in Sodom. Ironically, he was soon to run for his life from all that his hard heart had coveted. (Gen. 13:5–13.)

845 *JABEZ' PRAYER*   The prayer of Jabez surely ranks among the most selfish in literature: "Oh that thou wouldest prosper me and enlarge my lot! Oh that thine hand might aid me! Oh that thou wouldest ward me from evil, that no hurt may befall me!" (1 Chron. 4:10, MOFFATT).

846 *SELF-SERVERS*   Micah upbraided prophets who misled people by crying " 'Peace' when they have something to eat, but declare war against him who puts nothing into their mouths" (Mic. 3:5, RSV). In any profession there are self-servers who place their personal welfare above truth and service, but within the ministry is any behavior more reprehensible?

SERVICE

847 *ROLE OF SERVANT*   "He, who had always been God by nature, did not cling to his prerogatives as God's equal, but stripped himself of all privilege by consenting to be a slave by nature and being born as mortal man" (Phil. 2:6–7, PHILLIPS). Divine love expresses itself primarily in the humble role of a servant.

848 *HE TOOK A TOWEL*   To be a Christian means willingly and uncomplainingly to assume the role of a servant. Jesus effectively portrayed this when he "laid aside his garments; and took a towel . . . and began to wash the disciples' feet" (Jn. 13:4–5). Chief seats, position, prestige, and power were not claimed by Jesus, nor are they the portion he assigns to his followers.

849 *PURPOSE OF HEALING*   After Jesus had healed Peter's mother-in-law, "immediately she arose and ministered unto them" (Lk. 4:39). She did not dash to and fro among her neighbors to tell of the wonderful thing that had happened to her, but she turned to the needs of the members of her household. God heals us so that we may continue to fill our roles as servants.

850 *NOT SENTIMENT BUT SERVICE*   The mother of Zebedee's sons made an understandable request of Jesus: "Grant that these my two sons may sit, the one on thy right hand, and the other on the left, in thy kingdom." (Matt. 20:21). Selfish? Yes, but in a motherly way. Without condemning her, Jesus showed that kingdom citizenship was based not on sentiment but on service.

851 *WHO WOULD BE CHIEF*   Reading with a keen discernment the chronicle of human experience, the ancient Preacher concluded, "I saw that all the labor and all the hard work is due to men's jealousy of one another" (Eccl. 4:4, AT). By attempting to keep abreast or ahead of the Jones family, a man becomes poisoned and the only antidote which will cure is Jesus' prescription, "Whosoever will be chief among you, let him be your servant" (Matt. 20:27).

SHARING

852 *BENEATH HIS PURPLE ROBE*   During the siege of
Samaria, the plight of the people had reduced them to cannibalism.
"When the king heard what the woman said, he tore his clothes.
. . . (The people noticed that he was wearing sackcloth next his
skin.)" (2 Kings 6:30, MOFFATT.) The king shared their sorrow,
though unpretentiously he wore sackcloth beneath his royal garments.

853 *COME WITH US*   Christians wish to share the promises
of Christ with all who are receptive, even as did Moses who said to
Hobab, his father-in-law, "Come thou with us, and we will do thee
good" (Num. 10:29).

854 *THE SHARED LIFE*   To parcel out some small token
from our abundance in response to the desperate needs of our human
brethren is hardly an adequate Christian discipline. In their hour
of crisis, the early Christians disclaimed personal possessions and
joined their hearts and their hands. "Not one of them considered
anything his personal property, they shared all they had with one
another" (Acts 4:32, MOFFATT). The Christian life is the shared life,
in which not only material possessions, but also energies, talents,
and spiritual experience are contributed to the strengthening of
one another.

855 *IF THOU WILT GO*   When Deborah summoned Barak
to go into the field against the Canaanites, he replid, "If thou wilt
go with me, then I will go: but if thou wilt not go with me, then I
will not go" (Judg. 4:8). Deborah was a prophetess, and her presence would be an assurance of the presence of God.

SIGHT

856 *HEAVENLY CHARIOTS*   So often was the king of Syria
defeated by Israel that he determined to capture Elisha who had
been informing Israel's king of Syrian plans. Elisha's servant, be-
holding the Syrian horses and chariots which surrounded Dothan,

exclaimed, "Alas, my master! What shall we do?" The prophet replied, "Fear not, for those who are with us are more than those who are with them." (2 Kings 6:15–16, RSV.) The prophet saw the mountains swarming with God's forces. When the servant could not see what Elisha saw, the prophet prayed that his eyes might be opened to see the heavenly horses and chariots.

857 *SPIRITUAL VISION*   When Paul rose from the dust of the Damascus road after his life-transforming and faith-creating conversion, "though his eyes were open he could see nothing" (Acts 9:8, MOFFATT). For a season physical sight was denied to him, but the eyes of his spirit saw with a perceptiveness he had not previously known. Only by being blinded could he see those things which make for peace and promise.

858 *EYES FOR OTHERS*   Moses urged his father-in-law Hobab, who was knowledgeable concerning the wilderness, to accompany the Israelites. When Hobab resisted his solicitations, Moses pleaded further, saying, "Do not leave us, I pray you, for you know how we are to encamp in the wilderness, and you will serve as eyes for us" (Num. 10:31, RSV). To be eyes for the less experienced and to guide the untried steps are among life's richest privileges. "I was eyes to the blind, and feet was I to the lame," said Job (29:15).

859 *ELYMAS' BLINDNESS*   On Cyprus Paul's work was impeded by a false prophet, Elymas the magician. Paul upbraided him, saying, "Will you not stop making crooked the straight paths of the Lord?" (Acts 13:10, RSV). And Elymas became blind. What greater blindness is there than the attempt to frustrate God's work?

SIN

860 *FLIGHT TO BABYLON*   Zechariah asked an angel where winged creatures were taking a barrel containing a woman who personified the sins of the people. The angel said that they were flying to Babylon. (Zech. 5:5–11.) Would that we might as readily be rid of our sins! But the sins which do so easily beset us remain to plague, harass, and condemn. Only "the blood of Jesus Christ . . . cleanseth us from all sin" (1 Jn. 1:7).

861 *AGAINST WHOM WE SIN*   Censured by the prophet Nathan for his sin against Bath-sheba and for ordering the death of her husband Uriah, David made a fundamental and universal declaration of truth: "I have sinned against the Lord" (2 Sam. 12:13).

862 *WE SIN KNOWINGLY*   "And thou his son, O Belshazzar, hast not humbled thine heart, though thou knewest all this" (Dan. 5:22). Daniel said that the king, like most sinners, knowingly did that which was wrong.

863 *MY NAME IS LEGION*   Jesus asked the Gadarene demoniac, "What is thy name?" "My name is Legion," was his reply, "for we are many." (Mk. 5:9.) Like him, we come to Christ conscious of the innumerable sins which inhabit our hearts and lives; but in Christ we are made whole and single-minded—and we are given the name of the redeemed.

864 *FRIEND OF SINNERS*   The Pharisees became indignant when they saw Jesus consorting with persons of ill repute at the home of Levi. (Lk. 5:29–32.) Jesus identified his mission as one which served those whose need for salvation was greatest, and this has ever been the emphasis among those who correctly read the Master's mind.

865 *DOUBLE JEOPARDY*   One sin begets another. After his brothers had sold Joseph into slavery, they dipped his multicolored coat in blood and so intimated to Jacob that the boy had been killed by wild beasts. (Gen. 37:34.) The brothers then attempted to comfort their father, but their cruelty toward Joseph gave way to an even greater cruelty toward Jacob whose heart would bear the scars of pain for a lifetime.

866 *THE WEB OF SIN*   "By one man's disobedience many were made sinners" (Rom. 5:19). After David had sinned against Bath-sheba, he required that Joab be linked to him in sin, for he sent word to Joab that Uriah should be so stationed in battle that he would surely be killed. (2 Sam. 11:14–17.) The web of sin is such that, voluntarily or willy-nilly, others become complicated.

867 *WEEDS AMONG THE GRAIN*   In any worthy endeavor, so it would seem, at least one person behaves according to an evil purpose or an inferior motive. The good work is not altogether corrupted, but there is less harmony and strength than might otherwise have been possible. What to do? In his parable of the enemy who sowed weeds in a wheat field, Jesus indicated that the weeds could not be removed without uprooting the good grain. But at harvest time a separation is possible. (Matt. 13:24–30.)

868 *SUFFERING OF THE INNOCENT* Sin seldom is a solitary experience. Sin causes others to suffer and not infrequently links the innocent in a chain of evil. When Abraham identified his wife Sarah as his sister, Abimelech innocently took her into his house. After he had been enlightened concerning Sarah's true state, Abimelech censured Abraham, saying, "In the integrity of my heart and innocency of my hands have I done this" (Gen. 20:5). (See also Gen. 12:11–19; 26:7–10.)

869 *HE SOUGHT TO REDEEM* Sinful acts elicit a variety of responses. When Ham found his father in a shameful and drunken condition, his impulse was to inform his brothers. Shem and Japheth, however, "covered the nakedness of their father" (Gen. 9:23). The one brother gossiped; the others sought to redeem the sinner.

870 *INDIVIDUAL RESPONSIBILITY* However much we speak of corporate sin, each man must accept individual responsibility for his own sins. Judas returned the thirty pieces of silver to the high priests and elders, but they brushed him off, saying, "What does that matter to us? . . . it is your affair, not ours!" (Matt. 27:4, MOFFATT). They couldn't care less: "You've made your bed; now sleep in it." And Judas—alone—hanged from a bending limb, and only a patient, loving God attended his funeral.

871 *UNCHECKED SINS* "Catch us the foxes, the little foxes, that spoil the vineyards, for our vineyards are in blossom" (S. of S. 2:15, RSV). Many a life has been destroyed because small sins have been left unchecked.

872 *NO SECRET SINS* Angered when an Egyptian struck with a heavy hand one of his Hebrew brethren, Moses, after first looking furtively to the right and left lest anyone see him, then killed the Egyptian. (Ex. 2:11-14). Did Moses not know that there are no secret sins, no hidden evils which will not somehow, someday, come to light?

873 *POISONED ARROW*   During one of the darkest moments of Israel's history—when King Hazael of Syria and his son Ben-hadad completely dominated the lives of the children of God—Israel's king Jehoahaz besought the Lord to hearken unto the pleas of his people. The Lord responded by giving them a deliverer, Jeroboam II, Jehoahaz' grandson. But the relief was short-lived, for the people refused to abandon the sins of the house of Jeroboam. As a consequence, the Syrians destroyed the once-powerful armies of Israel and made them like the dust at threshing. (2 Kings 13:3-7.) For this ancient people and for any people sin is the poison which destroys a nation's freedom and corrupts her power.

874 *NET AND TRAP*   The tinsel joys of the wicked are transient and their achievements illusory. "Yea, the light of the wicked is put out, and the flame of his fire does not shine. . . . His strong steps are shortened and his own schemes throw him down. For he is cast into a net by his own feet, and he walks on a pitfall. . . . A rope is hid for him in the ground, a trap for him in the path" (Job 18:5, 7-8, 10, RSV).

875 *HARVEST OF THORNS*   "You have been ploughing evil, and you reaped disaster; you had to eat the harvest of your lies" (Hos. 10:13, MOFFATT). The pattern is inescapable. Evil cannot bring beneficent results, only a harvest of thorns.

876 *HUMAN DILEMMA*   Paul spelled out the dilemma of man in these words: "I do not understand my own actions. For I do not do what I want, but I do the very thing I hate. . . . I do not do the good I want, but the evil I do not want is what I do. Now if I do what I do not want, it is no longer I that do it, but sin which dwells within me" (Rom. 7:15, 19-20, RSV).

877 *THE STONE CASTERS*   The ancient law provided punishment for such sinners as the woman taken in adultery, but Christ, who sought always to conserve and redeem human life, appealed to a higher law. "Let him among you that has never sinned cast the first stone at her. . . . Go now, and sin no more" (Jn. 8:7, 11, RIEU).

SLEEPING

878 *BUT JONAH SLEPT*   When their ship had become a victim of stormy seas, each mariner cried to his god, but Jonah, who was fleeing from the Lord, continued to sleep. The shipmaster awakened Jonah and begged him to call upon God, but Jonah had deliberately shut God out of his life. (Jon. 1:4–6.)

879 *COULD YE NOT WATCH?*   "And he cometh unto the disciples, and findeth them asleep, and saith unto Peter, What, could ye not watch with me one hour?" (Matt. 26:40). Does it seem incredible that the disciples slept during so portentous an hour? Rip Van Winkle slept through the American Revolution. And we? Are we not spiritually lethargic in a period fraught with danger and potentiality?

880 *THE FALL OF EUTYCHUS*   Even Paul could not always claim the alert attentions of all members of his congregation, for we read of a young man named Eutychus who, sitting on the window ledge "as Paul's address went on and on . . . was overcome with drowsiness, went fast asleep, and fell from the third storey" (Acts 20:9, MOFFATT).

SORROW

881 *ALL MEN ARE ONE*   In sorrow all men are one. Death brings grief without respect to race or creed. After the death of Sarah, Abraham appealed to an understanding that is more than skin deep. To the Hittites he said, "I am a stranger and a sojourner with you: give me a possession of a buryingplace with you, that I may bury my dead." And responsive to his sorrow and need, they replied, "None of us shall withhold from thee his sepulchre." (Gen. 23:4, 6.)

882 *I KNOW THEIR SORROWS*   The loving-kindness of God is such that he is aware even of the fall of a sparrow. At the commissioning of Moses, God said, "I have surely seen the affliction of my pople which are in Egypt, and have heard their cry by reason of their taskmasters; for I know their sorrows" (Ex. 3:7).

883 *CORONALS FOR CORONACHS*   Isaiah proclaimed that God would give to them that mourn "beauty for ashes" (Isa. 61:3), or "a garland instead of ashes" (RSV), or "coronals for coronachs" (MOFFATT). And Jesus said, "How happy are those who know what sorrow means, for they will be given courage and comfort!" (Matt. 5:4, PHILLIPS).

SPEAKING

884 *THE BETRAYING ACCENT*   Does a Christian's manner of speech indicate that he has communed with God? Does his vocabulary express Christian love, confidence, and conviction? Those in the courtyard knew of Peter because of the manner in which he spoke: "You too are certainly one of them. For quite apart from other things, your accent betrays you" (Matt. 26:73, RIEU).

885 *VOICE OF A GOD*   After Herod had finished speaking, the people shouted, "It is the voice of a god, and not of a man," but the truly authentic accent is identified in the verse which immediately follows, "But the word of God grew and multiplied" (Acts 12:22, 24).

886 *SACRAMENT OF SPEECH*   Speech, too, is a sacrament and the lips should be controlled and directed by Christ. "Take my voice, and let me sing, always only, for my King" (Havergal). "If we put bits into horses' mouths to make them obey our will, we can direct their whole body. Or think of ships: large they may be, yet even when driven by strong gales they can be directed by a tiny rudder on whatever course the helmsman chooses. So with the tongue" (Jas. 3:3–5, NEB).

887 *DIVINE INSTRUMENT*   The gift of speech is an instrument worthy of divine service. "The Lord, the Eternal, has given me a well-trained tongue, that I may rightly answer the ungodly" (Isa. 50:4, MOFFATT), or "The Lord God has given me a tongue for teaching that I may know how to succor the weary with a word" (AT).

888 *THE PART OF GOD* Moses complained to God that he could not speak effectively, and God said that Aaron should do his speaking for him. "You must speak to him, and put the words in his mouth; I will help both you and him to speak, and I will instruct you both what to do. He shall speak for you to the people; he shall serve as a mouthpiece for you, and you shall act the part of God to him" (Ex. 4:15—16, AT). To act the part of God to another is the Christian's awesome responsibility.

889 *WORDS THEY UNDERSTOOD* Charged with desecrating the temple and dragged into the street, Paul claimed the right of defending himself. When the bloodthirsty mob "heard him speaking to them in their own language, they listened . . . quietly" (Acts 22:2, NEB), for he spoke words they understood.

STEWARDSHIP

890 *THE CONSECRATED SPINNERS* When furnishing the tabernacle, the Israelites gave according to their means and substances. Some offered gold objects, others brought linens and skins, and "all the women who had confidence in their ability spun the goats' hair" (Ex. 35:26, AT).

891 *WHAT THE KING GAVE* When soliciting funds for the temple, David was not satisfied to formulate plans and devise means, but he himself became an example of generous stewardship. "I have prepared with all my might for the temple of my God, gold for the golden objects, silver for the silver, bronze for the bronze, iron for the iron, and wood for the wooden, with jewels of beryl, jewels for setting, jewels for inlaid work, jewels of all colours, with gems of all sorts, and plenty of marble. Furthermore, in my devotion to the temple of my God, as I possess a private treasure of gold and silver, I give it to the temple of my God, over and above what I have prepared for the sacred temple." Having first given himself, he appealed to his people: "Now who will make a freewill offering to-day in devotion to the Eternal?" (1 Chron. 29:2–3, 5, MOFFATT.)

892 HE OWNED THE NILE   Ezekiel condemned Pharaoh for saying, "My Nile is my own; I made it" (Ezek. 29:3, RSV). But the Judaeo-Christian heritage declares, "The earth is the Lord's, and the fulness thereof" (Ps. 24:1) and "All things come of thee, and of thine own have we given thee" (1 Chron. 29:14).

893 MISSION OF PROFIT-MAKING   In the name of the budget and fiscal solvency, the churches too often resort to money-making schemes—even bingo!—and thereby have transformed the mission of soul-saving to that of profit-making. Jesus' words to the pigeon dealers in the temple were harsh and rightly so: "Take those things out of here. Don't you dare turn my Father's house into a market!" (Jn. 2:16, PHILLIPS).

894 DIVINE CREDIT   Financial support, too often thought of as an obligation enjoined—and too frequently—upon church members, is rather a privilege to invest in eternally meaningful adventures. "It is not the money I am anxious for; what I am anxious for is the interest that accumulates in this way to your divine credit!" (Phil. 4:17, MOFFATT).

STRANGER

895 SPIRITUAL REFUGE   Solomon stretched wide his heart and petitioned that strangers who might enter God's house to pray should be heard by the Eternal. "Hear thou from the heavens, even from thy dwelling place, and do according to all that the stranger calleth to thee for; that all people of the earth may know thy name, and fear thee, as doth thy people Israel, and may know that this house which I have built is called by thy name" (2 Chron. 6:33). God's house should always be a spiritual refuge which brings "peace to him that is far off, and to him that is near" (Isa. 57:19).

896 ONE OF YOUR OWN   The heart of Israel was large enough to embrace sympathetically all strangers in their midst. This social obligation came to them as a directive from God: "The stranger that dwelleth with you shall be unto you as one born among you, and thou shalt love him as thyself" (Lev. 19:34). Our casual and sometimes discriminating attitudes toward strangers stand as a judgment against us.

897 WELCOME TO OUTSIDERS   An ecumenical welcome to "outsiders" who willingly accept spiritual disciplines is suggested by the Lord's injunction to Moses: "If a stranger shall sojourn among you, and will keep the passover unto the Lord; according to the ordinance of the passover, and according to the manner thereof, so shall he do: ye shall have one ordinance, both for the stranger, and for him that was born in the land" (Num. 9:14).

898 NO SEPARATION   The love of God is broader than the measure of man's mind, or prejudices, or social yardsticks. The Kingdom embraces all men of faith. "Let not the foreigner who has joined himself to the Lord say, 'The Lord will surely separate me from his people'" (Isa. 56:3, RSV).

899 ABIDE WITH US   In the spirit of him whose loss they were mourning, the Emmaus travelers invited the Stranger who was with them to "abide with us: for it is toward evening, and the day is far spent" (Lk. 24:29). Not infrequently does the hospitable man entertain angels unaware and even him who is the Guest divine.

STRENGTH

900 STRENGTH FOR THE JOURNEY   Having fled a day's journey into the wilderness and so beyond the wrath of Jezebel, Elijah lay down to sleep under a juniper tree. An angel bade him arise and eat food which God had miraculously provided. Then again he slept and a second time the angel told him to eat and continue on his journey. Strengthened and nourished, he went to Mount Horeb, a forty-day trip. (1 Kings 19:4–8.) And the Lord strengthened not only his weak hands but also confirmed his feeble spirit.

901 CONTINUING STRENGTH   After an action-filled life of forty-five years, Caleb said, "I am as strong this day as I was in the day that Moses sent me: as my strength was then, even so is my strength now, for war, both to go out, and to come in" (Josh. 14:11). God had sustained him, Caleb said, for the work yet to be done.

902 *SOURCE OF STRENGTH*   The fellowship of Christ has ever been buttressed by men of humble and contrite hearts. To the children of Judah, who craved foreign alliances, the Lord said, "Your strength is quiet faith" (Isa. 30:15, MOFFATT).

903 *UNBRIDLED STRENGTH*   God gives to every man strength in proportion to his need. Samson was superlatively endowed with physical strength, but he used his prowess not in the service of God but in vindictive pursuits. So with a jawbone of an ass, he slew a thousand men and boasted of his capacity to retaliate against his enemies. And at last his unbridled strength brought his destruction. (Judg. 15:15–16.)

904 *THE DEVOURING JUNGLE*   Our strength is exhausted by lack of direction, confusion, and unclear purposes. In the onslaught by David's men upon the forces of Absalom, "the jungle devoured more than the sword that day" (2 Sam. 18:8, MOFFATT).

SUNDAY

905 *TO SAVE OR DESTROY?*   Certain Pharisees, seeking reasons for accusing Jesus of defiling venerated traditions, watched closely to see if he would heal a man having a useless right hand on the sabbath. Reading correctly their thoughts, Jesus asked, "Is it lawful on the sabbath days to do good, or to do evil? to save life, or to destroy it?" (Lk. 6:9). Not to have helped a needy person would have rendered meaningless God's day.

906 *KEEPING THE SABBATH*   When foreigners tempted the Jews with the advantage of engaging in commerce on the Lord's day, Nehemiah restated for his generation the Mosaic law: "If the natives of the land brought any wares or food to be sold on the sabbath, we would not buy from them on the sabbath or on a sacred day" (Neh. 10:31, MOFFATT).

907 *CLEAR CHANNELS*   The Lord's day is more than an occasion in which to refrain from the week's ordinary chores or to relax and be amused. By keeping the sabbath we keep clear the channels of grace whereby God is permitted to speak, not by fits and starts, but with a healing regularity. "I gave them my sabbath, to mark the tie between me and them, to teach them that it is I, the Eternal, who sets them apart" (Ezek. 20:12, MOFFATT).

TALENT

908 *LAW OF LIFE*   It is a law of life that our skills and capabilities, like our money, increase through wise use and employment. After the nobleman had taken the pound from the indolent servant and given it to the prudent servant, the people complained that the latter already had ten pounds. "I tell you, that to every one who has will more be given; but from him who has not, even what he has will be taken away" (Lk. 19:26, RSV).

909 *UNTAPPED RESOURCES*   Gideon was threshing wheat when an angel of the Lord said to him, "The Lord is with thee, thou mighty man of valour" (Judg. 6:12). Gideon may not have realized that the angel spoke to him, but the generous salutation was an appeal to the latent resources within Gideon which God would use.

910 *NO TALENT IS USELESS*   Jephthah was cast from the home of his father Gilead by his half-brothers who scorned his illegitimate birth, but later, when the brothers were sorely pressed by the Ammonites, they asked him to help. Jephthah consented on the condition that they name him as their leader. (Judg. 11:1–10.) In an emergency no man is "worthless," and God, who is "no respecter of persons" (Acts 10:34), deigns to use the talents of the most miserable sinner.

911 *LEFT-HANDED WARRIORS*   Among the Benjaminite warriors were "seven hundred picked men who were left-handed; every one could sling a stone at a hair, and not miss" (Judg. 20:16, RSV). Here is encouragement for handicapped persons who wonder whether they can skillfully serve God and man.

912 *MORE THAN ABLE* Only three hundred Israelites marched with Gideon against the Midianites. What they lacked in strength of arms, they more than compensated with imagination and cunning. Divided into three companies, they surrounded the enemy and at a given signal they sounded trumpets and broke pitchers. So successful was their "psychological warfare" that the enemy, fearful that they were being attacked by massed armies, were completely routed. (Judg. 7:16–23.)

TEMPERANCE

913 *COUNTERFEIT RELIEF* Bottled and packaged "spirits" are a beguiling tonic for weariness and fatigue; at best they bring a counterfeit and temporary relief. "Don't get your stimulus from wine (for there is always the danger of excessive drinking), but let the Spirit stimulate your souls." For genuine refreshment Paul prescribes singing spiritual songs and "making music in your hearts for the ears of God!" (Eph. 5:18–19, PHILLIPS.)

914 *FAITHFUL HERITAGE* Offered pitchers full of wine and cups, the Rechabites said, "We will drink no wine: for Jonadab the son of Rechab our father commanded us, saying, Ye shall drink no wine, neither ye, nor your sons for ever" (Jer. 35:6). And they proved faithful to their heritage.

915 *SOCIAL PRESSURE* Perhaps a lesson may be gleaned even from so ignoble a person as Ahasuerus who, having spread a sumptuous banquet, did not bring social pressure upon abstainers to indulge in drinking. "The rule about drinking was this, that no one was forced to drink" (Es. 1:8, MOFFATT).

916 *HUMAN WEAKNESSES* Of all the sons of men Noah only found favor in the sight of God. He "was a just man and perfect" (Gen. 6:9), yet Noah shared the weaknesses common to mortal man, and having left the ark, he "planted a vineyard: and he drank of the wine, and was drunken" (Gen. 9:20–21).

917 *EXTRAVAGANT REQUEST* Delighted by the erotic dancing of Salome before his guests, Herod promised to grant even her most extravagant request. When she demanded the head of

John the Baptist, Herod was forced to concur, for in his intoxicated condition he had sworn to do whatever the girl asked. (Matt.
14:1–12.)

918 *THE KING'S FEAST*   After she had interceded with
David in behalf of her foolish husband Nabal, Abigail returned to
tell him that David would not punish him; but her message of
such great portent could not be related, for "he was holding a feast
in his house, like the feast of a king. And Nabal's heart was merry
within him, for he was very drunk; so she told him nothing at all
until the morning light" (1 Sam. 25:36, RSV).

919 *CENTER OF ATTENTION*   He who is the center of attention at a cocktail party may well be a villain to those at home
who depend on him for love and sustenance and he may be a
liability to his employer. "Woe to those who are brave—at drinking!
mighty at—mixing a bowl!" (Isa. 5:22, MOFFATT).

920 *TOO BUSY FOR GOD*   Isaiah said of those "who get up
early for a drinking bout, who sit far into the night, heated by
their wine," that "they heed not what the Eternal has in hand, they
never see what he is doing" (Isa. 5:11–12, MOFFATT). Serving one
master, they have neither time nor inclination to serve the Master
of life.

TEMPTATION

921 *THE SIFTING OF PETER*   In our times of trial and
temptation there is One who prays for us. "Simon, Simon, take
heed: Satan has been given leave to sift all of you like wheat; but
for you I have prayed that your faith may not fail" (Lk. 22:31–32,
NEB).

922 *ENTICED BY A BAIT*   To blame God for our human
weaknesses and to beseech him not to lead us into temptation fails
to recognize the origin or our sinfulness. "A man's temptation is due
to the pull of his own inward desires, which can be enormously
attractive" (Jas. 1:14, PHILLIPS), or "Anyone is tempted to do evil
when he is allured by his own evil desire and enticed by a bait"
(WILLIAMS).

923 *WHEN WE ARE VULNERABLE*   Only after Jesus had fasted forty days and nights did the devil fling at him the words, "If thou be the Son of God, command this stone that it be made bread" (Lk. 4:3). Such is the subtlety of sin that we are tempted when we are most vulnerable.

TESTING

924 *THE HEART'S ACCENT*   The Gileadites tested the fugitives who said they were not Ephraimites by requiring them to say "shibboleth," for thereby the Ephraimites, who could not pronounce "sh," revealed their true identity. (Judg. 12:4–6.) Every man has an accent, not of the tongue only, but also of the heart, by which he is known.

925 *ULTIMATE QUESTIONS*   Having been told of Solomon's wisdom, the Queen of Sheba "came to test him with puzzling questions. . . . She opened out all that was on her mind, and Solomon answered all her questions; there was not a single thing hidden from Solomon, which he could not explain to her" (2 Chron. 9:1–2, MOFFATT). But there is no hint that the queen, who was adept at asking tongue twisters, even broached life's ultimate questions or that Solomon gave her an assurance concerning him whom his people affirmed to be the Answer to eternal salvation.

926 *TESTING OF ABRAHAM*   God, who surrendered his only-begotten Son upon a cross, "tested" the faith of Abraham by requiring that he sacrifice his beloved son Isaac. The real meaning of this story is not to be found in the obligation God placed upon Abraham but in Abraham's spontaneous, unquestioning, and unqualified willingness to do whatever God might desire. (Gen. 22:1–13.) Did Abraham expect to find an escape clause in the covenant? Probably not. Did he believe that God would sustain him in his hour of greatest grief? Emphatically yes.

927 *CHANGE OF DIET*   Having resolved even at the Babylonian court to honor the Jewish dietary laws, Daniel proposed a test to determine whether vegetables and water or the king's meats and wines were more nourishing. At the end of a ten-day period those who ate what Daniel preferred were in more robust health. (Dan. 1:8–16.) By remaining loyal to his principles Daniel persuaded the court to change the diet for all of the young men.

928 *THE FLEECE TEST*   Wanting to be certain what was God's will, Gideon proposed a test whereby God, by making a fleece of wool wet or dry, would indicate that he should deliver Israel, as God had promised. (Judg. 6:36–40.) Although we may question the creditability of Gideon's method, we admire his determination to know for a certainty what was God's will.

929 *TESTING GOD*   In an hour of great peril the Lord told King Ahaz to ask for a propitious sign or omen "from the deep underworld, or from high heaven," but the wicked king replied with a pious hypocrisy, "No . . . I will not put the Eternal to any test" (Isa. 7:11–12, MOFFATT). What sign did he reject? The birth of Immanuel.

930 *THE DEVIL'S PROPOSAL*   The devil tempted Jesus to cast himself spectacularly from the pinnacle of the temple and thereby test God's power miraculously to save him; but Jesus rejected the opportunity to be spared danger and trials and gave himself willingly to those demands which God might require of him. (Lk. 4:9–12.)

931 *FINAL EXAMINATION*   After Christ's elevation into heaven, his followers returned "unto Jerusalem from the mount called Olivet, which is from Jerusalem a sabbath day's journey" (Acts 1:12). As much as they may have longed to remain on this hill of spiritual inspiration, they had to return to the city where their exhilaration would be tested and proven as they undertook the work which Christ had commissioned.

THANKFULNESS

932 *FORGET NOT GOD*   Our goodly heritage represents the faith and labors of men of many generations. Speaking words of enduring pertinence, Moses reminds us of our need for appreciation toward those who have blazed trails along which we travel in relative comfort: "When the Lord thy God shall have brought thee into the land which he sware unto thy fathers, to Abraham, to Isaac, and to Jacob, to give thee great and goodly cities, which thou buildest not, and houses full of all good things, which thou filledst not, and wells digged, which thou diggedst not, vineyards and olive trees, which thou plantedst not; when thou shalt have eaten and be full; then beware lest thou forget the Lord, which brought thee forth out of the land of Egypt, from the house of bondage" (Deut. 6:10–12.)

933 *HE GAVE THANKS*   Adrift on the Sea of Adria and having little hope for survival, Paul bade the members of the crew to eat some food, and he "took bread, and gave thanks to God in the presence of them all; and when he had broken it, he began to eat" (Acts 27:35). In whatever exigency Paul found himself, he practiced the simple piety of thanksgiving.

934 *ONLY ONE RETURNED*   After Jesus had cured ten lepers, only one—"And he was a Samaritan" (Lk. 17:16), a foreigner who was beyond the pale—returned to express his gratitude.

TOLERANCE

935 *MUCH-MALIGNED WORD*   When the indignant members of the Sanhedrin sought to slay the apostles, Gamaliel interceded in behalf of reasonableness and tolerance. The much-maligned word "tolerance" rightly understood does not mean the pampering of an unpopular point of view because it doesn't much matter what one believes. Rather, genuine tolerance recognizes the possibility that at least a kernel of truth may be found in the honest expression of another's ideas. Gamaliel wisely counseled, "If this project or enterprise springs from men, it will collapse; whereas, if it really springs from God, you will be unable to put them down. You may even find yourselves fighting God!" (Acts 5:38–39, MOFFATT).

936 *WANTED: MORE PROPHETS*   When Moses had gathered seventy elders at the tabernacle where the Spirit rested upon them and they prophesied, two men, Eldad and Medad, remained in the camp where they also prophesied. Their prophesying distressed Joshua who complained concerning them and asked Moses to make them cease. But Moses looked kindly upon the two and said, "Enviest thou for my sake? would God that all the Lord's people were prophets, and that the Lord would put his spirit upon them!" (Num. 11:29). The Spirit "bloweth where it listeth" (Jn. 3:8), and none to whom the Spirit speaks should be restrained.

937 *PROVINCIAL ATTITUDE*   When the neighbors of Judah, testifying to their worship of God, wished to help in the building of the post-exilic temple, the Israelites curtly replied, "You have nothing to do with our building a house for our God; we will build it ourselves for the Eternal the God of Israel." The result of their provincial religious attitude? "Whereupon the people of the land thwarted the people of Judah and were a trouble to them as they were building; they hired agents against them, in order to defeat their purpose." (Ezra 4:3-4, MOFFATT.)

TRADITION

938 *THAT WHICH IS HANDED DOWN*   In Jesus' day—and in our own—some men are so zealous to transmit handed-down traditions that they close their minds to new truth. "You are so busy holding on to the traditions of men that you let go the commandment of God!" (Mk. 7:13, PHILLIPS).

939 *PRIORITY BY NEED*   Adhering to a tradition only because it formerly had meaning was, according to Jesus, inadequate. When his disciples plucked grain to eat, the Pharisees reprimanded them for disrespecting ancient laws concerning sabbath observance. Jesus responded by saying that the needs of men must take priority over mere legalism. (Lk. 6:1-5.)

TROUBLE

940 *DOOR OF HOPE*   Whatever the buffetings of the moment, God provides a way through the valley of the shadow, a turning of night into day, and a transforming of tragedy into victory. This is

God's promise: "I will . . . make the dale of Trouble a door of hope" (Hos. 2:15, MOFFATT).

941 *SHARPENED WEDGE*   Trouble is often the sharpened wedge which opens untried doors. After the generation of Joseph had passed, the Egyptians conscripted the Israelites into labor gangs, "but the more they oppressed them, the more they multiplied and expanded" (Ex. 1:12, AT).

942 *THE ONLY ANSWER*   The prophet Azariah said to Asa, "Now for a long season Israel hath been without the true God, and without a teaching priest, and without law. But when they in their trouble did turn unto the Lord God of Israel, and sought him, he was found of them" (2 Chron. 15:3–4). These words bear the imprint of human experience. "They that seek the Lord shall not want any good thing" (Ps. 34:10), be it a loving God's concern for them, instructors in spiritual truth, a content of belief to be affirmed. God, so long neglected, is the only answer for troubled lives. And one wonders, "Are not these evils come upon us, because God is not among us?" (Deut. 31:17).

943 *WITH THE TIDE*   From the chronicle of Paul's passage by ship to Rome comes a formula for those who must face circumstances which can be conquered by neither heart nor hand: "And when the ship . . . could not face into the wind, we gave way to it and were carried along" (Acts 27:15, C. S. C. WILLIAMS).

944 *PHYSICIAN, HEAL THYSELF*   Eliphaz explained that although Job had nurtured others in their troubles, he was apparently unable to find healing in his own medicines. "You have yourself set many right, and put strength into feeble souls; your words have kept men on their feet, the weak-kneed you have nerved. But now that your own turn has come, you droop; it touches you close, and you collapse" (Job 4:3–5, MOFFATT). "Physician, heal thyself" (Lk. 4:23). One reason for the persuasiveness of some spiritual advisers is that they have themselves passed through troubled waters.

945 *LARGER THAN LIFE*   The troubles which plague us almost always seem larger than their true dimensions. The chronicler records that the Philistine champion, Goliath, was of monstrous height and arrayed in the most formidable armor. "And the staff of his spear was like a weaver's beam" (1 Sam. 17:7).

TRUTH

946 *BETWEEN THE LINES*   Ifs, and, and buts do not diminish the transparent honesty of Paul: "You don't have to read between the lines of my letters; you can understand them" (2 Cor. 1:13, MOFFATT).

947 *SHADOWS OR MEN?*   Observing the approach of Abimelech's soldiers, Gaal said, "Behold, there come people down from the top of the mountains." The beguiling Zebul, seeking to disguise the truth, said, "Thou seest the shadow of the mountains as if they were men." (Judg. 9:36.)

948 *LYING TO GOD*   Lying not only disrupts harmonious relationships among men, but it also violates the nature and character of the universe. When Ananias lied concerning the money he had turned over to the early Christian community, Peter rebuked him and said, "Thou hast not lied unto men, but unto God" (Acts 5:4) to whom and for whose purposes the collection was taken.

949 *WHITEWASH*   Ezekiel likened prophets who see delusive visions and give lying divinations, who cry peace when there is no peace, to builders who camouflage flimsy walls with whitewash. Lies are unsubstantial and whitewash will not long disguise their inadequacy. (Ezek. 13:8–12.)

UNITY

950 *KNIT TOGETHER*   After perverted men in Gibeah committed a heinous crime, "all the men of Israel were gathered against the city, knit together as one man" (Judg. 20:11). Erstwhile divided peoples unite against a common foe. Why cannot a corresponding spirit mold hearts and hands in ordinary circumstances?

951 *NONE INFERIOR NOR SUPERIOR*   Paul's plea on behalf of Christian unity and harmony is vividly related in an analogy of the human body in which diverse parts, though serving their individual functions, are so interrelated that none may be described as either inferior or superior to another. "If the whole body were an eye, where were the hearing? If the whole were hearing, where were the smelling? . . . But now are they many members, yet but one body" (1 Cor. 12:17, 20).

952 *PARTY-CRIES*   Urging harmony within the Corinthian church, which was torn by conflicting loyalties, Paul wrote, "Brothers, for the sake of our Lord Jesus Christ I beg of you to drop these party-cries. There must be no cliques among you; you must regain your common temper and attitude." For a competitive Christendom his question is still pertinent: "Has Christ been parcelled out?" (1 Cor. 1:10, 13, MOFFATT.)

VALUE

953 *BARTERED FOR TRINKETS*   A topsy-turvy world in which, as Emerson said, things are in the saddle and ride mankind is a world where true values are bartered for trinkets and where we "have seen slaves on horses, and princes walking on foot like slaves" (Eccl. 10:7, RSV).

954 *ALIVE TO TRUE VALUES*   "A material man will not accept what the Spirit of God offers." Unable to detect the value of that which cannot be weighed, possessed, or exchanged, he clings to those things he covets. "But the spiritual man is alive to all true values." (1 Cor. 2:14–15, GOODSPEED.)

955 *POOR SUBSTITUTES*   After Shishak, the king of Egypt, took from the temple "all of the shields of gold which Solomon had made. King Rehoboam made shields of bronze in their stead" (1 Kings 14:26–27, AT). Similarly we substitute that which is inferior and sometimes go so far as to conclude that bronze, after all, is as good as gold.

VISION

956 *APPOINTED HOUR* God speaks in the fullness of time and according to his own reckoning of what best serves his children. To the prophet who had gone to the watchtower to await God's word, the Lord said, "The vision has its own appointed hour, it ripens, it will flower; if it be long, then wait, for it is sure, and it will not be late" (Hab. 2:3, MOFFATT).

957 *EYES FOR INVISIBLES* When Elijah asked Elisha if there was anything he could do for him, the young man asked that he, too, might have prophetic vision: "I pray thee, let a double portion of thy spirit be upon me." Elijah responded, "Thou hast asked a hard thing," but also added, "If thou see me when I am taken from thee, it shall be so unto thee; but if not, it shall not be so." (2 Kings 2:9–10.) Elisha did possess eyes for invisible realities, for when the heavenly chariotry came for Elijah, he saw Elijah's ascent.

958 *LINES OF COMMUNICATION* Under the guidance of Eli, Samuel was being prepared to do God's work at a time when "the word of the Lord was rare . . . there was no frequent vision" (1 Sam. 3:1, RSV). Samuel would one day repair the lines of communication between man and his Creator.

959 *THRESHINGFLOOR VISION* One might perhaps expect to see a divine vision only when he visits a shrine or holy place. But it is not always so. "And Ornan turned back, and saw the angel. . . . Now Ornan was threshing wheat" (1 Chron. 21:20). The angel appeared to him at the least likely place and at the least expected hour, and Ornan's threshingfloor became David's altar and the site on which Solomon's temple was later erected.

960 *UNCOMMON REVELATION* Zecharias was fulfilling routine priestly duties in the temple when the angel appeared unto him. (Lk. 1:8–11). No doubt he had considered this to be just another day of wearisome responsibilities, but into so common a circumstance came an uncommon revelation.

961 *I SAW THE LORD* "In the year that king Uzziah died I saw . . . the Lord sitting upon a throne, high and lifted up" (Isa. 6:1). Mortal kings die, and confusion, turmoil, and uncertainty follow; but the prophet's vision was of One who reigns eternally.

WAR

962 *FAITH IN ARMAMENTS* So confident were the Jebusites that they could withstand David's attack on their seemingly impregnable fortress of Jerusalem that they jeered, "You will not come in here, but the blind and the lame will ward you off" (2 Sam. 5:6, RSV). But David took the city whose inhabitants thought the blind and the lame could easily defend. Such has often been the fate of those who place their faith in armaments. Stronger is he who puts his faith in the Lord: "In him will I trust: he is my shield, and the horn of my salvation, my high tower, and my refuge" (2 Sam. 22:3).

963 *THIS WORK MUST CONTINUE* In a generation when armaments are given priorities, the work of building good will among peoples is even more imperative. Enemies threatened the work of raising the walls of Jerusalem, but that important work could not be delayed. "The labourers were armed; each of them worked with one hand, and held a weapon in the other" (Neh. 4:17, MOFFATT).

964 *BLOODSTAINED HANDS* The Lord deprived David of the privilege of building the house of God. "You have shed much blood and have waged great wars; you shall not build a house to my name, because you have shed so much blood before me upon the earth. Behold, a son shall be born to you . . . a man of peace. . . . He shall build a house for my name" (1 Chron. 22:8–10, RSV). Men of war must sometimes destroy that others may build, and to the men of peace is given the privilege of constructive endeavors.

WATCHFULNESS

965 *THE WAKE-TREE* When Jeremiah was commissioned as a prophet, the Lord assured him of divine watchfulness by calling his attention to a shoot of a wake-tree. "I am wakeful over my word, to carry it out" (Jer. 1:12, MOFFATT).

966 *ROLE OF SENTINEL*   The Lord said to Ezekiel, "I have made thee a watchman unto the house of Israel: therefore hear the word at my mouth, and give them warning from me" (Ezek. 3:17). The role of the pastor is that of a sentinel who discerns the signs of the times and mediates the pertinent and applicable word of the Lord.

967 *WATCHMEN A-DREAMING*   Isaiah's condemnation of Israel's leaders is not without relevance to Christ's ministers who renege at their posts of responsibility: "My watchmen are all blind, they know not how to guard; dumb dogs, every one of them, they cannot bark—there they lie, a-dreaming, in the sleep they love" (Isa. 56:10, MOFFATT).

968 *WHAT OF THE NIGHT?*   The pastor should read the signs and seasons so that he may communicate to less sensitive ears and eyes what might otherwise remain undetected. "Watchman, what of the night?" (Isa. 21:11), or "Watchman, what hour of the night is it?" (AT), or "How far has the night gone, watchman?" (MOFFATT).

WIFE

969 *A WIFE'S COUNSEL*   After an angel of the Lord appeared to Manoah and his wife, Manoah was greatly agitated and said, "We shall surely die, bcause we have seen God." But his wife, having considered reasonably all of the circumstances, counseled, "If the Lord were pleased to kill us, he would not have received a burnt offering and a meat offering at our hands, neither would he have shewed us all these things, nor would as at this time have told us such things as these" (Judg. 13:22–23).

970 *HER WARNING*   Only once do the Evangelists mention the wife of Pilate. When her husband sat in judgment, she sent word to him: "Have thou nothing to do with that just man" (Matt. 27:19). And then she and Pilate pass into oblivion. Pilate was not

the first man to realize too late that he might better have listened
to his wife's counsel.

971 *THE WIFE OF ANANIAS*   When a husband and wife are
in complete agreement, the one may be no more than a doormat
over which the other's steamroller moves, or they may indeed have
found harmony in emphasis and perspective. Better than agreement
is the willingness at times of a spouse to shore up the moral resolution of the other and so bring out the best that is to be gleaned. At
least a measure of the tragedy of Ananias lies in the fact that short-
changing of the early Christian community was done "with his
wife's knowledge" (Acts 5:2, RSV) and apparently her concurrence.

972 *MARRIED TO A FOOL*   Abigail interceded with David
in behalf of her witless and selfish husband Nabal, whose name
literally means "fool." Like many another wife who rightly reads
her husband's weaknesses, Abigail explained, "Let not my lord, I
pray you, take seriously this worthless individual, Nabal, for as his
name is, so is he; 'Fool' is his name, and folly his boon companion"
(1 Sam. 25:25, AT).

973 *AN EXAMPLE FOR WOMEN*   After Vashti refused to
appear at Ahasuerus' banquet, the king inquired of those experienced in court etiquette concerning proper disciplinary measures.
Fearful that Vashti's independent manner might be emulated by
their own wives, the court attendants through Memucan counseled,
"This behavior of the queen will come to the ears of every woman,
and they will look down upon their husbands. . . . This very day,
the ladies of Persia and Media who have heard of the queen's conduct are talking proudly and petulantly enough to all the king's
officials!" (Es. 1:17–18, MOFFATT).

974 *HIS WIFE'S HOUSE*   When Solomon married Pharaoh's
daughter, he built a separate house for her, saying, "My wife shall
not dwell in the house of David king of Israel, because the places
are holy, whereunto the ark of the Lord hath come" (2 Chron. 8:11).
Apparently Solomon had no desire to convince this foreign princess
—who was suitable as a wife but unsuited to live within his house—
of the veracity of his father's faith.

975 *ADAM'S COMPANION* Adam without Eve was little more than a shadow, for he was without companionship or a real reason for living. God—the irreplaceable third partner in every marriage—recognized Adam's deficiency: "It is not good for man to be alone; I will make a helper to suit him" (Gen. 2:18, MOFFATT).

WITNESS

976 *JONAH'S CREDENTIALS* When their ship was threatened with destruction, the mariners sought out their passenger Jonah and bombarded him with questions: "What is thine occupation? and whence comest thou? what is thy country? and of what people art thou?" Jonah unequivocally offered his credentials: "I am a Hebrew; and I fear the Lord, the God of heaven, which hath made the sea and the dry land." (Jon. 1:8–9.) The forthrightness of Jonah's self-identification should put to shame those Christians who boast of their professional activities, their political affiliations, and their golf scores, but hide their Christian convictions behind the transparent plea that a man's religion is a private affair.

977 *AUTHENTICATED TESTIMONY* Paul no doubt dictated the letters which he circulated to his beloved church friends, but he signed them personally. "I, Paul, write this greeting with my own hand" (Col. 4:18, RSV). His signature authenticated his testimony. Have we a witness to which we could as proudly affix our names?

978 *LETTER OF RECOMMENDATION* Paul claimed that his parishioners were his "letter of recommendation" (RSV). "You yourselves are our testimonial, written in our hearts and yet open for anyone to inspect and read" (2 Cor. 3:2, PHILLIPS).

979 *SAINTS IN CAESAR'S HOUSEHOLD* It is easy enough to maintain nominal Christianity in circumstances conducive to and encouraging Christian living, but more valiant are those to witness for Christ where everything contrives to extinguish the light of faith. "All the saints salute you, especially those who are Imperial slaves" (Phil. 4:22, MOFFATT), or "chiefly they that are of Caesar's household."

980 *DESERT ROAD*   An angel of the Lord sent Philip to the least likely of places to witness for Christ: the road that goes down from Jerusalem to Gaza. "This is a desert road" (Acts 8:26, RSV). But it was in that woebegone place that he conversed with an Ethiopian official whom he led down into the waters of baptism.

981 *SEEN AND HEARD*   Evidences of the Spirit's miraculous power caused consternation in the hearts of the elders of Israel who, unable to deny what their eyes had beheld, tried to silence Peter and John by threats and intimidations. To the command that they abstain from further speaking, the apostles energetically replied, "We cannot but speak the things which we have seen and heard" (Acts 4:20).

982 *RING OF CONVICTION*   "Forasmuch as many have taken in hand to set forth . . . those things which are most surely believed among us . . . it seemed good to me also . . . to write" (Lk. 1:1, 3). Every Christian has a testimony, and another's will never have the same ring of conviction as the one we volunteer. "Come and hear, all ye that fear God, and I will declare what he hath done for my soul" (Ps. 66:16).

983 *SECONDHAND TESTIMONIES*   Secondhand testimonies offer at best only a secondhand satisfaction. When the Samaritan woman told of the Christ, her neighbors sought him out for themselves. And to their informer they said, "We no longer believe on account of what you said; we have heard for ourselves, we know that he is really the Saviour of the world" (Jn. 4:42, MOFFATT).

984 *EXCEPT I SHALL SEE*   When the disciples excitedly told Thomas that they had seen the risen Lord, Thomas—understandably —said, "Except I shall see in his hands the print of the nails, and put my finger into the print of the nails, and thrust my hand into his side, I will not believe" (Jn. 20:25). Too good to be true, the experience was one which Thomas refused to accept on another's say-so. And Jesus fulfilled Thomas' wish even as he has confirmed his resurrection to all latter-day disciples who desire more than a secondhand testimony.

985 *SUSPENDED ANIMATION*   A tepid Christian witness, comprised of concessions and compromises, is in a state of suspended animation. The Spirit reprimanded the church in Laodicea as being ingloriously neutral in things that matter most: "You are neither cold nor hot. Would that you were cold or hot! So, because you are lukewarm, and neither cold not hot, I will spew you out of my mouth" (Rev. 3:15–16, RSV).

986 *PRISON WITNESS*   Paul felt that there were advantages to be reaped even from his confinement in prison: "Friends, I want you to understand that the work of the Gospel has been helped on, rather than hindered, by this business of mine. My imprisonment in Christ's cause has become common knowledge to all at the headquarters here, and indeed among the public at large; and it has given confidence to most of our fellow-Christians to speak the word of God fearlessly and with extraordinary courage" (Phil. 1:12–14, NEB).

WOMEN

987 *CONGREGATION BY A RIVER*   An apparently unpromising gathering of women at the side of a river near Philippi on a Sabbath day "was the foundation of a church renowned for its courage, generosity, and truly Christian spirit, for whose members the Apostles had only praise, gratitude, and love" (Foakes-Jackson). No occasion to proclaim God's Word is expendable. Christians are still inspired by the consequences of Paul's words spoken to that unlikely congregation. (Acts 16:13–15.)

988 *WHAT MEN MIGHT SAY*   During Abimelech's attack against the tower of Thebez, a woman dropped upon him a millstone that crushed his skull. To avoid complete humiliation, Abimelech ordered his armor-bearer, "Draw thy sword, and slay me, that men say not of me, A woman slew him" (Judg. 9:54).

989 *RESTRAINING INFLUENCE*   The valiant plea of Abigail on behalf of her husband Nabal turned the thoughts of David from mortal revenge. David said to Abigail, "Blessed be your discretion, and blessed be you, who have kept me this day from bloodguilt and from avenging myself with my own hand!" (1 Sam. 25:33, rsv). Women have often represented a restraining influence which is conducive to intelligent behavior.

WORK

990 *WHAT IS YOUR WORK?*   Joseph told his brethren that when Pharaoh asked, "What is your occupation?" they should respond, "Thy servants' trade hath been about cattle from our youth even until now, both we, and also our fathers." To acknowledge their vocation would not make them popular, "for every shepherd is an abomination unto the Egyptians." (Gen. 46:33–34.) More important than the kind of work to which a man is called is the quality of work he achieves. "I . . . beseech you that ye walk worthy of the vocation wherewith ye are called" (Eph. 4:1).

991 *WHILE TENDING FLOCKS*   To common shepherds, who were tending their flocks near Bethlehem, was given the glorious announcement of the birth of our Lord. (Lk. 2:8–9.) A night like a thousand others. Who knows a shepherd's heart, his loneliness, and his tedious labors? Yet to them came the best news mankind has ever heard.

992 *HUMDRUM WORK*   While serving the Lord in the temple, where of all places he should have most expected a heavenly vision, Zecharias became troubled and fearful when an angel did in fact appear. (Lk. 1:11–12.) Had his work become so humdrum and monotonous that he was indifferent to divine visitations?

993 *COMMON LABOR*   During the building of the walls of Jerusalem, the Tekoites worked with the other peoples, "but their nobles put not their necks to the work of their Lord" (Neh. 3:5). They desired the walls as much as anyone, but they were unwilling to engage in the common labor.

994 *THE WORK AT HAND*   The beauty and upkeep of our communities is possible when everyone attends to that work which is nearest at hand. In the rebuilding of Jerusalem, each of the exiles had a particular responsibility. "Jedaiah, the son of Harumaph, made repairs opposite his house" (Neh. 3:10, AT).

WORLDLINESS

995 *THE DESERTER*   Paul persevered triumphantly in the vocation to which Christ called him: "The hour for my departure is upon me. I have run the great race, I have finished the course, I have kept the faith." By contrast, Demas, his faith having ingloriously languished, "deserted [Paul] because his heart was set on this world." (2 Tim. 4:6–7, 10, NEB.)

996 *MIMICKING THE PAGANS*   While visiting in Damascus, Ahaz made a detailed copy of a pagan altar and sent specifications to Urijah the priest so that a similar altar might replace the one in the temple. (2 Kings 16:10–16.) Venerated traditions and hallowed convictions of God's people are sometimes substituted for appealing secular ideas. But the church is true to her Lord when she resists worldly encroachments. Although Jesus counseled against a meaningless clinging to ancient truth, we ought also to recall the salubrious words, "Remove not the ancient landmark, which thy fathers have set" (Prov. 22:28).

997 *HUMAN LEVELS*   In but not of the world, Christians have been called by Christ to a way of life which the world for the most part neither comprehends nor appreciates. The worldly behavior of the Corinthian Christians caused St. Paul to write with indignation, "With jealousy and quarrels in your midst are you not worldly, are you not behaving like ordinary men?" (1 Cor. 3:3, MOFFATT), or "living on a merely human level" (GOODSPEED).

WORRY

998 *ONE THING IS NEEDFUL*   Too encumbered with domestic chores to realize the rare privilege she was missing, Martha protested that Mary was not doing her part in the household work. Jesus answered, "Martha, my dear, you are worried and bothered about providing so many things. Only a few things are really needed, perhaps only one" (Lk. 10:41–42, PHILLIPS). The cares and concerns of life should not choke the one thing which is needful: the growth of the Spirit in our lives.

999 *AN INCH OR AN HOUR*   Faith in God, Jesus believed, must replace the worries which preoccupy men's minds and sap their strength. "Can any of you make himself an inch taller however much he worries about it?" (Lk. 12:25, PHILLIPS), or "Which of you with all his worry can add a single hour to his life?" (GOODSPEED).

1000 *UNNECESSARY WORRIES*   Many of the things we most worry about do not materialize. As the women went to the sepulchre of Jesus, they needlessly anticipated trouble: "And they said among themselves, Who shall roll us away the stone from the door of the sepulchre?" (Mk. 16:3).

WORSHIP

1001 *SUN WORSHIPERS*   Ezekiel saw men whose backs were "toward the temple of the Lord, and their faces toward the east; and they worshipped the sun toward the east" (Ezek. 8:16). Such is the posture and perspective of so-called Christians, who sunning themselves on the porch of the church look toward other lights by which to walk.

1002 *KEY TO WORSHIP*   Ostentation is inappropriate in worship where sincerity is the key to rich spiritual benefits. "When you pray, don't be like the play actors. They love to stand and pray in the synagogues and at street corners so that people may see them at it" (Matt. 6:5, PHILLIPS).

1003 *MANUFACTURED ALTARS*   "You must no longer worship things you manufacture" (Mic. 5:13, MOFFATT). The prophet spoke to those who reverenced idols which their skill and imaginations had wrought, but his message to us is no less pointed. Our danger is that we give priority to appliances, gadgets, and labor-saving devices which seem at times to have become the altars in our homes.

1004 *THE CALVES WE WORSHIP*   The stupidity of idolatry was vividly portrayed by Hosea. "And still they go on sinning, making metal gods of silver, idols in human form, the craftsman's work—and these they call their 'gods'! And men at a sacrifice, men offer kisses to calves!" (Hos. 13:2, MOFFATT). Sophisticated modern men no longer carve idols or worship calves, but are more likely to worship prowess, profit, and pleasure.

1005 *HIS TO BARGAIN WITH*   The devil offered Jesus the power and the glory of the kingdoms of the world "if thou . . . wilt worship me." Perhaps the kingdoms of the earth were—and are—the devil's to bargain with, but Jesus answered, "Thou shalt worship the Lord thy God, and him only shalt thou serve." (Lk. 4:7–8.) Nothing can long belong to him who surrenders his allegiance to evil.

1006 *DRAW NEAR TO LISTEN*   Modern worshipers need to consider an ancient admonition: "Never enter God's house carelessly; draw near him to listen" (Eccl. 5:1, MOFFATT).

YOUTH

1007 *THE YOUNGEST SON*   None of the sons of Jesse who were presented to Samuel were qualified to succeed Saul as king. "Are all your sons here?" Samuel asked. Jesse replied "There remains yet the youngest, but behold, he is keeping the sheep." (1 Sam. 16:11, RSV.) Then the boy David, whom his father had perhaps considered without the commendations of experience and maturity, was anointed.

1008 *BOY WITH A SLINGSHOT*   Goliath was greatly insulted when the boy David, a slingshot in his hand, came forward to do battle, but David was more than a match for the champion of the Philistines: "Thou comest to me with a sword, and with a spear, and with a shield," David said, "but I come to thee in the name of the Lord of hosts, the God of the armies of Israel, whom thou hast defied" (1 Sam. 17:45).

1009 *I AM TOO YOUNG*   When the Lord called Jeremiah, he recoiled from so formidable a work and said, "Ah, but, O Lord Eternal, I cannot speak, I am too young!" And the Eternal replied, "Say not, you are too young; to whomsoever I send you shall you go, and whatever I command you, shall you speak. Be not afraid

at the sight of them, for I am with you to succour you." (Jer. 1:6–8,
MOFFATT.)

1010 *THE MAN HE MIGHT HAVE BEEN*   The anointing of
Saul as king of Israel seemed propitious, for he was "a choice young
man . . . and there was not among the children of Israel a goodlier
person than he: from his shoulders and upward he was higher than
any of the people" (1 Sam. 9:2). Not only was he head and shoulders
above all others, but he apparently possessed every other requisite
for leadership. The fact that he subsequently became one of the
colossal failures in biblical history only the more emphasizes his
potentials as a young man.

INDEX OF TEXTS

References are to item numbers

INDEX OF BIBLICAL NAMES

References are to item numbers

Aaron 370, 503, 541, 554, 778, 888
Abednego 288, 360, 373, 507
Abel 80
Abigail 347, 918, 972, 989
Abihu 653
Abijah 242
Abimelech, king of Gerar 201, 687, 868
Abimelech, son of Gideon 17, 209, 947, 988
Abishai 186, 451
Abraham
   altar of 11
   amicability of 438
   bosom of 798
   censure of 868
   children of 302, 665
   faith of 286, 629
   generosity of 844
   hospitality of 448
   intercession of 501
   laughter of 539
   legacy of 422
   plea to 790
   promise to 79
   servant of 351
   sin of 201
   son of 219, 504
   sorrow of 881
   testing of 926
   well of 421
Absalom 55, 282, 299, 324, 415, 451, 493, 698, 904
Achish 204
Achsah 739
Adonijah 42
Adam 592, 754, 779, 975
Agrippa (*see* Herod Agrippa)
Ahab 92, 244, 377, 423, 494, 517, 582, 688, 726, 774
Ahasuerus 33, 58, 403, 775, 805, 839, 915
Ahaz 929, 996
Ahaziah of Israel 405
Ahaziah of Judah 466, 481, 610
Ahijah 242

Amaziah of Judah 366
Amaziah, priest of Bethel 371, 669
Amnon 300, 744
Amon 298
Amos 172, 371, 699
Ananias of Damascus 86, 710
Ananias of Jerusalem 207, 948, 971
Ananias, high priest 549
Anna 24
Aquila 542
Araunah 13
Asa 404, 942
Asenath 318
Athaliah 481, 610
Azariah 942

Balaam 77, 492, 535, 641
Balak 77, 492
Barabbas 108, 550, 700
Barak 855
Barnabas 122, 327, 328
Barsabas 95
Bath-sheba 84, 300, 459, 516, 609, 861, 866
Belshazzar 427, 808, 862
Ben-hadad II 726, 774
Ben-hadad III 873
Benjamin 440
Bezaleel 647

Caesar 189, 312, 526, 979
Cain 80
Caleb 9, 441, 739, 901
Christ (*see* INDEX OF TOPICS)
Cyrus 22, 178

Daniel 862
   faith of 287
   integrity of 178, 497
   interpretation of 808
   loyalty of 581
   test of 927
   vision of 22
   warning of 725
Darius 581

SPECIAL DAY AND OCCASION INDEX

References are to item numbers

INDEX OF TOPICS

References are to item numbers
Main entries are listed in boldface type